FIRST AID
TO THE
BATTLEFRONT

FIRST AID
TO THE
BATTLEFRONT

*Life and Letters of
Sir Vincent Kennett-Barrington
(1844–1903)*

EDITED BY
PETER MORRIS

ALAN SUTTON

First published in the United Kingdom in 1992 by
Alan Sutton Publishing Ltd · Phoenix Mill · Stroud · Gloucestershire

First published in the United States of America in 1992 by
Alan Sutton Publishing Inc · Wolfeboro Falls · NH 03896-0848

British Library Cataloguing in Publication Data

First Aid to the Battlefront.
 I. Morris, Peter, *1943–*
361.77092

 ISBN 0–7509–0016–4

Library of Congress Cataloging in Publication Data applied for

Typeset in 10/12 Times.
Typesetting and origination by
Alan Sutton Publishing Limited.
Printed in Great Britain by
The Bath Press Ltd, Avon.

CONTENTS

ILLUSTRATIONS

MAPS

PREFACE

The hard work of deciphering and transcribing these letters was undertaken by Alice Lascelles, to whom a large share of the credit for this volume is due. It is typical of her modesty that she should underestimate the importance of her contribution and the value of her constructive comments as the work progressed. The editor wishes to place on record his own appreciation of both. He also wishes to acknowledge an especial debt to Dr J.M. Alberich for permission to draw on his notes and use material from his introduction to the Exeter Hispanic Texts edition of the letters from Spain, reproduced in the present volume. It was impossible to improve on them.

Extracts from Sir Vincent's reports to the National Aid Society and the original maps reproduced in the present volume are by courtesy of the Museum of the Order of St John. All errors of fact and of judgement are the exclusive responsibility of the editor.

Peter Morris

Sir Vincent Hunter Barrington Kennett-Barrington

INTRODUCTION

On 12 May 1886 Prime Minister Gladstone amid the turmoil of the Home Rule crisis wrote to the grandson of a former Irish opponent of Union:

> I have much pleasure in proposing to you, with the Queen's permission, that you should receive the honour of Knighthood in recognition of the service you have rendered, in many countries and many campaigns, in aid of the sick and wounded, and I trust that this proposal, in which Her Majesty has been graciously pleased to express a special interest, may prove agreeable to you.

It did and the recipient of the letter became Sir Vincent Hunter Barrington Kennett-Barrington. The honour was well earned. Vincent's record of active involvement in the burgeoning charitable medical relief work made him an early pioneer. His involvement started in the Franco-Prussian War 1870–1 and ended only with his death as the result of a ballooning accident in 1903. He played a significant part in the embryonic organizations which grew into the present-day Red Cross and St John Ambulance movements, coming into contact with many of the leading figures of those early days.

Like most of his contemporaries, he was an inveterate letter-writer. While absent from his family on his charitable work, he sustained a substantial correspondence and kept notes and fragmentary diaries. On his death in 1903 the letters were stored at the family house at Dorchester-on-Thames, consigned to the attics and in well-sealed tin boxes, with the sole exception of several bundles relating to his time in Spain which were burned unread in keeping with the wishes of his widow. The undisturbed boxes were transferred in the early 1950s, when the house was sold on the death of Vincent's only son, Guy, to the Lascelles family home at Woolbeding and into the safekeeping of Vincent's only daughter Leila, who had married into the Lascelles family. Leila began the process of reading through the letters, prompted by Alice, her daughter and Vincent's grand-daughter. It was the latter who was the first to disturb the neatly folded, orderly and very dusty bundles. Only Vincent's letters remained, written in a difficult and hurried hand which requires acquaintance, on paper often torn hurriedly from his sketch-book and like his contemporaries often crossed in his anxiety to use paper economically. His spelling was erratic and his variations on foreign names amusingly idiosyncratic, and the editors have striven to retain the variety which he employed. The letters are from time to time illustrated by drawings, for Vincent was an enthusiastic amateur sketcher. The laborious work of decyphering and transcribing them was undertaken by Alice Lascelles, who in collaboration with J.M. Alberich published those letters written from Spain during the Carlist Wars between 1874 and 1876.[1] In the present volume some are reprinted, together with letters from France, the Balkans, and Egypt while further correspondence from India and South America has been drawn upon in the introduction. The present editor has also added extracts from Vincent's official reports to the National Aid Society (NAS) and the Stafford House Committee, originally published in the official accounts of those organizations.

Vincent's letters reveal the private man and add a gloss to the sometimes constricting requirements of official reporting. They show a man far removed from the Victorian stereotype. His political opinions led his family to consider him a radical, while his views on religion and the competing claims of rival sects were in advance of many present-day ecumenicists. The letters chart his career from relatively obscure family origins to moderate fame at his death, without much by way of formal qualifications. As his letters reveal, Vincent was able to persuade doctors and nurses, soldiers and officials to co-operate with him and do as he asked. Yet he had no medical skills or qualifications, no military rank apart from a lieutenancy in the militia, and neither experience of public life nor an official position apart from that which he was able to fashion for himself.

Vincent Hunter Barrington Kennett was born on 3 September 1844 in Italy at Bagni di Lucca, then 'a flourishing English watering place'.[2] He was always sentimental about his birthplace. Family legend claimed that his wet nurse ran off with him for three days, leading to the idea that he might be a changeling. By then the Savoy operas had begun and the idea was popular. Vincent had a sly sense of humour and encouraged the notion. He certainly believed his birthplace had a lasting effect on him, claiming it gave him some immunity against sunstroke, though his later experiences belied this.

His enthusiasm for ballooning, which made him a founder member of the Royal Aero Club, was a safer guide, for the first balloon ascent in Britain had been made in 1785 by Vincenzo Lunerdi, a native of Lucca.

When he revisited his birthplace forty-three years later Vincent described his journey as a pilgrimage and sought out the villa where he had been born. He wrote to his wife:

> I have visited some old churches and other spots where I know my good parents would have often been: strolled about the terraced garden where I first saw the blue bright sky of Italy and reluctantly drove away with a setting sun and rising new moon.

He brought back with him a bottle of water for the baptism of future generations from the mountain stream which ran by the house. He met and talked with Miss Stisted who had lived there all her life and remembered his parents and other members of the family, including his maternal grandfather, Sir Jonah Barrington. She particularly remembered the exciting stories of India told by Vincent's father.

Vincent Frederick Kennett was a retired captain in the East India Company army. Born in 1799, he had displayed a talent for languages and as an administrator though he never saw active service. He acted as aide-de-camp to his older cousin, John Brackley Kennett, who on retiring with the rank of lieutenant-general in 1851 stayed on in India. Even before retiring early on half pay in 1839, Vincent Frederick seems to have spent long periods in Europe, where, in September 1837, he married Arabella Henrietta, Baroness Calabrella, at the Anglican church in Geneva. Two months later he married her at St James's Church, Westminster.[3]

Arabella Henrietta was a strong character. She was the youngest daughter of Sir Jonah, an Irish protestant Judge in Admiralty who had been deprived of office in 1830 for misappropriation of funds. Sir Jonah took his large family to live abroad permanently. Arabella was a baroness by virtue of her first marriage to Edward Hughes Lee, about whom little can be found. Whatever the origins of the title, she was every inch a baroness and remained fiercely proud of her father. Each of her four children was given the Barrington name: Patricia Barrington baptized at Geneva in 1838, Arabella Barrington baptized at Naples in 1843, Vincent Hunter Barrington born at Lucca in 1844, and Brackley Herbert Barrington born near Calais in 1846. The Kennetts moved frequently which may explain why there is no trace of them in the records of Lucca. Arabella Henrietta died in Kensington in 1884. In accordance with the terms of her will, Vincent added Barrington to his surname to become Vincent Hunter Barrington Kennett-Barrington.[4]

The Kennett family finances were meagre. Vincent Frederick had his halfpay and little else while Sir Jonah was not given to economies as his *Personal Sketches of his Own Time* reveals.[5] The baroness may have inherited something from the complex family trust from which her first husband derived his income. Money was, however, clearly short and it was cheaper to live abroad than in Britain. The family's financial position improved in 1857; General Kennett was stabbed in India by a disgruntled servant and on his deathbed made a will leaving his property at Dorchester-on-Thames to Vincent Frederick, and disinheriting his only daughter who had deeply offended him by becoming a Roman Catholic.

The Kennetts returned to live at Dorchester-on-Thames. There was enough money to send young Vincent to Eton, though not without some sacrifices from the rest of the family as his father told him. From Eton Vincent secured a scholarship in 1863 to Trinity College, Cambridge, to read the mathematics tripos. He passed out with the equivalent of a first class honours degree in 1867, being 34th in the list of wranglers for that year. Attracted by his grandfather's avocation, he remained at Trinity to take a law degree in 1868, then moved to the Inns of Court, and was called to the Bar in November 1872. By then his brother Brackley had left Rugby School, taken his BA at Trinity and had been purchased a commission to the 51st Foot. By then the direction of Vincent's life had also changed. He may have found legal work unsatisfying, and he had certainly found a far more congenial outlet for his energies in humanitarian relief work.

Vincent was connected with two main philanthropic organizations during his career. The first was the English branch, or 'langue', of the Order of the Hospital of St John of Jerusalem, which in 1878 established an ambulance department, which in its turn secured a Royal Charter in 1888, becoming known as the St John Ambulance. The langue had been revived in 1831 as a 'dilettante charitable association'[6] of nobility and well-connected clerics. After involvement with the lifeboat movement, its modern profile as an organized and professional relief body developed under the guidance of Sir Edmund Lechmere.[7] He became its secretary in 1867 and continued to play a major part in the Order's affairs until his death in 1894 when he was its chancellor in England. In 1874 he was instrumental in securing part of the Order's medieval complex at St John's Gate in Clerkenwell as the Order's English headquarters. It is not clear when or how Vincent became associated with it. He was also closely connected with the St John Ambulance Association on whose central executive committee he served from 1879, becoming deputy chairman in 1883. In the same year, during a visit to India on behalf of the Edison Indian and Colonial Electrical Company, he helped organize branches at Calcutta and Bombay. He remained deputy chairman until his death in 1903. Elected a Chevalier of Grace in 1887, he was a member of the committee of the Order's opthalmic hospital in Jerusalem from 1889. His obituary in the annual report for 1903 noted his long association with the Order and commented:

> Sir Vincent Barrington's genial and amiable characteristics, his deep interest in everything which concerned the relief of the sick and wounded in war, and in the amelioration of the condition of the working classes, had greatly endeared him to all those who knew him.

The other organization with which he was associated, and for which he worked in France in 1870–1, in Servia in 1876, in Egypt in 1885, and in Bulgaria in 1885–6, was the Society for Aiding and Ameliorating the Condition of the Sick and Wounded in Time of War, known more concisely as the National Aid Society and later as the Red Cross. The Red Cross was the product of two rather different impulses and its often uneasy stance, as in the Balkan crisis between 1876 and 1878, reflected this. The initiative to create an English branch of the rapidly developing international Red Cross movement came from members of the Order of St John, seven of whom, including Lechmere, formed a provisional committee in 1868. Two of its members attended the 1868 Berlin International Conference where they met Baron Mundy and Baron von Langenbeck who feature in Vincent's letters. Both were later elected honorary associates of the English Order of St John. On the outbreak of the Franco-Prussian War in 1870, John Furley, a member of this provisional committee, approached Colonel Loyd-Lindsay and asked him to help in forming an English branch of the Red Cross.

Loyd-Lindsay, later Lord Wantage, knew Furley through their common involvement in the military volunteer movement in Kent. Furley, along with another St John's stalwart Captain, later Major, C.J. Burgess, had worked closely with Loyd-Lindsay since at least 1866. The latter had a distinguished army career, in which he had won the VC, before resigning on his marriage to the only child of the banker, Lord Overstone. He then became a keen supporter of the volunteer movement and a lesser political figure as Tory MP and peer after 1885. His experiences led him to believe the systematization of voluntary aid for wounded soldiers was essential. He was convinced that the army medical service could not meet the sudden needs of a largely expanded army in any future conflict and that voluntary organizations, unimpeded by official restrictions, could respond more quickly.[8]

The Franco-Prussian War aroused a deep charitable response in Britain to both sides. On 4 August 1870 the British National Aid Society was formally established and a public subscription launched. With the queen as patroness and the Prince of Wales as its president, the new society's social position and respectability, and consequently its economic success, were assured. It was able to raise the enormous sum of £294,455. From the start it established the principle of direct control over funds through the appointment of responsible commissioners who lived on the spot. It was a model to be copied later by other bodies. At the end of the war the National Aid Society still had £73,212 unexpended. This was invested in Government stock and its administration entrusted to three trustees, HRH the Duke of Connaught, the Earl of Shaftesbury and Colonel Loyd-Lindsay. They controlled over £1,800 in annual interest. The future of the Society then became a cause of controversy. Was it to retain its organization in peacetime ready for a further call in the event of a new war, was it to be mothballed, or should it be active in a civil capacity in accidents or natural disasters within and without Britain? This led to a split in 1872 between those who, like Loyd-Lindsay, believed the Society should retain its organization but not be involved in civil emergencies and a more activist group led by John Furley which urged the creation of a standing peacetime organization to provide medical assistance in civilian disasters. This latter group created the St John Ambulance.

How Vincent became involved in the newly emerging organization for the relief of the sick and wounded is unknown. The decision to retain control over the distribution of funds and supplies required the recruitment and dispatch of convoy agents, of which Vincent was one, to accompany the goods to be distributed on behalf of the National Aid Society. From October 1870 until mid-November Vincent acted with the French forces on and around the River Loire where Tours had become the focal point of French resistance after the investment of Paris on 20 September. After a brief return to England, he was sent back to operate from Meaux and after March 1871 from Vesoul. He served his apprenticeship in the tiring, unglamorous and frequently exasperating business of moving heavily laden carts over damaged roads in frequently bad weather conditions while undergoing the scrutiny of both sets of combatants.

Vincent's letters reflect the practical preoccupations of someone in his position, as well as his lively appreciation of what he witnessed. The continuing enthusiasm of the French for the war, the relative comfort of life, the position and influence of the traditional leaders of French society, lay and cleric, were all observed by him during the first months of his work. There were hints, too, of the deeper passions stirring, which animated the *francs-tireurs* and German reprisals.[9] Vincent's first experiences of hospitals and working with the wounded brought out his compassion for the 'poor fellows' as he was repeatedly to call them during the coming years. He found this unnerving, and it was not until after repeated exposure that he was able to stand the sight of wounds. It said much for his fundamental humanitarianism that he never lost that sympathy and compassion.

His lively correspondence with his family and especially with his mother reflects his sustained interest in family affairs and the well-being of relations. In it he also displays the enthusiasm of a young man for collecting memorabilia and a concern for sartorial proprieties which never quite left him even in later life. But continually breaking through these comfortable and domestic concerns is the reality of the first modern European war between nations. The work was both physically strenuous and nervously oppressive and his health began to suffer. Not for the last time in his career, he found that relief work entailed a considerable strain on his health. The experience, however, was personally satisfying and obviously uplifting morally: as Vincent came face to face with deprivation and misery inflicted by man on man he found a purpose and sense of commitment. His resulting enthusiasm was sufficiently infectious for Brackley to volunteer as a convoy agent, operating from St Malo after 11 February 1871. The experience of witnessing the effects of invasion at close quarters had another effect on Vincent. It led him to accept the responsibilities of service and he joined the Middlesex militia as a lieutenant on 9 September 1871. It may be doubted, however, whether he ever found the role of part-time soldier congenial as his letters to his wife during 1878 show. Indeed, he found himself in increasing embarrassment as the Eastern Crisis steadily developed and Prime Minister Disraeli prepared to call out the reserves. He resigned from the militia in May 1878.

The Vincent who returned to London in April 1871 was more mature, more compassionate and more rounded. He obviously relished independent action and thrived on the opportunity to take responsibility and make decisions free from the enmeshment of the red tape he so dreaded. His organizational capacities and powers of leadership were emerging and his innate tact and diplomatic skills were developing. His particular combination of qualities had found a natural outlet and he was to devote much of his time and nervous energy during the next fifteen years to relief work in foreign wars.

The immediate cause of the Franco-Prussian War had been the search for a king for the Spanish throne, vacant since the expulsion of Queen Isabel II in October 1868. Within Spain the vacant throne had consequences no less profound than the war itself. Isabel had had to fight for her throne between 1833 and 1840 against her uncle Don Carlos and his Carlist supporters. After 1868 his successor and grandson Don Carlos de Borbón Austria-Este believed the moment had come. His cause was pressed in newspapers and periodicals, his picture widely distributed, and his claims advanced as the champion of traditional Spanish values. The interim military government of General Juan Prim, however, selected Prince Amadeo, second son of the King of Italy. His reign lasted two years, ending in his abdication in February 1873. By then the Carlist forces were in open rebellion as their initial expectations of a peaceful accession for Carlos through parliamentary elections in 1871 and 1872 were dashed, it was claimed, by electoral management. In April 1872 Carlos decided to fight.[10]

In the ensuing war there were few major engagements but many skirmishes. The centre of Carlist support was in the Basque Provinces and Navarre, with outposts in Catalonia. Carlist support from France was important, for the common frontier permitted the relatively free flow of arms and money. Bayonne, centre of France's Basque district, acted as a Carlist organizational centre, and Vincent travelled regularly to and from France. Despite the ideologies involved, it was a very modern war, technically and militarily speaking. The Carlists organized a miniature modern state within the confines of the Basque Provinces where they cast cannon and made ammunition at the Eibar foundaries, ran a postal service, and printed money. They fought the war with modern armaments and according to the rules of modern strategy. This aspect of the war attracted the attention of many foreign observers and explains the presence of so many Englishmen, mostly army officers, on or near the Franco-Spanish frontier. It was far more humane and 'civilized' than the first war, despite the occasional ferocity of the fighting. In some ways the belligerents of 1872–6 treated each other with a degree of mutual consideration and respect which contrasted strongly with Vincent's later experience in other wars, most notably in the Balkans where savagery, inflamed by religious zeal, went far beyond that seen elsewhere. In the Carlist Wars the task of looking after the wounded and sick was mostly carried out by the religious orders, such as the Brethren of San Juan de Dios or the Sisters of St Vincent de Paul. Patronage and fund-raising became fashionable among the upper classes. The Duchess of Medinaceli presided over the Red Cross, while, on the other side, Doña Margarita, Don Carlos's wife, showed an untiring interest in the welfare of hospital inmates cared for by the rival society La Caridad.

On the outbreak of war in 1872 the National Aid Society felt unable to assist in what was a civil war and thus a society was formed in England and, apparently, in France, with the object of helping in the care and hospitalization of the wounded in both sides. It was to be supported by voluntary contributions and by the disinterested assistance of its members, and took the name Society for the Relief of the Sick and Wounded of the Spanish War. Vincent became one of its representatives at the battlefront. Very little documentation exists about it, but its unpublished Final Report of the Executive Committee has partly survived in proof form. Together with the letters, it permits some informed guesses as to its membership, activities and finances. Some names suggest business families engaged in trade between Spain and England, such as the chairman, Manuel Misa, Cristóbal and A. de Murrieta Carlos de Larrea and Señor Quintana of Santurce, and Mme de los Heros, who ran a hospital for government soldiers in Castro Urdiales. A Mr Batters, owner of the ship *Somorrostro* normally used for the export of iron ore from Bilbao, lent his ship for the transport of wounded men and for the ferrying of medical and hospital supplies such as mattresses, blankets and furniture between Biarritz and wherever they were needed. Vincent and his friend Allen Young[11] were the two most active and dedicated representatives of the Society at the front. As there is no list of the Society's subscribers and agents, it is often impossible to distinguish between its members and the many helpers and co-workers from other institutions who were also engaged in ambulance work with the Society's men. Vincent's two closest associates at Yrache in the Carlist camp, Monsieur Guillaume Bourgade, a French legitimist, and the priest Don Manuel Barrena, director of the hospital, were both in the service of La Caridad, the Carlist counterpart of the Red Cross.

The Society's money was spent on relief operations and the exchange of prisoners and often on substantial donations to sister societies like the Madrid Red Cross or the French *Comité des Secours aux Blessés Espagnols*. Its finances seem to have been very sound. In September 1874, for instance, the total subscriptions received amounted to £6,218 and £699 still remained. It was only at the very end of the war, when Vincent wrote anguished letters to his friends asking them for a few pounds to keep the hospital at Lesaca going for a short time, that money appears to have run short.

Vincent made three visits to the scene of war, the first between April and May 1874, the second between October 1874 and May 1875 and the third between September 1875 and May 1876. As befitted his greater prominence as compared with his role during the Franco-Prussian War, he now had to write reports to the Society in London, extracts of which are included here. He also kept a fragmentary diary in note form for his own use. Also in 1870 and 1871 he found time to keep up a correspondence mainly with his mother and with various friends. Also included in the present collection are letters to his wife from Madrid when he revisited Spain in more peaceful circumstances in 1887. For the first time during this war Vincent also began to indulge his favourite pastime of sketching, contributing drawings of military scenes to *The Illustrated London News*, *The Graphic* and *Le Monde Illustré* of Paris. He was to sketch while in the Balkans between 1876 and 1878. This interest in novelty and science was another of Vincent's characteristics and led him to his passionate interest in ballooning.

Vincent left Spain in May 1876 and scarcely set foot in England before being drawn into the Balkan crisis which began in 1875 with local uprisings in Bosnia and Hercegovina. As Ottoman forces strove to put down the revolt, others thought the end of the Ottoman Empire was at hand, in particular Bulgarian nationalists based in Moldavia and Wallachia, the modern Romania. The insurrection they inspired in the Rhodope mountains in May 1876 provoked an excessively violent Turkish reaction. Short of regular troops, the Ottoman authorities resorted to irregular local muslim militias, known as Bashi-bazuks, whose fanatical response was massacre and pillage as they toured the region seeking insurrectionists. Events in Bosnia, Hercegovina and the Rhodope mountains fired the ambitions of Prince Milan who governed the autonomous province of Servia. Eager to take advantage of the situation and under the strong promptings of Russian pan-slavic officers such as Chernaiev he declared war on 18 June 1876. His government lacked money and his army of untrained peasant conscripts unenthusiastic for war was short of officers. Initial success ended in early July when Ottoman forces rallied and from then until the final collapse on 17 October the Servian position became increasingly desperate.[12]

Scarcely surprisingly medical facilities were almost totally lacking. Writing from Belgrade in February as the war momentum increased, the British consul noted 'nothing has been done as yet either as regards commissariat or ambulances' and while Milan's government adhered to the Geneva Convention in April 1876 the outbreak of war starkly revealed the inadequacies of the Servian medical system. In July, Consul White reported some two thousand wounded and a great need for medical appliances and surgeons and in August an English cleric, the Revd Hopkins of Trinity Hall, visited the battlefield and reported on the appalling conditions of the Servian field hospitals.[13]

By then knowledge of the situation had aroused a response in Britain. The lead was taken by the Order of St John, a number of whose members gathered at Lechmere's house where they met two long-time charitable workers in Servia, Miss Irby and Miss Johnston.[14] These ladies had already begun to collect funds from their own friends and acquaintances and this formed the nucleus of the subscription list of the Eastern War Sick and Wounded Relief Fund, set up at the July meeting. Vincent, fresh from his experiences in Spain, became one of the two honorary secretaries. A public meeting was organized for 15 August at which an appeal was launched. At that meeting Loyd-Lindsay reluctantly agreed to involve the National Aid Society which would provide £20,000 from its reserves. Having made this commitment, he moved rapidly to take over the whole operation. On 16 August the National Aid Society proposed the creation of a joint executive committee on which two-thirds of the places would be taken by its representatives. Vincent's brief period as secretary thus came to an end, although he and his fellow officers of the Eastern Fund were able to state quite truthfully that it was their initiative which provoked the National Aid Society into action. They had also used the money raised by the Misses Irby and Johnston to send to Servia a body of surgeons and dressers including Dr Laseron, an honorary associate of the Order of St John, and seven surgeons. Responsibility for supporting these was assumed by the new committee.

The ending of his secretarial function freed Vincent to undertake work probably more congenial to him. The new Turco-Servian Relief Committee sent out its own party at the end of August. Loyd-Lindsay went himself as chief commissioner, taking with him a private secretary and an aide-de-camp. The sad history of disputes in Belgrade and criticisms of Loyd-Lindsay there and in Britain suggests his presence was at best unhelpful. He arrived with the reputation of being pro-Turkish and seems to have viewed his role as essentially political. His strong pro-Turkish and anti-Russian opinions were reflected in the letters cited in his biography which mention medical relief work only perfunctorily. On his return he made strongly anti-Russian public speeches.[15] Much more important and significant were the six additional surgeons and the party of deaconesses from Laseron's Tottenham Deaconesses' Institution who went out. Vincent was appointed Director of Transport Services. Absent mostly from Belgrade, he avoided the ill-will and acrimony which Loyd-Lindsay quickly attracted.

While in Servia, Vincent kept a notebook in which he made periodic jottings on which he drew when compiling his official reports. Extracts are included from letters to the secretary of the committee in London and to a close friend Fleetwood Sandeman, soon to become Vincent's brother-in-law. His activities and the difficulties confronting him are vividly portrayed. Most of his time was spent in the creation and oversight of a system of transportation of the wounded from the battlefield to hospital facilities far in the rear. It involved almost continual travelling over roads little better than tracks. There were no sprung carts for the wounded and great difficulties in the securing and maintaining of a supply of animals. Vincent developed a system of river barges equipped with medical facilities which took the wounded from Semendria, the modern Smederevo, to Belgrade. It was no sinecure, and at times Vincent's good humour deserted him when confronted by oafishness, drunkenness and mere obdurate obstruction. Yet he remained free of rancour and unconcerned for his personal safety. His ability to establish good working relations with different nationalities, to avoid tedious moralizing and to ignore discomfort were in striking contrast to Loyd-Lindsay.

With the armistice in October, Vincent agreed to cross the frontline to seek out and offer assistance to Servian prisoners in Ottoman hands. Such missions across battlelines were something of a speciality of his whether during the Franco-Prussian War, in Spain or, later, in the Servo-Bulgarian War. On this occasion the principal danger lay in the terrible difficulties of travel in the Balkans in winter. After completing this mission, he joined the prominent philanthropist Lady Strangford who was active in organizing relief on the Turkish side. Together they visited the sites of Bashi-bazuk atrocities, especially Batak, the scene of the worst incidents and required viewing for foreign travellers. During this period he kept a diary, part of which has survived. In it he recorded the real perils he encountered, which he consistently played down in his letters home to his mother in which he laid stress on the romantic aspects of his experiences. After leaving Lady Strangford he made his way to Constantinople and home.

The deepening crisis between the Russian and Ottoman Empires compelled the latter to seek foreign assistance in making good its deficiencies which included medical facilities.[16] Captain Herbert, who volunteered to join the Ottoman army in the spring and who fought at Plevna, noted the medical organization was practically non-existent in peacetime and was hastily improvised when the need arose. Frantic efforts were made to recruit foreign surgeons. The process was haphazard. C.S. Ryan was given a perfunctory interview by the son of the Ottoman ambassador in London before being signed on at the age of twenty-one. He knew no Turkish and only a little German. He needed the money, was attracted by the adventure and liked to travel. He went out in a party which included George Stoker who had served with the Ottoman forces during the Servian campaign. In his case there is little doubt as to the attractions: the lure of the exotic East, harems, slaves. His memoirs may have been spiced for his Victorian audience and his brother was Bram Stoker, playwright, actor-

Dr George Stoker

manager and creator of Dracula. Yet there must be a question mark over the real value of such recruits. Men like Ryan were still apprentices, learning their craft. As he himself later admitted:

I will candidly confess that if I had possessed my present knowledge at that time, and if I had had command of all the best appliances, I could have saved many lives which unfortunately flickered out.

Ryan was competent, Stoker was not. His medical treatment of Vincent as shown in the letters was not encouraging. In his own memoirs he records an event which did him little credit. After bemoaning at length the lack of medical skill of native doctors and belittling their notions of diet and hospital order, he commented:

I took the knife and was going to cut, when the chief of the hospital stopped me, saying –
'You will tie the arteries.'
I said, 'No, it is my case. I am going to amputate.'
He replied that he would not allow me to do so. 'Vous n'êtes pas capable.'

He spent his time treating fevers and skin diseases and dysentery and complaining about not being paid or receiving travelling expenses. Ryan cast serious doubt on the value of many foreign recruits. He recalled one with especial loathing:

> he had spoiled his life and ruined his chances with drink. He was the most awful drunkard I have ever met. In fact, he was never sober, and in his habits he was perfectly filthy.

Other nations provided recruits as unimpressive. Herbert found at Widdin:

> a small, crooked, shabby, spectacled German surgeon, Doctor Schmidt by name, who looked withered and broken down and somewhat pathetic. He wore as yet his threadbare civilian attire, as they could not find a uniform sufficiently small for him.

Paradoxically the best surgeons were often natives. Herbert found the best one at Plevna to be a Bulgarian doctor from Sofia, who, as a loyal muslim, had established a hospital at his own and his friends' expense. The best surgeon Ryan met was a Turk, while Williams at Kars had nothing but praise for the Turkish hospital there while being contemptuous of the performance of the foreign, mainly German, doctors who he commented 'skimp their work' while receiving pay and status higher than those of an Ottoman colonel.[17] Such skilled native talent was, however, in short supply and the Turks were compelled to accept whatever foreigners came forward regardless of whether they were getting value for money.

The British societies took considerable trouble to avoid recruiting unsuitable personnel. The key figure in the process was William Mac-Cormac, who acted as agent for the National Aid Society and also for the Stafford House Committee. His distinguished career, which later took him to the offices of President of the Royal College of Surgeons between 1896 and 1900 and honorary sergeant-surgeon to King Edward VII at the time of his death in 1901, was underway when he first became drawn into the National Aid Society in 1870. Using his position as surgeon and lecturer at St Thomas's Hospital, with which Florence Nightingale was associated, he selected surgeons for its work in the Franco-Prussian War and later acted in a similar capacity for the Eastern War Committee in 1876 and for Stafford House, on which committee he also served. Like so many others he was also a member of the Order of St John, whose principal medical officer he subsequently became. He recruited two rather different categories of surgeons. Some were experienced practitioners willing to leave well-established consulting rooms for a period of charitable work. Others were either unregistered, having just completed their training, or men who had been registered within the past year. For them the experience must have been valuable and to judge from their later careers and addresses of their practices it was no hindrance to professional development.[18] In addition, the societies offered pay and travelling expenses which were generous. By far the largest items in the published accounts of the societies were the salaries paid to doctors. Of the total expenditure of the National Aid Society in the Turco-Servian War, for example, thirty-one per cent went on the wages and allowances of its employees while in the later Servo-Bulgarian operation it amounted to nearly twenty-nine per cent.

The work of the local commissioner of a British charitable committee was a serious and responsible one, involving the oversight of personnel and the control of supplies provided from Britain or obtained locally. It also carried a heavy financial responsibility as the commissioner had to account for monies expended in circumstances of turmoil and confusion, in which exact accounting was difficult and the securing of receipts troublesome. It speaks much for the growing reputation which Vincent enjoyed that he was to return to Constantinople in this capacity. The weight of his duties was later noted by the English Chapter of the Order of St John, which congratulated him:

> Although he was assisted by a very efficient staff, Mr. Kennett's labour and responsibility were of no ordinary nature, as may be realized from the fact that during the year which has elapsed since June last [1877] he has carried out the organization and direction of hospitals in no less than nine places in European Turkey and Asia, as well as field ambulances, a sanitary service, and the railway transport.[19]

These services were rendered to an *ad hoc* organization brought into being by the escalating crisis which aroused strong passions in Britain.

As the National Aid Society procrastinated, in December 1876 the Duke of Sutherland invited some friends to his London home at Stafford House where they agreed to set up a committee to raise money to ease suffering among the Turkish troops. Membership of the Stafford House Committee was a roll call of leading peers, distinguished soldiers and sailors and men associated with existing charitable organizations, such as Sir Edmund Lechmere and Dr MacCormac. It launched a public appeal and created its own independent administration. This remained separate even after the National Aid Society belatedly launched its own parallel operation. It was to the Stafford House Committee that Vincent offered his services in the late spring. He was warmly welcomed and on 11 June set off back to Constantinople where he took over as commissioner, replacing the Ottoman dignatory Vefik Pasha who had hitherto represented the committee. There Vincent presided over the rapid expansion of its work and personnel which finally numbered eighty-two, with additional assistants. His work there was regularly reported to London and when the committee finally wound itself up his reports were published along with other papers in 1879.

Of Vincent's private letters only those from February and March 1878 remain. Historically and personally, however, they were probably the most interesting in the collection. Vincent was at the centre of momentous events when the Ottoman empire seemed about to disintegrate and Britain and Russia were on the brink of war. The letters cover the events leading up to and including the Peace of San Stefano on 3 March 1878. They also date from the weeks immediately following Vincent's marriage on 19 January 1878 to Alicia Sandeman. The combination of love letters with moving accounts of human misery is very touching.

His marriage brought him into the ranks of the important wine producing and shipping family of Sandeman. The firm had been founded in 1790 by George Sandeman, who continued to control it until his death in 1841 when he was succeeded as head of the firm by his nephew George Glas Sandeman who died in 1868, aged seventy-six. His youngest daughter, born in 1848 was Alicia, Vincent's bride and known to him as Alice. Though her father was dead, her English mother, referred to by Vincent with the appropriately Spanish title of *madre*, was still alive and she and other members of the extensive Sandeman family were often mentioned in Vincent's letters. He was closest to Fleetwood, Alice's brother. It is unclear how he and the Sandeman family had met, but Vincent and Alice had at one time been neighbours in Oxfordshire where the Kennett home had been sufficiently close to that of the Sandemans at Chislehampton for Alice to ride over to meet him in the fields. By the late 1870s the Sandemans were firmly etablished in their London home at 15 Hyde Park Gardens and they also owned a substantial part of Hayling Island. Vincent was thus brought into a family far wealthier than the Kennetts and it was Alice's money which provided for him and their children. There is every indication that Vincent was conscious of this and rather uneasy about it.

Immediately after his wedding Vincent returned to Constantinople but in fulfilment of his undertaking to his wife's family he did not take Alice with him. Instead, she settled at Menton in southern France until such time as the situation would enable her to join him. The separation was to prove increasingly painful to Vincent. Initially he put on a brave face but the pressures of loneliness grew until he felt unable to accept the situation. The

Vincent with his wife, Alice

letters he wrote to Alice reveal Vincent's romantic streak and show a tender solicitude for the smaller matters of personal, private business which mingles with descriptions of life in Constantinople and comments on public affairs. As was his usual habit, he played down the dangers in which he found himself although they must have been considerable. Alongside the problems of securing accommodation suitable to a European lady and the appropriateness of first or second class cabins on board steamers for personal maids are references to the outbreak of cholera and its ravages, and reflections of the tensions arising from the proximity of Russian armies and from the presence of the British fleet in Besika Bay. Always present was the flood of diseased and destitute Muslim refugees from the European territories of the Ottoman Empire, whose administration had virtually collapsed under the strains. Vincent found doing business with Turkish officials decidedly difficult. Not only were they demoralized, they were venal, too.

Despite these preoccupations, Vincent found time to write to Alice almost daily and at times twice a day. He included with his letters little gifts in the form of books, examples of local dress, the wrappings of bonbons dedicated to her by his fellow-diners, small parcels of her favourite sweetmeats (sent by a trusted messenger) and violets upon which he had slept. The latter was perhaps the most unexpected demonstration of the impact of marriage and separation on him. The reader may detect a slight awkwardness in manner when Vincent came to express his feelings but that may well have been due to his desire not to express them too fully, and he was certainly not above a little flattery. But once his guard was down and he dropped the constraint and artifice he could be painfully open and direct.

Like most Europeans in the Ottoman Empire, Vincent lived a life isolated socially from the great majority of native peoples, with whom he came into contact only in matters of business. He moved in a relatively narrow social circle, whether dining on board the yacht of wealthy visitors or at the Club, whether meeting the wives of members of the local diplomatic and naval community or whether seeking out a place of residence for himself and for Alice. It was this, no doubt, which led him to urge Alice that, while she should severely restrict her baggage, she should include one or two good dresses suitable for dining out and her diamonds, as well as her saddle and all her riding equipment.

With Alice settled at Therapia, there was no need for further letters. They were to remain to oversee the gradual winding down of the Stafford House Committee's operations before leaving by ship on 5 June 1878, ending two year's work in the Balkans. He was not to be involved in work on the battlefield for a further six and a half years. However, his Balkan activities had brought him into the public eye and were probably the most important he undertook. Typically, he himself exercised a self-denying ordinance and did not rush into print as did so many of the other British volunteers in the Balkans. But he flits through the pages of their memoirs. The twenty-one-year-old Lieutenant Salusbury who had never seen active service and volunteered to fight with the Servians met Vincent amid the mud in the disorder of retreat in October 1876:

> Kennett jumped out to greet us. How could he keep so neat and tidy? I wondered, for he was just as well dressed as he would be at home.[20]

The war correspondent Frederick Villiers remembered a different aspect of Vincent. When he came to write his memoirs he recalled being persuaded to conduct a less than satisfactory Servian servant of Vincent back to his home. He regretted being swayed by Vincent's eloquence just as he was 'rather irritated' when Vincent told him that Hafez Pasha, the Turkish commandant at Alexinatz, had threatened to hang *The Graphic*'s correspondent. The intrepid Villiers took the threat seriously and it made him edgy, in contrast to the light made by Vincent of the dangers amid which he worked.[21] Indeed his unostentatious bravery, personal neatness and modesty allied with his powers of persuasion and formidable physical energy made him extraordinarily good at his self-imposed duties.

The outburst of charitable relief characteristic of the 1870s in Britain brought with it a multitude of public appeals and the emergence of dominant, not to say domineering personalities who saw their operations in personal terms and who wished to have sole control, with the minimum of accountability, over the disbursements of the monies and resources donated by a charitable public. Such activities became an extension of their combative personalities and the suffering their personal property. Unlike others engaged in relief work in the Balkans, such as Lady Strangford, Miss Irby, the Quaker James Long or American missionaries,[22] Vincent recognized the need for co-operative endeavour and combined it with an absence of public self-assertiveness and vain glory. He was well aware that others did not share this catholicity of outlook, as is shown by his obvious pleasure and surprise in July 1877 when he wrote from Constantinople:

> All the societies, the National Aid, Red Crescent, Stafford House, and Lord Blantyre's surgeons, are working hand in hand. It is the first time I have seen so much good feeling and sensible cooperation, from which immense benefits for the great end, the good of the wounded, will inevitably result.

This plea for co-operation and mutual assistance became his personal crusade. Within two months in 1879 he was able to repeat it as *the* lesson to be learned by all involved in relief work. In his forward to the published report of the Stafford House Committee he wrote of 'the great advantage of establishing a principle of co-operation in the work of voluntary societies' as being one of the keys to successful operations. Speaking to the General Assembly of the Knights of St John of Jerusalem he commented:

> I also wish to call attention to the great advantage of a principle of co-operation in the work of voluntary societies, exactly opposed to that of exclusiveness and jealousy.[23]

His own commitment to the principle is well illustrated by the praise of those most unforgiving critics, the members of other charitable relief organizations, as well as by others on the spot. Lady Strangford's appeal to him speaks for itself and she was not the only one to look to Vincent. He was ready in 1877 to co-operate with the Turkish Red Crescent despite his privately recorded doubts about that body, while in the crisis of 1878, with Constantinople flooded with refugees and the local medical services virtually collapsed, he was quick to ignore the strict terms of his remit, which limited Stafford House to the relief of wounded and suffering Ottoman soldiers. He lent surgeons and made resources available to the Turkish Compassionate Fund, set up to relieve civilian suffering.[24] His explanation in his reports does not ring very convincingly as an argument though there is no doubting the passionate sincerity of the sentiment which underlay it:

> There was no proper staff of medical men attending the mass of refugees in the mosques of Sultan Achmet and St Sofia; small-pox and typhoid fever were rapidly on the increase, and great epidemic of these diseases appeared imminent . . . [it] would be a terrible danger to the troops, as it would be sure to extend to them.

The newspaper correspondent Williams, attached to Mukhtar Pasha's army in Armenia, wrote of the terrible scenes of the retreat of the summer of 1877. If only, he lamented, someone of Vincent's ability and competence had been in charge at Constantinople they might have been averted.[25]

Vincent was well aware of the need to improvise and to make the best use of available resources, human or material. He did not spurn offers of help, neither was he blind to the weaknesses of collaborators. When Coope found himself unable to assume his duties as a colonel of Turkish gendarmerie he approached Vincent and offered his services to organize a field-stretcher system to provide first aid on the battlefield. He was encouraged and offered funds and medical staff if he could provide the men required for stretcher-bearing. Vincent himself 'took steps in a powerful quarter to have the matter brought before the Grand Vizier'[26] but the whole scheme came to nothing. His gift for judging men and for tactful direction was apparent in his handling of George Stoker whom he met when crossing the Balkan mountains in December 1876 *en route* to meeting up with Lady Strangford. Vincent's own experiences at the hands of the virtually untrained Stoker led him to utilize the latter's services in the summer of 1877, but not as a surgeon. Under Vincent's guidance, Stoker went to Adrianople to organize the transport of the wounded from Shipka and their distribution among the hospitals. In an unspoken tribute to Vincent's tact, nowhere in his memoirs did the fashionable and disputatious physician on the 1880s and '90s give any evidence of being aware of this tacit condemnation of his surgical skills.

Allied to this belief in co-operation and his readiness to improvise and utilize whatever lay to hand was a marked ability to put himself in the shoes of others. Nowhere was this sympathetic empathy shown better than in his report to the British ambassador about insults allegedly offered to British surgeons who entered the besieged fortress of Plevna with Shevket Pasha's column in September 1877. Vincent quietly rebuked their wounded vanity:

> Foreign Surgeons . . . entering a fortified position of the importance of Plevna in the middle of the night, and without previous notice being given of their arrival, must be prepared to put up with little annoyances . . . so trifling in comparison with the momentous events occuring around them.[27]

Not many British contemporaries were as ready to see the Turks' point of view. This imaginative insight made Vincent a forceful advocate. A rare glimpse of his persuasive talents was provided by Charles Ryan. He describes in his memoirs how, while recuperating in Constantinople, he was persuaded by Vincent to go to Erzerum to take charge of the ambulance work there. Offering better terms than the Turks, Vincent also proffered a free hand. Although Ryan declined, Vincent asked him not to make an absolutely final decision. Next morning while Ryan was still in bed Vincent returned with his deputy Stoney who had previously treated Ryan with the greatest kindness. They emphasized 'the condition in Erzeroum was desperate. The town was full of wounded men, and supplies of all

Dr Charles Ryan

kinds were urgently needed.' The combined appeal to pocket, personal obligation and professional pride had its effect and Ryan was on the noon boat that same day.[28] This tactful shrewdness recommended Vincent to British diplomats, while his reputation was enhanced by his quietly efficient and diplomatic administration of the Stafford House Committee's funds at Constantinople. Fife-Cookson, one of the additional military attachés at Constantinople, commented:

> From the very commencement of the War I had been struck by the very efficient organisation and working of this Society [the Stafford House Committee], the credit of which must be greatly attributed to Mr. Barrington Kennett.[29]

His reputation in the British Embassy must have been confirmed by his solicitude during the illness of the wife of another military attaché, Major Francis de Winton, whose life he was instrumental in saving. His work in Constantinople confirmed his reputation and laid the foundations for his two subsequent tours of duty with the National Aid Society, both of which gave ample opportunity for the display of his diplomatic skills.

In the interval of six and a half years between returning from Constantinople in 1878 and setting off for Suakin in March 1885 Vincent's career began to develop in new directions. His marriage had brought financial security, but Vincent evidently found his position difficult and was eager to carve out for himself and his wife an independent position in the world. He did not take up a legal career in earnest but instead branched out and became a free-lance business agent. He had already had some experience of the business world while serving on the commission for the Brussels Exhibition of 1876 and was to be a member of the commissions for the Melbourne Exhibition of 1887, the Paris Exhibition of 1889 and of the second Brussels Exhibition of 1898. By then he had become a man of affairs who served on committees in the uncertain world where the commercial ended and the official began. In 1883 his new business career was launched when he was elected to the London Chamber of Commerce, but as yet there was no stark division between his professional and his charitable activities.

In 1883 he also travelled to India on behalf of Edison's Indian and Colonial Electrical Company to encourage the development of electrification there and to interest the appropriate authorities in the Edison Company. In the occasional spare time available to him he took the chance to promote the St John Ambulance, but his visit was essentially a business one. He was away from February to April and as was his custom kept up a steady correspondence with Alice. The letters were purely private and are not reproduced here. They do, however, shed interesting light on various aspects of Vincent's personality and help illuminate his success in ambulance work. His organizational prowess rapidly surfaced. Spontaneously chosen by his fellow railway travellers as group treasurer for the journey across Europe he set about getting value for money. Typically he enjoyed the challenge, writing to Alice on 7 February:

I could not see why we should not get *hot* dinners in the sleeping car as well as cold ones. I took 12 francs off the joint dinner account of the car because it was cold the first day, and we were rewarded with three courses of warm, well cooked provisions the second! Great triumph and many thanks.

At Alexandria, he was once more chosen by his fellow travellers as 'the paymaster and arranger of the programme' of the group, while once in India he slipped into the role of leader of the small party of Edison representatives. His social skills too were deployed. He was skilful enough to perform creditably as a singer in amateur entertainments on board ship – and sensible enough to keep his talents under wraps whenever possible; he met a shockingly naughty child – and confirmed his liking for rogues, describing his encounter on 2 April:

I have made friends with a dear little girl of about 9, such a romp. She bites and scratches and does everything which she ought not to do, and of course in my perverse way I like her better than the good children.

As on his other trips, he kept a close interest in events at home. He was now closely involved in the work of his local St John Ambulance branch of which he was an instructor. While he was away Alice, a Lady of Grace in the Order, deputized for him. Family matters also concerned him and he deployed his formidable powers of charm and persuasion in the role of matchmaker, advising Alice on 16 March:

> You know how much I have Brackley's happiness at heart. I want *very much* to see him settled down and I only wish that I had pushed on his affair with Eleanor more. . . . Do not ask Eleanor on a visit until my return. I am determined to make a match of it if I can. . . . I have written to him what my wishes are, *if* he has a really old affection for Eleanor I hope that he will act on my letter . . .

He was to get his way, even though it took a further two years. His own career too received attention, as the possibilities of his securing a place on the Metropolitan Asylums Board were considered. He weighed the possible ways of achieving this in his letter of 31 March, deciding that it was unlikely that he could secure election by the Poor Law Guardians and opting instead to seek nomination by the President of the Local Government Board, the radical Liberal MP Sir Charles Dilke. Vincent decided to 'try to work it', and he did, being nominated by Dilke later that year.

In many ways the most interesting feature of his letters from India are the revelations of his personal doubts and insecurities. His trip was undertaken amid a sense of personal failure. He wrote to Alice on 27 February:

> I have been in some ways so unfortunate and to my own mind such a failure. . . . I am determined to devote myself more directly in making life more pleasant to you when I return though, God knows, that the chief aim in all I have at present undertaken has been that object. . . . Had I been successful, we ought by now to have been in a far more independent position . . .

and returned to the theme on 17 March, bemoaning his lack of success in adding 'to my share of the gold sovereigns with which comforts in life are bought' and continuing:

However I must not grumble as you must take the whole of a life to tell whether a man has been fortunate or not. . . . I feel that I owe a great deal to you, and I recognize it. A great deal of my struggling etc was perhaps owing to the feeling which prompted me to try and do more to be in a position to do something for you! I do not know whether this is a high feeling but to an independently minded man it is a natural one.

Perhaps this sense of personal deficiency added to Vincent's religious awareness which was heightened by his exposure to India. That he was religious is shown by his letters, but the nature of his commitment was clarified. His was a broad and tolerant faith, deprecating narrow sectarianism and suspicious of the exclusivity and dogmatism of Roman Catholicism. His letters reveal him poking quiet fun at both though his inherent tact prevented him from offending the strongly held religious beliefs of his Sandeman relations. To Alice he confided his belief in the efficacy of prayer as provocative of quite unexpected developments in everyday life. His, however, was a universal view of God. On 1 April he confined to Alice:

The Bishop [of Calcutta] is a very good man and an energetic worker. I only regret that his good example and blameless life should not do even more good if his views were on our broad basis. I feel so sure at times that it would be good to have some church where people of all religions could worship God in perfect simplicity, and pray to be kept from temptation and sins which their reason and education tell them are wrong. Hindoos, Christians and Mahommedans would meet in such a temple on a common humanitarian platform. They all agree that theft, immorality, lying, slandering, false witness are wrong; they all worship one God under different names. . . . I suppose that all these suggestions are really absurd and would only shock people. I should like to worship at such a temple and also to attend my own Church. I do not see that the two need necessarily clash.

This inherently warm and humane faith informed many aspects of Vincent's life and coloured his responses to appeals to place his skills at the disposal of the sick and wounded.

It is in the light of this that he responded to the last two calls upon him by the National Aid Society, setting aside his business work for the short but frantic interludes of the Sudan campaign and the Servo-Bulgarian War. The latter was to earn Vincent his knighthood, but the former was the most trying and disappointing of all his war relief activities. Both were to place considerable demands on his tact and finesse.

Egyptian control over the Sudan, first asserted by Mehmet Ali in the 1820s and enhanced after 1865, had led to increasing resentment under the guidance of locally influential religious figures. The most striking was Muhammad Ahmad, son of a carpenter, but convinced of his religious mission as mahdi or rightly guided leader of the faithful. By 1882 he had succeeded in putting together a religiously inspired movement of formidable proportions. In face of the mounting challenge to his authority Tawfiq, the Khedive of Egypt, sent an expeditionary force which was annihilated on 5 November 1883 south of Khartoum after which Egyptian officials and garrisons in the whole of the Sudan came under attack. By then the Khedive's independence had factually ended with the British bombardment of Alexandria in July 1882 and the destruction of the Egyptian army at Tel al-Kabir in September. British officials, in their role of advisers, effectively controlled Egyptian policy and the responsibility for framing a suitable response to the Mahdi fell on the Cabinet, advised by its officials in Cairo.

The ensuing muddled policy was based on the decision to withdraw Egyptian officials and garrisons from the Sudan, and in January 1884 a former Governor-General of the Sudan, General Charles Gordon, offered to go to Khartoum and was accepted. Gordon was one of the most glamorous of the late nineteenth-century imperialists. He had made his name in China between 1860 and 1865, when he had played the leading part in suppressing the Taiping uprising. Subsequently he served Ismail, Tawfiq's predecessor, as Governor of the Sudan between 1874 and 1879. He became the darling of the British public. Instructed to organize an orderly withdrawal from the Sudan, he decided to stay and to reassert British authority and prestige. He soon became a prisoner in Khartoum, cut off from Egypt by mahdist forces. By August 1884 the British Government under the pressure of popular clamour was forced to agree to the dispatch of an expeditionary force under the most prominent British general of the time, Sir Garnet Wolseley.[30]

The utter failure of the expedition to achieve its objective was to lead to serious political repercussions in Britain, but it was due in part at least to the dissensions and scarcely veiled animosities of the various British commanders. Disagreement centred about the best strategy to follow: whether the best line of advance was down the Nile or via the port of Suakin on the Red Sea and thence by the caravan route to the town of Berber on the Nile. This became a struggle between officers stationed in Egypt, virtually unanimous in their opinion that the Nile route was impracticable owing to the cataracts on the river, and Wolseley and his circle who, after a rapid and superficial review, adopted it. The former group favoured the Suakin–Berber route as shorter and more accessible. Wolseley remained sceptical of the merits of it and thought the Suakin field force a sideshow, a distraction from the real struggle. By the time it was sent it was February 1885, Gordon was dead and the Mahdi's forces in full spate. The original purpose was gone, but the weight of public fury in Britain at the perceived humiliation rendered impossible any immediate abandonment of the Sudan expedition. As the Nile route indeed proved slow and difficult, on 17 February 1885 the British Government signed a contract with the firm of Lucas and Aird for the construction of a standard gauge railway from Suakin to Berber.

The port of Suakin, with its population of about six thousand, already had a British military presence. Since 1882 British warships had periodically visited the harbour to strengthen the hands of the local Egyptian officials and the position of the British consul. In December 1883 command of the garrison had passed to a British officer while Herbert Chermside Pasha had been appointed civil governor. In October 1884 the latter was promoted to the post of Governor-General of the Red Sea Littoral and his place as civil governor of Suakin passed to General Fremantle. In March 1885 there assembled a force of over thirteen thousand to open the route to Berber and protect the railway construction teams. Command was once more given to Lieutenant General Sir Gerald Graham, proponent of the scheme and commander of the earlier, slighter force which had checked the mahdists in the vicinity of Suakin in February and March 1884. He arrived on 12 March as units of the Suakin Field Force began to assemble, drawn from the Indian as well as the British army and including a contingent of Australians from Queensland. The National Aid Society decided to send teams to both the Nile and Suakin and appointed Vincent as its commissioner to the latter. For a brief moment British public opinion focused on the remote spot.

It was an extremely delicate assignment. The military operation was suspect to the commanders of the Nile-based force and the commanders of the Suakin force were divided. Graham himself was a *bête noire* of Wolseley, whose protégé, General Sir John McNeill, commanded the British infantry brigade. Relations between the two men were poor. The climate was bad: hot and humid, the fetid atmosphere sapped resolve, shortened tempers and induced lassitude.[31] The harbour was difficult, its shoals and reefs a constant source of danger to shipping which had to travel over 720 miles from Suez. For the NAS contingent and for Vincent personally there were the treacherous reefs of personal feelings and professional judgement, no easier to negotiate. He had simultaneously to identify a satisfactory role for the NAS to play, thus justifying the decision to send the contingent, while avoiding giving offence to the Army Medical Department by suggesting it was inadequate. Despite his appreciation of the dangers and his well-known personal charm and tact Vincent ran onto those reefs. Significantly, the cause of the dissension was a press release by Loyd-Lindsay in which he misleadingly quoted from Vincent's dispatches to London. With the passage of time the trouble caused by what now seems an innocuous reference looks disproportionate. It can only be explained by the deep suspicions of the National Aid Society held by military medical men who thought it cast a slur on their professional capabilities, and by the personal animosity of many of those in authority toward Loyd-Lindsay.[32]

Symptomatic of the confusion of the expedition was the uncertainty over the name of the port. There was disagreement as to whether it was Suakin or Suakim and Vincent shared that uncertainty. Like them he was unclear as to the objectives of the operation and like the soldiers he found the climate increasingly trying. His usually generous attitude to those about him faltered under the strains and by May 1885 his letters spoke of them with a wholly untypical acerbity. For the first and last time he revealed his deeper opinions of others. There was one further, deeply personal factor. Vincent was about to become a father for the second time. His first child, Guy, had been born in 1883 and now Alice was expecting their second child. His absence during this period clearly caused Vincent considerable unease and he may have suffered from a guilty conscience as his duty to his wife conflicted with the duties freely assumed toward the sick and wounded. He seems to have gone to Suakin under the impression that he could get back in time for the birth and his letters suggest he had so promised Alice. He was in fact still away when his daughter was born on 15 May. The event moved him to verse: certainly not great verse, but an unexpected literary effusion repeated neither before nor after. Despite his obvious attraction to the name Desiree, and his efforts to insinuate the name in Alice's mind, the girl was named Leila Winifred Leonor.

The NAS contingent with the Suakin Field Force was small. It consisted of five surgeons, the choice of whom, by the ubiquitous Sir William McCormac, Vincent criticized, two nursing sisters who soon went back to Britain accompanying the war wounded, a clerk whose unsuitability he lamented but who was his own choice, and two other servants. In addition, there was Sir Allen Young, mysteriously appointed 'Commissioner afloat'. The explanation of the latter is far from obvious. It may have owed something to his friendship with Lord Charles Beresford, the commander of the Royal Navy's detachment on the Nile and Wolseley's aide-de-camp, who was a fellow Conservative MP of Loyd-Lindsay, and more to Sir Allen's ownership of a steam yacht, the *Stella*, on which he travelled to Suakin and which he was expected to use for the Society's needs. The potential problems latent in the appointment of two commissioners did not materialize as Vincent was a friend of long standing and able to work with him. He was not a great asset, however. His yacht was but little used, he suffered from dysentery and Vincent was unable to pass on to him much of the administrative burden. The whole incident illustrated the casual inconsequentiality of much of the organization of the still evolving National Aid Society.

Vincent was appointed on 6 March and travelled by rail via Brindisi and steamer to Cairo where he met all the significant figures in the government of Egypt. He also met the Khedive, Tawfiq, whose domestic quarters he penetrated when he visited the Princess Nasri. His approach to informing Alice was typical of his indirect manner, first alluding to his visit and giving a fuller description later once the ground was prepared. From Cairo he travelled to Suakin via Suez, mainly on an Egyptian tramp steamer. That voyage produced one of the most delightful of all the letters, written, as so many were, in daily instalments and posted as a whole from Suakin. Pulsing with life, it reflected Vincent's lively response to his surroundings, half fascinated, half repelled, capturing the moment as in a short story. Once at Suakin, he plunged into a busy round of organization, unwisely relying on his self-proclaimed immunity from heat until going down with a mild form of sunstroke as a result of excessive hours spent out of doors. His health indeed underwent a serious strain, until on the eve of his departure in early June he collapsed with what seems to have been heat exhaustion. He was to spend much of the time between his arrival and departure planning ways to hand over his supplies and to organize affairs so as to be able to leave as soon as possible. In fact he was unable to do so until 5 June.

By the time Vincent arrived, the heavy fighting was over and a sense of futility progressively engulfed the force, well illustrated in his letters. It is not clear whether the decision to evacuate the Sudan, announced in Parliament on 21 April, was known at Suakin, but by the end of the month it was apparent that all enthusiasm for the fighting had gone. The arrival of Lord Wolseley in early May was eagerly awaited. There was little to do and the activity that did occur was scrappy and inconsequential. For Vincent his work was little more than that of a commissary sergeant and a porter and he obviously found it unrewarding to be restricted to the counting and handling of stores. His spirits soared when he could visit the front to spend time with the troops there, even if there was no action. He too welcomed

Wolseley's recommendation of the withdrawal of the bulk of the forces, leaving only a small garrison at Suakin, yet despite his readiness to be off he was in fact among the last to go. The evacuation began on 17 May with the departure under a cloud of General Graham, whose handling of the fighting was criticized by Wolseley and his friend McNeill, and of the Brigade of Guards and the Australian contingent. Between 20 and 21 May the majority of the force followed them, leaving only a small contingent of British and a somewhat larger one of Indian troops.

It had been a short and unpleasant little campaign. The fighting had been desultory but quite sanguinary, with relatively high casualty rates. Most of the engagements were guerilla attacks on small, isolated parties or at night on encamped soldiers. The whirlwind surprise attacks of Uthman Digna's forces and their equally sudden disappearances resulted in desperate close-quarter engagements as at the battle of McNeill's zariba on 22 March. Vincent noted on 6 May that it was hard to see heavily equipped British troops catching Uthman Digna. 'Certainly no great army, struggling slowly through thorny scrub in its cumbersome square formation, could catch and destroy such darting raiders.'[33] Some of the measures taken to try to combat this mode of attack are mentioned in the letters. In the light of this, it was reckless of Vincent to agree to ride back alone to Suakin from a forward post, in the late afternoon, for a distance of ten miles. His admission to carrying his revolver at the ready shows he knew this perfectly well. His attempts to explain it away were unconvincing and it is clear that he repented such foolhardy behaviour. This and other journeys to the advance posts were, however, a break from the tedium of life in a military encampment suffused by lack of purpose. Small wonder that the most useful activity of the National Aid Society was the provision of newspapers and other recreational aids.

To the tedium and sense of futility had to be added strains in his personal relations. These were new, for in previous and subsequent assignments he had always found his associates not uncongenial. Dr Newby he found distasteful and embarrassing, without ever quite explaining exactly what it was which caused this reaction in him. He recognized the man's professional merit and presence of mind, and it was Newby who saved him from a nasty accident on board the *Calabria*. Yet despite Vincent's broadmindedness and relative freedom from the snobberies of his time and class, even he was prone to look for 'gentlemanly' qualities and displayed a certain aloofness in dealings with those identified as social inferiors. Dr Newby failed on both counts.[34] Some army oficers, too, Vincent found uneasy company, especially engineers. Indeed, he was clearly disappointed in many of the British with whom he came into contact. Newby was not a gentleman, Burrell whom he specifically asked Alice to seek out from his bankers Cocks Biddulph turned out to be both lazy and incompetent while Dr Squire was jealous of Newby and refused to work under him. Add to that disappointment with General Ewart, whom Vincent thought a time-server, and with British sailors who, like the General, thought only of personal advantage, and the disillusion was complete. It was the only time Vincent was active in a campaign involving British forces and it brought him a timely reminder that what was for him an heroic hobby with a noble purpose was to others work for which they were hired and for which they expected reward. As a last straw came the letters to the *Standard* levying allegations against the National Aid Society. For the first and last time he lost his temper. As the letters were anonymous there was little he could do, but they showed that Britons, and even British officers, were not necessarily gentlemen. He left Suakin in an unhappy frame of mind.

There was to be only a short interlude before he was recruited once more, this time to return to the Balkans. The settlement imposed by Russia at San Stefano and modified by the Powers at the Conference of Berlin had within it the seeds of trouble. The dispositions made in respect of 'Bulgaria' were particularily suspect. The large, independent state created at San Stefano was divided into the small principality of Bulgaria and the province of Eastern Roumelia. The former became an autonomous, self-governing principality under the suzerainty of the Ottoman Sultan, while the latter remained within the Ottoman Empire but under the inspective oversight of the Powers who undertook to ensure the good treatment by the Ottoman authorities of all their Roumelian subjects. The emergence of the new, Christian, Bulgaria aroused the suspicions and jealousies of Milan, now King of independent Servia. The two countries had conflicting territorial ambitions in the region of the Ottoman Empire known as Macedonia, inhabited by an ethnic mix, inextricably intermingled. The two states were also the focus of Great Power rivalries. Milan was the friend of the Dual Monarchy and drew closer to it during the 1880s, becoming the Habsburgs' closest Balkan client. The new Bulgaria owed its existence to Russia who devised its constitution and provided its first government. The election of the German Prince Alexander of Battenberg as Prince of Bulgaria reflected this close relationship, for he was the cousin of Tsar Alexander III and had served in the Russian armies in the Russo-Turkish War. Relations between him and his Romanov kinsman soon became strained, and the tactless behaviour of Russians in Bulgaria, many of them officers in the Bulgarian army whose Minister of War until September 1883 was the Russian General Kaulbars, led to increasing tension. Alexander was both determined and ambitious and his attempts to lessen Russian influence and extend his *de facto* control over government and armed forces alienated the Tsarist Government. By mid-1885 he was openly at odds with the Russians who were intriguing against him, while he enjoyed the sympathy and esteem of Britain and Germany.[35] Against this background of growing internal pressure within both Bulgaria and Servia a coup took place on 18 September 1885 at Philippopolis, capital of Eastern Roumelia. The Bulgarian Government ritualistically denied involvement or prior knowledge but no-one believed it and its own rapid response suggested advance planning. By the end of the month Bulgarian forces had concentrated in Roumelia ready to meet an Ottoman military response which never came. The challenge to the Bulgarian action came not from Constantinople but from Belgrade.

The crisis of mid-September found King Milan on holiday in Budapest, from where he was able to make easy contact with the Government of the Dual Monarchy, travelling to Vienna for discussions. Servia mobilized its army and talked of the need to re-establish the Balkan balance of power and secure compensation. It was generally assumed that compensation would come from the Ottoman Empire and that Servia would demand historic 'Old Servia', the district around Kossovo then part of Macedonia. By the second week of October it had become clear that the Servians intended an attack on Bulgaria, whose capital Sofia lay close to the Servian frontier, separated from it by the strategically important Dragoman Pass. Despite this, and despite the delay of a month before the Servian attack was launched, Alexander and his army remained in southern Roumelia and the defence of the Servian frontier was left to ill-trained, ill-equipped and hastily assembled levies.

The Servian army attacked on 14 November. Initially successful, little stood between them and Sofia but thanks to the heroic efforts of small Bulgarian forces they were sufficiently delayed to permit Alexander to return with the bulk of his army. Checked, the Servian forces began a retreat which quickly turned into collapse as in October 1876 before the Turks. By the last week in November Milan was ready for peace but his efforts to secure international backing for an imposed armistice were not immediately successful. It was not until the end of the month, with the Bulgarian forces at Pirot in Servia, that international intervention secured a suspension of hostilities.

War found the combattants ill-prepared for the sick and wounded. The Servians at least had their experiences of 1876 to guide them and had learnt sufficient to make some advance preparations, though on an inadequate scale. The Servian Red Cross began to make extensive purchases of medicines and other requirements in Vienna at the end of September, securing there the services of volunteers from among young doctors and medical students. The continuing friendly attitude at Vienna was further demonstrated a month later, when the Servian Red Cross tried to borrow ambulance carts. Rebuffed by the Hungarians at Budapest, where the Red Cross organization declined to aid one side only, it succeeded at Vienna. Once the fighting began, the Servians asked for doctors and medical assistance from the Dual Monarchy on 22 November. The next day both the Vienna Red Cross and the Austrian Order of the Knights of Malta announced they were sending aid to Servia.[36] There were no similar preparations in Bulgaria. The Bulgarian Red Cross was only founded in the last week of October 1885 and it had to improvise as best it could with the help of the foreign community at Sofia. They did so with determination and a success on which Vincent commented. Among others, the British Agent and Consul General at Sofia, Frank Lascelles, was notably active, collecting funds to assist the hospitals which mushroomed. On 21 November his sister, Mary Lascelles, wrote to *The Times* appealing on behalf of her brother for money for the Bulgarian Red Cross. Four days later a second appeal was made by Malcolm Maccoll, the secretary of the pro-Servian and pro-Bulgarian Society for the Relief of the Wounded in the War against the Turks which had been set up in 1876. He now proposed that the unexpended balances be used as the nucleus of a new appeal for the current conflict. Simultaneously with this renewal of the charitable impulse in Britain came a public appeal by the Red Cross in Germany which called for aid for both countries. Launched on 24 November, its first relief party left on 26 November. Headed by the eminent Baron von Langenbeck, it included other, younger surgeons of later fame. Vincent's involvement in the relief operation must be seen against the background of this formidable international effort.

The National Aid Society announced on 26 November that in keeping with its commitment to aid both parties in conflicts it was sending missions to both Servia and Bulgaria. In his letter to *The Times*, Wantage named Vincent as the commissioner for Bulgaria. This new mission placed Vincent in a particularly delicate position, for it was one in which Queen Victoria took a personal interest. Her Majesty had first learnt of Vincent's activities in 1877 from his correspondence with Sir Henry Layard and his report on the Plevna incident. The connection was sustained by Alice's work with the Princess of Wales Branch, the ladies' wing of the National Aid Society. Alice sat on its committee. Through this she and Vincent were brought into contact with the queen's youngest child, Princess Beatrice, who took a close personal interest in the work and who was married to Prince Henry of Battenberg, brother of Alexander, Prince of Bulgaria. It was partly under the auspices of the Princess of Wales Branch that the Suakin mission had been organized and Vincent was in direct contact with Princess Beatrice. He sent her an account of his work at Suakin, detailing the distribution of the preserved milk, jams and fruit and of the soup powder, tobacco and oranges which the branch sent out. On his return he reported personally to her at Windsor and presented her with copies of his reports of his work in the Carlist, Turco-Servian and Russo-Turkish Wars. In return the princess accepted the Presidency of the third district of the St John Ambulance Association, of which Vincent was chairman. As he later wrote to her, 'we have never had so successful a year both in regard to the number of certificates gained and finance.'[37] Vincent enjoyed a degree of royal patronage and was to sustain a friendly correspondence with the Battenbergs after his return from Bulgaria.

The intense interest displayed by the royal family produced an immediate problem requiring tact and delicacy. It centred on the person of Miss Henrietta Stewart. She had first attracted royal attention when employed in the Army Medical Department, being commended for her nursing work on board the transport ship *Carthage* on its voyage to Egypt in 1882, and in July 1884 she was one of the first ladies to receive the newly instituted decoration of the Royal Red Cross, an honour shared with Viscountess Strangford and Lady Loyd-Lindsay. Her career seemed assured when in late 1883 she was appointed sister-in-charge at the Royal Naval Hospital at Haslar, Gosport where she was to introduce the new system of nursing by trained sisters. There, however, she ran into trouble. As she bitterly complained to Lady Ely, the queen's lady-in-waiting, she had been treated in a disgraceful manner. Bad relations with her insubordinate staff with whom she had no power to deal had led the Admiralty to ask for her resignation. As a holder of the Royal Red Cross she solicited the queen's intervention. She got it. On royal insistence an enquiry was held. It emerged:

> the young nurses were rather flirtatious with the young doctors and played at Lawn Tennis in the Hospital Grounds together – Miss Stewart stopped this . . .

and from the Admiralty Sir Frederick Richards explained on 14 May:

> Miss Stewart is a Lady of very winning and agreeable manners, possessing many admirable characteristics but she is unfortunately of a highly contentious spirit and irritable temperament.

The Admiralty declined to reinstate her despite the queen's warm advocacy.[38]

Events in Bulgaria provided a new opportunity. It was proposed that the National Aid Society should utilize Miss Stewart's services, much to Wantage's alarm. He telegraphed on 27 November 'do not think nurse would be desirable' and followed this up with two letters on 28 November. To Sir Henry Ponsonby, the queen's Private Secretary, he wrote that Miss Stewart's past record was unfortunate and that he desired 'to protect Kennett Barrington'. She spoke no foreign languages and it was NAS policy to send out nurses in pairs. To Princess Beatrice he claimed that Vincent objected to taking Miss Stewart as the journey would be rough. She was not employed by the National Aid Society. But she was by Queen Victoria, who appointed her 'The Queen's Nurse', paying her at the rate of one hundred pounds a year and providing her with a uniform and travelling expenses. Vincent was asked to take her with him and to ensure her services were suitably utilized. They set out together on 28 November 1885.[39]

The forebodings were not unjustified. Vincent was able to establish a good personal relationship with her, as his regular letters to Alice show. But it was difficult to find a suitable role for her. His original intention had been to use her to run a small hospital and train Bulgarian nurses but this Miss Stewart rejected as unsuitable, and on better acquaintance Vincent agreed with her. The problem was solved by placing her under the wing of Dr Gluck, the able young German surgeon, and fitting her out with a Bulgarian nurse who could act as interpreter. Once professionally settled, Miss Stewart turned her talents for dispute to her domestic surroundings. The Hotel de Bulgarie selected by Vincent as the best in Sofia and thus most suited to the needs of a lady was judged by her far too expensive. It was not just Miss Stewart who was a problem, the entire NAS party was dogged by misfortune. Dr Featherstonehaugh broke a bone in his foot while Dr Lake injured a finger treating patients and contracted blood poisoning. Vincent too was once more a patient.

Having survived injury in war, avoided shot and shell, escaped from falling horses and damaged carriages and dodged cholera and smallpox, Vincent fell victim to the joys of celebration. In an aberrant moment while escorting the wife of the British Minister at the celebrations to mark the triumphant entry of Prince Alexander to Sofia on 26 December, Vincent passed in front of a jubilatory cannon and was hit by the debris of the *feu de joie*. From his sick bed he wrote home reassuringly as usual playing down the seriousness of his condition to avoid alarming loved ones. By then the heavier part of his work was over and he could submit to the hands of the disputatious medical fraternity with a more or less easy mind. He was not the only member of the family to endure medical attention. His son had problems with his legs and details of the treatment proposed to rectify these were regularily sent to Vincent. Taken together, details of the experience of father and son shed interesting light on late nineteenth-century medical practice.

In early December, however, the pressure on Vincent had not eased. Though the first part of the journey to Widdin on the Danube was accomplished quickly, Balkan travel was as difficult as ever and the snow as deep. He arrived to find the Bulgarians had performed prodigies of improvisation to meet the demands of the wounded and that a plethora of hospitals had sprung up. There was also the now customary medley of competing relief organizations. His usual level-headed self, he immediately decided no good would be achieved by setting up yet another hospital and that the best use of the Society's funds would be the disbursement of them through existing outlets, whatever their nationality. His arrangements for Miss Stewart and donations to various hospitals showed Vincent was no narrow nationalist anxious to wrap relief in the national flag. The performance of the German surgeons in particular aroused his admiration for their 'extraordinary operations'. This broad approach to the relief of suffering and dislike of narrow-minded nationalism led him into a polemic at second hand with a Dr Evatt who wished to keep National Aid Society funds for the exclusive use of the British volunteer movement in time of war. In his usual co-operative spirit, he did not permit his distaste for the competitive approach of many would-be relievers of suffering or suspicion of their motives to prevent him from attempting constructive utilization of their services, as was shown in his response to the petulant complaints of American missionaries at Samakov. He would have been unimpressed had he read their annual report for 1886 in which they freely admitted that kindly offices among the wounded and sick gave an entrée to many otherwise inaccessible households and could be accompanied by scriptures and sacred texts. As it was he neatly skirted the problem by responding to Dr Kingsbury on 27 December that he should 'find out any cases of convalescents who are feeble and have long distances to go. A night's rest in your prepared hospital at Samakoff, and a good breakfast in the morning, would be a great help to them.'[40]

Vincent's position in Sofia bore a quasi-official character. As a result of the intervention of the queen's Private Secretary he was able to utilize the regular diplomatic courier service provided by Captain Lumley, the queen's Messenger. Characteristically he suggested Alice should invite him to dinner when in London. It was Lumley who brought out the surgical instruments of which there was so much need. He worked closely and easily with the British Minister, Frank Lascelles, re-establishing that link with the diplomatic service which he had forged at Constantinople. In a happy irony Vincent's only daughter subsequently married Edward Lascelles, nephew of the Minister. That was to happen, however, after Vincent's death and the previous connection between him and his posthumous son-in-law's family only came to light long after. His previous services in Servia were still gratefully remembered and proved to be valuable, for as in his other operations he found it necessary to cross from one side of the fighting to the other. On this occasion he passed from the Bulgarian to the Servian side, going direct to Belgrade to obtain blankets and other items more speedily procurable from the NAS depot there and thus avoiding a long detour. His personal links with King Milan facilitated this. As the British Minister at Belgrade reported, Milan gave Vincent his personal permission to take back whatever he needed for the Bulgarian wounded.[41]

The simplicities of Bulgarian society were congenial. Confronted by them Vincent gave expression to his personal attitudes with a new freedom. He was impatient of the antics of politicans and their two-faced duplicity. While his personal religious faith and the strong sense of the divine presence in his own life came close to a sense of predestination, his dislike of cant and humbug gave him a marked contempt for the self-proclaimed protagonists of organized religion. He clearly had little time for the professionally godly and even less for the amateurly so. Disliking titles and social divisions, he found the egalitarian nature of Bulgaria to his taste. Lacking an aristocracy, the natural simplicity of its peasant society appealed to him. He positively warmed to Prince Alexander personally and displayed a partiality for the Bulgarian cause absent from his reactions on other missions.

Vincent's activities aroused keen interest in Britain. He became something of a national figure with reports regularly appearing in *The Times*. His letters to the National Aid Society were sent to Osborne where they were read by and acknowledged on behalf of the queen and her son-in-law Prince Henry of Battenberg. By the time he left Bulgaria on 15 January 1886 he was an established figure. Yet as his letters show he was starting to doubt his continuing fitness for the life. Though in robust health, he was more interested in creature comforts and at the age of forty-two felt himself to be growing old. On leaving Sofia he also said good-bye to the life of representative in the field for which he was knighted in May.

His business career now assumed major proportions. His work for the London Chamber of Commerce intensified as he joined the council of the

Association of Chambers of Commerce in 1886 and became deputy chairman of the London body in 1889. His work for the Metropolitan Asylums Board too grew heavier as Vincent utilized his mathematical skills to become chairman of its Statistical Committee and a member of its Cholera Committee. He continued to travel widely, especially in South America, where his knowledge of Spanish and French was valuable. In 1889 his knowledge of those countries was recognized and he became chairman of the Chamber of Commerce's South American section. Before then he had had the opportunity to revisit his haunts during the Carlist Wars, during a trip made between August and November 1887 on behalf of the Melbourne Centennial Exhibition, with the object of securing foreign participation. For the first time in his life he was being paid a regular salary of six hundred pounds a year and travelling expenses on which he carefully subsisted, saving as much as possible of his salary to enable Guy to go to Eton. Amused at being assured he was worth ten times his weight in gold he calculated he ought to be paid at the rate of £3,275 a year. More serious were the encounters with old friends, principally in Vienna and Spain. He was always sentimental on such occasions as he admitted, and he found the meetings affecting. Memories were also kindled when he passed Menton on the train, *en route* to Spain from Italy. He wrote to Alice on 23 September:

> Need I tell you that I thought much of you as we passed Mentone? I remembered our first separation which I really felt far more than you thought. Then on arrival at Marseilles I remembered that horrid goodbye in the cabin of my ship. . . . This is the same hotel where we stayed at Marseilles and tomorrow I shall make a pilgrimage to the spot where we said goodbye.

There was an unexpected opportunity to exercise his first aid skills when his arrival at Pisa coincided with a railway accident. Almost with regret he wrote to Alice that three doctors were on the spot and plenty of bandages were available so that his own services were not required.

His new eminence opened doors to him as he wryly acknowledged. *Sir* Vincent had a ready reception from British consular and embassy officials: but everyone expected large tips from him. As ever, Vincent was careful whenever he mentioned meeting other ladies on anything more than the most casual basis. Conscious of Alice's sensitivities, he carefully ascribed his liking for the Spanish Duchess of Medinaceli to her looking like Alice, while of his meeting with the Marchioness of Anglesey 'and her exceedingly pretty niece' he hastened to explain:

She must *have been* a most beautiful woman and her features are still finely chiselled but bear the traces of sorrow and temper. The American niece, about *18* fresh from a New York School is (or would be to anyone else than myself!) simply charming.

Crafty old Sir Vincent!

The decade of the 1890s saw him in South America, mainly in Brazil, Argentina and Venezuela. Of his letters to Alice only scattered fragments survive, too few to be included. From them, however, emerges a picture of patient negotiation and incessant travel as Vincent built for himself a career as an agent for companies with interests in need of defence or assertion in the turbulent and politically changeable atmosphere. Railway companies, estates with ranching interests and harbour companies employed him and though he sometimes had trouble collecting his fees he was able to boast of steady success, even if it often took longer to achieve than he first anticipated. He was appalled by the casual brutality and easy assumption of superiority of the local military, distinguished then as now by ferocious treatment of their cowed peoples and by a lively sense of self-preservation and moral cowardice. He found their claims to embody the national honour hard to stomach. In this sub-continent of more or less incessant strife he believed there was important work for medical relief agencies and devoted his spare time to the creation and firm establishment of Red Cross organizations.

He was instrumental in setting up the Buenos Aires branch of the Red Cross in April 1892, inspired by the political turmoil he witnessed. He wrote to Alice on 9 April:

> Why does an all-seeing providence allow the unjust to triumph? . . . High Mass is being celebrated with gorgeous pomp at the Caridad Church under my windows, while armed soldiers stand round to intimidate voters for the election as they pass through the iron gates to the voting place in the Church vestry. What a farce is the sham of Christianity. It makes my blood boil. I open my windows and there on the roof opposite and hidden among the bells of the Church are armed policemen ready to shoot down the population if they make any demonstration of indignant protest.

His greatest success came in Venezuela, where he spent a considerable time in 1894 and 1895. After helping to found the Caracas Chamber of Commerce he turned his attention to Red Cross work. He explained to Alice in a letter dated 6 February 1895 he had first persuaded the

Venezuelan Government to sign the Geneva convention and then set about organizing a grand meeting of all the Venezuelan ministers and of the diplomatic corps. The Secretary of the United States Legation, Bartleman, provided the diplomatic muscle, and Vincent summoned all his linguistic skills to make an eloquent plea in Spanish. With the Venezuelan branch more or less secured when President Crespo of Venezuela accepted the honorary presidency and the Archbishop of Venezuela agreed to become Vice President, Vincent extended his horizons:

> seeing the chance I determined to push the movement all over Central America where they fight like Greek v Greek, always fighting.

The idea was warmly received. Grand civil receptions followed and by June Vincent was able to tell Alice that his draft statutes for the Society had been accepted and that he had found a suitable successor to himself as president. It was a highly satisfactory outcome and Vincent was presented with the decoration of the bust of Bolivar.

From South America Vincent watched the unfolding of the drama of the Boer War. Despite his age, he was troubled by his own non-involvement. As always the thought of the 'many who are going to their 'long bye-bye' in the spring-time of their lives' deeply distressed him. He was limited to making donations and collecting money from the local British community for war widows and dependents, but thought of ways of ending his business commitments and going to South Africa to help. He never did so, and perhaps it was as well for as he wrote to Alice on 11 December 1899:

> I am rather too much of a free hand, too much inclined to my hobby of having a very elastic organisation untrammelled by red tape, in fact like the Boers – so that I could move rapidly, fill up gaps . . .

Wartime medical services and their organization had moved too far for there to be scope for the inspired amateur.

Vincent felt himself to be as fit at fifty-five as he had been at twenty-five. It was a testimony to his active life style. As is evident from his letters, some of the attraction of war work had always lain in the physical exertions and dangers, the tiredness after the accomplishment of a job worth doing. This aspect of Vincent's personality flourished unabated. During his time in South America he made provision in a busy schedule for exercise, playing tennis and especially mountain walking. When he climbed the Pico Naiguatá in Venezuela in March 1895 he proudly informed Alice both of the difficulties and exhilaration of the climb and that it was only the eighth

Vincent's balloon, *Shropshire*

time it had been made. When in Argentina he went mountain walking with members of the local Alpine Club. When in Britain he rowed actively, being on his death one of the oldest members of the Leander Club. It was this taste for adventure which was, literally, to prove has downfall.

By the 1890s ballooning had ceased to be the sensationalist entertainment of the early nineteenth century. As men strove to emulate the birds and fly and as exploration of the upper air gathered momentum ballooning acquired a respectable, scientific aura attracting serious men. It was perhaps not surprising that Vincent should have developed an interest in it. It appealed to his scientific and mathematical bent; it was also dangerous and strenuous enough to satisfy his adventurousness.[42] There is no record of his first introduction to ballooning. By 1890, however, he was a confirmed addict. He was making regular ascents with the Aeronautical Club, and his activities were regularly in the newspapers, as he and his fellow balloonists set off from the grounds of the Ranelagh Club. Particular companions were Percival Spencer, the well-known racing balloonist with whom Vincent made many flights, and Frank Butler, later to achieve fame for the first 'blind' flight through thick fog for a distance of 115 miles. By 1900 Vincent had his own balloon, called *Shropshire*. Among his papers are several examples of letters written to his family while aloft and thrown to earth to be posted. By the time he visited New York in November 1902 his fame as an aeronaut was sufficient for both the *New York Herald* and the *New York Daily News* to concentrate on it to the detriment of his activities with the Red Cross. Vincent was reported as having made many ascents in England, France and Germany and his opinion was canvassed on the merits of the most recent designs of powered heavier-than-air craft. His links with both ballooning and with South America led him to entertain the pioneer Brazilian aeronaut Senor Santos-Dumont in November 1901 when the Aeronautical Society fêted him on being the first to circumnavigate the Eiffel Tower in a powered craft under control. Vincent was the guest of the Brazilian Minister in London and sat at the top table at the Aeronautical Club dinner in honour of Santos-Dumont.[43] Indeed, his skill and standing as a balloonist, as well as his association with the royal family led to his assisting the Prince of Wales's children into a balloon car in July 1903. A few days later he was dead.

By far the most hazardous aspect of ballooning was the landing, and a succession of more, or less, distinguished and more, or less, skilled practitioners had died in accidents on landing or of injuries sustained in such accidents.[44] Vincent was no exception. The principal danger was an over-speedy, abrupt descent leading to a heavy landing. In extreme cases the luckless passengers might be thrown from the basket or dragged along

A violent landing, July 1902

the ground for a considerable distance as the balloon failed to collapse quickly enough or the grapples thrown out to act as brakes failed to grip the ground. Passengers could be seriously injured. In other instances the landing was so heavy as to cause more or less instantaneous death. By far the most common injuries were to the legs and lower abdomen, caused by the shock of the impact.

Vincent was no stranger to the violent and uncontrolled landing. The magazine *Black & White* on 19 July 1902 reproduced a drawing of him and fellow balloonists entangled in the branches of an oak tree at the Ranelagh Club as their balloon was caught in a sudden gust of wind, while on another memorable occasion which passed into family tradition Vincent fell through the roof of a conservatory while landing. The irate owner so far forgot his manners as to omit to invite his unexpected visitors to lunch. Vincent's own letters recorded the impact of landing. He wrote to Alice on 10 September 1890 describing a relatively good landing:

> nearer and nearer we got to the ground, then he [Percival Spencer] threw out the grapnel; it stuck fast at the first trial, and we came down with a bump, then a bound and second bump, then a third and we rested quietly in the car.

A heavy landing could be countered by climbing into the rigging connecting the basket to the envelope, or by kneeling down.

Vincent's last flight took place on 10 June 1903 from the Ranelagh Club grounds, the balloon landing near Erith. With Vincent was Frank Butler who later testified at the inquest into Vincent's death, and an unnamed lady passenger. Vincent disliked ascents with ladies as he believed it was necessary to give them considerable attention while landing in addition to overseeing the evolutions of the balloon. On this occasion a heavy landing occurred. Vincent remained standing, lifting his lady passenger so as to cushion the impact. In doing so he landed with stiff legs and sustained a severe shock. According to his doctor at the inquest, Vincent explained:

> He had omitted . . . to bend his knees, and was standing on his feet on the floor of the car, and had a bad shock. He also had a bad pain in his left ankle.

Massage was prescribed, but by 6 July the problems were back. They were not sufficient to prevent Vincent's attending a balloon rally on 7 July, though they were sufficient to deter him from an ascent. He later spent two days at Henley Regatta. His condition was steadily deteriorating, however,

Sir Vincent and Lady Kennett-Barrington with their children, Guy and Leila

and he had to be brought home from Henley suffering from what the doctor diagnosed as sunstroke. His death was ascribed to that cause. In fact, as a post mortem examination showed, he had died of blood poisoning arising from the injury to his ankle which had suppurated. The jury returned a verdict of accidental death.

At his death Vincent had accumulated many foreign honours in addition to his British knighthood. Spanish, Turkish, Servian, Bulgarian, Egyptian and French decorations attested official recognition of his services in war while unofficial medals such as his bronze and silver Royal Humane Society medals reflected personal bravery to save those in danger of drowning. It was an impressive testimony to widespread appreciation of his activities in so many varied aspects of humanitarian relief.

NOTES TO INTRODUCTION

1. Alice L. Lascelles and J.M. Alberich, (eds.), *Letters from the Carlist Wars (1874–1876)*, Exeter Hispanic Texts xliii, Exeter, 1987.
2. E.E. Whipple, *A Famous Corner of Tuscany (Bagni di Lucca)*, London, 1928, p. 199. For Lucca see also Mrs Henry Stisted, *Letters from the Bye-Ways of Italy*, London, 1845; W. Snow, *Bagni de Lucca*, Pisa, 1846; J. Murray, *Handbook of Central Italy*, 1st edition, London, 1843. Further material may be found in the Foreign Office consular archives for Italy in the F.O.70 series in the Public Records Office at Kew. These and other Crown copyright materials have been used and reproduced by permission of the Controller, HM Stationery Office.
3. Vincent Frederick's career may be traced through the archives of the India Office, Orbit House, which are Crown copyright and have been used by kind permission of the Controller, HM Stationery Office. His cadetship papers are in L/MIL/9/132 H 106–9 and his service record is in L/MIL/12/b8 p. 279; for details of his pension see L/AG/21/11/44. The service record of General J.B. Kennett is in L/MIL/12/67 p. 49.
4. Details of family births, marriages and deaths may be found in the papers of the Bishop of London at the Guildhall Library under the *Calendar of Baptisms, Marriages and Burials Overseas* in the Ms10,926 series. Further details may be found in the consular archives series in the Foreign Office archives at the PRO and in the files of the Registrar General of Births, Marriages and Deaths at St Catherine's House, Kingsway.
5. Sir Jonah Barrington, *Personal Sketches of his Own Time*, 2 vols., London, 1827 with a third voiume, London, 1832.
6. For the history of the Order of St John, see J. Gildea, *The Order of St. John of Jerusalem in England*, London, 1881; W.K.R. Bedford and R. Holbeche, *The Order of the Hospital of St John of Jerusalem*, London, 1902; St. John Ambulance Association, *The Origin and Development of the St. John Ambulance Association*, London 1898; from 1871 there is the annual *Report of the Chapter of the Order of St. John of Jerusalem in England*.
7. Sir Edmund Anthony Harley Lechmere (1826–94), Conservative MP for most of the period between 1866 and 1894. Joined Order of St John in 1865. Secretary 1867 and subsequently its Receiver and Chancellor in England. Founded the Order's first modern commandery at Hanley Castle. See E.W., *In Memoriam Sir Edmund A.H. Lechmere*, no date.
8. For the history of the Red Cross, see G. Moynier, *The Red Cross*, London, 1883; S.H. Best, *The Story of the British Red Cross*, London, 1938; Dame Beryl Oliver, *The British Red Cross in Action*, London, 1966. For the early days of the movement, see J. Furley, *In Peace and War*, London, 1905 and C. Graves, *The Story of St. Thomas's 1106–1947*, London, 1947.

9. For the Franco-Prussian War, see M. Kranzberg, *The Siege of Paris 1870–1*, Cornell, 1950; A. Horne, *The Fall of Paris*, London, 1965. The best account is M. Howard, *The Franco-Prussian War*, London, 1961. There are contemporary accounts in the *Daily News, War Correspondence of the Daily News, 1870–1*, 2 vols., London, 1871 and A. Forbes, *My Experiences of the War between France and Germany*, 2 vols., London, 1871.

10. On the Carlist Wars there is in English only E. Holt, *Carlist Wars in Spain*, London, 1967. The subject is not well covered.

11. Allen William Young (1827–1915), sailor and polar explorer who after a career in the mercantile marine made his reputation as an explorer after 1857. He was a Younger Brother of Trinity House. The Dictionary of National Biography comments that he had a strong dislike of publicity.

12. For the Balkan Wars see B.H. Sumner, *Russia and the Balkans 1870–1880*, Oxford, 1937; M.D. Stojanovic, *The Great Powers and the Balkans 1875–8*, Cambridge, 1939. A modern account of Chernaiev is D. Mackenzie, *The Lion of Tashkent*, Athens (Georgia), 1974. For a contemporary and hostile British view, see the *Quarterly Review*, vol. 142, October 1876. For an account by a Bulgarian insurrectionist, see Z. Stoyaneff, *An Autobiography*, London, 1913. A detailed account of the fighting is in A. Forbes, *War Correspondence of the Daily News*, 2 vols., London, 1878. The impact of the crisis in Britain may be traced through R.W. Seton-Watson, *Disraeli, Gladstone and the Eastern Question*, reprinted London, 1962.

13. See the correspondence of W.A. White, Consul-General at Belgrade, with Sir H. Eliott, Ambassador at Constantinople, during the spring and early summer 1876, in FO 260/1–5 in the PRO, Kew.

14. Dorothy Anderson, *Miss Irby and her Friends*, London, 1966. See also her *The Balkan Volunteers*, London, 1968.

15. H.S. L.-Lindsay, *Lord Wantage VC, KCB, a Memoir*, London, 1907. The author was his wife.

16. See C.S. Ryan, *Under the Red Crescent, 1877–8*, London, 1897; Captain F.W. von Herbert, *The Defence of Plevna, 1877*, London, 1911; G. Stoker, *With 'The Unspeakables', or, Two Years' Campaigning*, London, 1878; V. Baker, *War in Bulgaria*, 2 vols., London, 1879.

17. C. Williams, *The Armenian Campaign*, London, 1878.

18. The doctors' careers may be traced through the *Medical Register* and the *Medical Directory*, both of which may be consulted in the Library of the Welcome Institution.

19. *Annual report of the Chapter of the Order of St. John of Jerusalem in England*, 1878.

20. P.H.P. Salusbury, *Two Months with Tchernaieff in Servia*, London, 1877, p. 241.

21. F. Villiers, *Villiers: his Five Decades of Adventure*, 2 vols., London, 1921, i, pp. 48–50.

22. For these see American Board of Commissioners for Foreign Missions, *Reports at Annual Meetings* and *General Survey for 1875*; E.M. Pearson and M.E. McLaughlin, *Service in Servia*, London, 1877; W. Jones, *Quaker Campaigns in Peace and War*, London, 1899; J.O. Greenwood, *Quaker Encounters*, vol. 1, York, 1975.

23. *Some Ambulance operations during the Carlist, Turco-Servian and Turco-Russian Wars, an address to the General Assembly of the Knights of St. John of Jerusalem, 24 June 1879*, London, 1879.

24. Organized by the noted philanthropist Baroness Burdett-Coutts who mobilized a massive public subscription. For an account see H.M. Dunstan, edit. W. Burdett-Coutts, *The Turkish Compassionate Fund*, London, 1883. This details several examples of Vincent's interventions during 1877 and 1878 on behalf of destitute civilian refugees.

25. Williams, *op. cit.*, p. 291.

26. W.J. Coope, *A Prisoner of War in Russia*, London, 1878, pp. 14–15.
27. V.B. Kennett to Sir A.H. Layard, 27 November 1877, in *Report of the Stafford House Committee for the Relief of Sick and Wounded Turkish Soldiers*, London, 1879, p. 22.
28. Ryan, *op. cit.*, pp. 312–14.
29. J.C. Fife-Cookson, *With the Armies of the Balkans*, London, 1879, pp. 190–1.
30. On the Sudan expedition and for details of the operations at Suakin, see the official history of the campaign: Colonel H.E. Colvile, *History of the Sudan Campaign*, 2 vols., London, 1889; Earl of Cromer, *Modern Egypt*, 2 vols., London, 1908; M. Shibeika, *British Policy in the Sudan 1882–1902*, Oxford, 1952; edit. A. Preston, *In Relief of Gordon: Lord Wolseley's campaign journal . . . 1884–5*, London, 1967; A.B. Theobald, *The Mahdiya*, 8th impression, London, 1967; G.H. Tahhami, *Suakin and Massawa under Egyptian Rule 1865–1885*, Washington, 1975.
31. For a contemporary view see Anon., *Suakin 1885*, London, 1886.
32. The offending passage appeared in *The Times* on 21 April 1885. It claimed the work of the society's doctors and nurses was highly appreciated by the armed forces and stated 'Much inconvenience was also found in transferring the sick and wounded from the piers to the hospital ships until Mr Barrington purchased a steam launch . . .'
33. Theobald, *op. cit.*, p. 129.
34. This was surprising for Charles Henry Newby had served in the Turco-Servian War, for which he had been decorated, and was again to be involved with the National Aid Society during the Servo-Bulgarian conflict. MRCS, LRCP and FRCS, he had first been registered in 1875 after training at St Thomas's where he was surgeon-registrar. He was clearly a most competent surgeon.
35. See C. Jelavich, *Tsarist Russia and Balkan Nationalism*, Berkeley, 1958. The standard history of Bulgaria is R.J. Crampton, *Bulgaria 1878–1918*, Boulder (Colorado), 1983; see too the same author's *A Short History of Modern Bulgaria*, Cambridge, 1987. On the Battenbergs there is Count E. Corti, *The Downfall of Three Dynasties*, London, 1934.
36. See the reports in *The Times* between September and December 1885.
37. Materials relating to Queen Victoria and the royal family are taken from the Royal Archives, Windsor Castle. They have been consulted and references to them made with the gracious permission of HM The Queen. For Vincent's reports on the Plevna affair see RA H16/9 and H17/49 and 50. For Princess Beatrice's interest see RA 026/182.
38. Miss Stewart's earlier career and the Haslar incident are covered in RA 017/23, R53/124 and R53/2538.
39. For Miss Stewart's activities in Bulgaria, see RA R53/3267.
40. Report of F.L. Kingsbury, medical missionary at Samokov, in American Board of Missionaries for Foreign Missions, *Annual Report for 1886: European Turkey Mission*.
41. H. Wyndham, Belgrade, to Lord Salisbury, 217, 22 December 1885, in FO 260/36. Lascelles's dispatches from Sofia are in FO 78/3771.
42. For the history of ballooning, see J.E. Hodgson, *The History of Aeronautics in Great Britain*, Oxford, 1924; C.H. Gibbs-Smith, *Ballooning*, London, 1948; C.H. Gibbs-Smith, *A History of Flying*, London, 1953; L.T.C. Rolt, *The Aeronauts*, London, 1966. For an account by a nineteenth-century balloonist, see H. Coxwell, *My Life and Balloon Experiences*, 2 vols., London, 1887–9.
43. See *Senhor Santos-Dumont's reception in London, 1901*, London, 1902. A. Santos-Dumont, *My Airships: the Story of my Life*, London, 1904.
44. In every number of the *Aeronautical Journal* published from 1897 there is an account of at least one accident on landing leading either to injury or death.

ONE

Letters from the Franco-Prussian War, October 1870–April 1871

CHRONOLOGY OF THE FRANCO-PRUSSIAN WAR, 1870–1

1870

15 July	Declaration of war.
28 July	Napoleon III takes command of army at Metz.
4 August	German invasion of Alsace and victory at Wissembourg.
6 August	German victories at Spicheren and Froeschwiller.
14 August	French armies concentrated around Metz under attack from Germans leading to major battle at Gravelotte and St Privat after which French forces retired on Metz.
21 August	Newly assembled French army under Napoleon and Mac-Mahon sets off from Chalons to relieve Bazaine.
23 August	Siege of French army under Bazaine at Metz begins.
29 and 30 August	MacMahon's force encounter Germans at Beaumont and, defeated, withdraw to Sedan.
31 August and 1 September	Unsuccessful efforts to break out of Sedan leading to complete defeat and Napoleon is taken compelled to sue for terms.
2 September	Total surrender, and Napoleon into captivity at Wilhelmshöhe.
4 September	Empress Eugenie leaves Paris for Britain and Second

Map of part of northern France to illustrate activities in October 1870

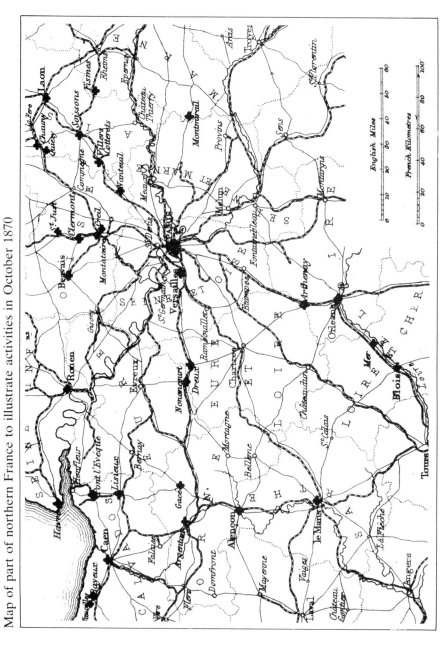

Empire ends; in Paris Government of National Defence created with Favre as Minister of Foreign Affairs and Gambetta as Minister of the Interior.

7 September	German advance on Paris begins.
15 September	Order given to invest Paris.
20 September	Paris surrounded and cut off from outside world – siege begins.
28 September	Strassbourg, besieged since 14 August, surrenders.
7 October	Gambetta quits Paris by balloon and joins other French officials at Tours to establish organization of resistance to Germans in which he is Minister of War as well as of Interior.
11 October	Germans captures Orleans.
29 October	Bazaine's capitulation at Metz.
31 October	First outbreak of radical unrest in Paris.
9 November	French retake Orleans.
November to December	Skirmishing and local engagements as French forces try to break siege of Paris from which unsuccessful sorties launched; irregular forces known as *francs-tireurs* harrass German lines of communication, especially in eastern and north-eastern France, leading to guerilla war with increasing claims of atrocities on both sides.
5 December	Germans retake Orleans.
19 December	Vincent arrives at Lagny.

1871

5 January	German bombardment of Paris begins.
22 January	Second outbreak of radical protest in Paris.
26 January	Bombardment suspended.
28 January	Government of National Defence signs armistice with Germans covering all France except for Jura region.
February	Elections to new National Assembly which meets for the first time on 7 February and opens peace negotiations.
26 February	Peace preliminaries signed.
13 March	Vincent arrives at Besançon.
21 May	Treaty of Frankfurt brings war to a conclusion.

Wednesday [13th October 1870]

My dearest Ma,

I sent you a telegram this afternoon to tell you about my having been chosen to convoy the stores through Belgium. I think that I am very *lucky* as I *shall* have the opportunity of seeing an immense amount of country and of doing good at the same time. I am not sent to where the fighting is so there is practically no more danger than in time of peace – scarcely – I go as an officer of the British National Society and will be comfortably lodged and fed at their expense; they will give me a cheque tomorrow and allow me one pound a day for food which is more than enough – I am so pleased. . . . I think that it will be a great advantage to me to see a new sort of life and to be doing some good . . .

Hotel Frascati   Monday, 17th October 1870
Havre

My dearest Ma,

I have had lots to do since I have been here [he had arrived on 15 October], but am much annoyed at the stupid mistake which was made by the authorities who sent me on to Havre without any bales for Tours; I cannot understand how they could have done anything so stupid. I have been working hard helping the ambulance which started for Paris today but there was no place in it for me, it having been made up before. Owing to the mistake I have conflicting orders which makes it very embarrassing for me, being told by one man to go back and not having any orders further from headquarters. I shall wait here until tomorrow for certain, when I may proceed to Tours with the bales or, if they do not then arrive, I shall proceed to London by the next boat which starts the day after tomorrow, as I have a commission for the French ambulance which I should like to do . . .

Every man in Havre seems armed, and you hear nothing else but a succession of trumpets and drilling; some of the French are still very confident and as far as men go they have plenty. The huge Paris Ambulance started today and reaches Rouen tonight. I only wish I was with them. 100 horses, 100 men and 20 or 25 surgeons etc. There was of course a certain amount of confusion but all went off well.

As the following extract from the official report to the National Aid Society by Surgeon Manley shows, Vincent's comments were a masterpiece of understatement:

The departure of the Ambulance being delayed by the steamer not being ready at the time appointed . . . the horses [were left] in charge of the English veterinary surgeon. This person appeared to have very little idea of what he had to do on the arrival of the Ambulance and his manner was such that it was quite impossible to do duty or work with him in any way. He commenced immediately to cause such confusion that . . . I began seriously to think that we should never be able to get further than Havre. . . . Only four [of the French drivers] . . . had been stablemen before; many of them had worked on the quay at Havre, and of those that came under my personal observation three were stonemasons, one was a florist, one a grocer, one an omnibus driver, and one an old postboy. They had been hired promiscuously about the town, without reference to their qualifications as drivers. . . . Pairs of horses appeared, one in wheel and the other in lead harness, reins and bridles, bits and curbs, arranged in a most fantastic manner . . . the tailboards of two of the ambulance waggons were broken through by the shafts of the ones in the rear being forced through them, the effect of bad driving, and from suddenly halting without warning. . . . As the whole was to proceed to Rouen by rail . . . and the remainder of the horses not coming to hand, some of those which had already brought waggons to the railway were sent back to bring up the remaining waggons which had no horses, and officers were dispatched about the town to hunt up the missing drivers and horses.

Hotel de Blois   Friday, 31st [*sic* 21] October

Darling Ma,

I have a few hours to spare for writing and so shall give you some news. I am now comfortably housed in the best hotel in this picturesque old town of Blois. I left Havre with the bales which arrived there on Tuesday morning. They would not have been sent off that day at all had it not been that I took upon myself the responsibility of cutting the red tape knot and carried off bodily the 31 bales addressed to Tours. There was a mistake about the invoices and perhaps the bales would have been there now had I not used my own discretion; the agent I expect is astonished but I have been warmly thanked by the committee here and shall be more than repaid for any risk by knowing that hundreds of poor wounded men will have their blankets etc a day or perhaps 3 days sooner.

I left Tours at 3 o'clock on Tuesday by the Honfleur boat, I had just two and a half hours to have the 31 bales landed from one steamer, passed through customs, and shipped on the other. The agent stupidly was not to be found anywhere so I had to see everything done myself. The poor agent had such an enormous amount of work to do for the Paris ambulance that very likely it was not his fault. I arrived at Honfleur at about 4 and was well received by the people there who were not a little astonished at my luggage! A cart was placed at my disposal and I had all my bales put in, climbed in on the top and off we started for the station. I had previously secured a requisition from the Prefect of Havre by means of which I secured a railway van for my bales and had a free passage to Le Mans with bales and all. Started from Honfleur at 7.20 p.m. The further we got south the more traces of war were to be seen. The station was crowded with Garde Mobiles and other regiments, and there were to be seen groups of wounded soldiers; the latter seemed very quiet and even happy, and did not seem to be suffering at all. The Mobiles and others were singing the Marseillaise and as lively as possible. I arrived at Lisieux at about 11.30 p.m., where we waited till 1.30 arriving at Mezidon at 2 a.m. of Wednesday; this is a small junction station and was crowded with soldiers, many of them wounded and lying asleep on the floors of the different waiting rooms of the station. There is no regular hotel as it is only a village so I hammered away at the door of a little inn and after about 20 minutes they let me in. I climbed up a steep staircase like a chimney, no banisters, and finally secured a room which had just been vacated by another traveller who was going back by some train. I started again at 10.30 next day. The station was literally crammed with soldiers, the officers spoke to me and were excessively polite; the chef de gare helped me to get my luggage van and all went right; we arrived at Le Mans at about 5 o'clock p.m. The station master said it was absolutely impossible for me to get on by the 5.30 train to Tours as my van had to be attached etc., but I was very polite, took my hat off 20 times to master, sous chef, inspector, and I believe even to the porters and finally my endeavours were crowned with success and my waggon shunted onto our train. The Ambulance Francais which came with me from Mezidon had to leave half of their things behind! I arrived at Tours at about 9.30 p.m. and after chalking in huge letters over my waggon that it was to be left at the station, I reported myself to our committee. They were delighted to see me, one insisted upon my staying with him after that night etc. I, however, for that night had a great difficulty in finding a bed in a hotel; at last I found one that had some room so I slept there that night. I was rather astonished when the next morning there was fever or some malady in the hotel, so I immediately proceeded to light a large cigar, pack up my things and bundle out to go and stay with Mr Campbell who had asked me to visit him; the greater part of my things are now at Mr Campbell's.

On Thursday morning I was introduced to the French Protestant Curé, and the Viconte de Flavigny,[1] president of the Société Francaise. He gave me papers and instructions. The English Committee urgently requested me to take 8 of the bales to Orleans, and 1 of the bales of the Société Francaise. I consented and have got as far as here. I arrived here at 10.30 p.m. yesterday and cannot get any further as the line is cut. I have got a 'sauf conduit' from the French General and have just been to the Mayor for an order for a cart and 2 horses to take me and my bales to Orleans; we shall very likely start at 4.30 or 5 a.m. tomorrow morning. I hear that they are fighting today between here and Orleans so I shall most likely pass over the battlefields there. I was stopped last night by a soldier in the street which was quite deserted at about 12 p.m. He asked me how I came to be there, where I came from and all about me. I answered all his questions calmly and requested him to take me to the post, where the guard was that my papers might be seen; however he was quite satisfied and told me to 'allez me couchez' which I did promptly. As a rule all the soldiers and officers are extremely civil and respectful; they like to see us as they know we come for their good.

I have to call on the Bishop of Orleans from the V. de Flavigny and the Conte de la Touanne the secretary, and have been entrusted with a most important mission to his Société: they gave it to me as the English Société is very much respected by both sides.

I am so anxious to go on to Orleans tomorrow, I could not get on today and must not travel on the roads at night. I wear a uniform cap of the Société; black forage cap with a patch of white and red cross, this and the brassard pass me through most places but I have often to show my papers.

I have met several very nice fellows of the Société Francaise, they are helping me to try to get away tomorrow morning and I hope one of them will come with me, he says he will very likely, we are all at the same hotel.

I am perfectly well. I had the first good nights rest last night since I left England; I *did* sleep slightly. All my flannels etc are *so* useful, changing them as Alfred told me is an intense luxury. I was never much more dusty and dirty in my life than last Wednesday night, but I had a huge hot bath this morning, and then a cold one and am once more clean. It has been very interesting to see the curious old towns of Normandy etc.

It was a touching sight to see at one of the stations all the ladies and people brought out cigars, coffee, wine, grapes etc for the poor wounded soldiers in our train and also for the others, they are *so* grateful for the slightest kindness. While waiting at Tours I found two poor chickens, legs tied; I went to the buffet and got some water and bread for them. The two ate nearly all a large lump of bread! Goodbye I have no more time to spare as I have to write a long letter to the committee.

Bishops Palace   Tuesday [24th October 1870]
Orleans

My dearest Ma,
The Viconte de Flavigny (President of the French Société) gave me letters of introduction to the Bishop of Orleans etc.[2] I accordingly called at the Palace and he, after our talk, asked me to stay with him. I have just come from dinner; the Bishop and five or six priests were the only people present. I never met a more agreeable and polished man than the Bishop . . .

I had my first experience of a hospital today. There were 31 wounded, and one poor fellows wound had mortified and he must die in a few days. You have no idea how grateful the poor wounded are for any attention shown them. I only wish I could buy 1,000 cigars for them, but you cannot as there are none to be had.

It was very interesting passing from the French to the Prussian lines, I slept at a little village exactly half way between them last night. Nearly all the Prussians and Bavarians are dressed in blue and are very fine men, they are nearly all fair and have all the same cut. They make themselves quite at home here.

This is a fine old town and has a splendid cathedral and the celebrated statue of Jean d'Arc. A battle took place just outside the walls not long ago and they were actually fighting in the suburbs.

This is a fine old Palace, there is a huge salon with painted walls and frescos, and lines of windows looking out on a wild little plantation. Everything is done in a very good style, my little room has a sitting room and third room for my washing stand. The carpet is very soft and everything that one can possibly want at hand. There is a wood fire burning brightly in the hearth but I remember that there are 40 wounded men sleeping tonight under the same roof.

I drove from Blois to Beaugency yesterday on the top of a country cart with my bales and a huge flag with red cross as it is not quite so safe as Oxford Street, although with precautions there is no real danger. I was stopped once at Blois and asked for my papers by a soldier and have of

Felix Dupanloup, Bishop of Orleans

course been stopped by several posts etc. I was so curious to see the first Prussian. He had a dirty black coat and helmet but very fine chest and face, some are remarkably handsome.

I have met with the greatest kindness from all with whom I have had any transactions. My bales contained articles *most wanted*, viz blankets, shirts and slippers and socks etc. I am so pleased that they were just the right things and that I hurried on their departure.

Hotel de Chateau   Wednesday, 26th October 1870
Blois

Dearest Ma,

I have had a very adventurous day and night. The Bishop of Orleans and Marquis de la Touanne succeeded in obtaining the release from the Prussian Commandant of 43 wounded French prisoners. Touanne asked me to accompany him and the prisoners from Orleans to Blois and thus pass through the Prussian and French lines again; of course I agreed and we were to have started at 9 a.m. yesterday; at the last minute there were no horses! However, he obtained a requisition for 6 and off we started in following order.

No. 1   Carriage Touanne and myself with red + flag and French flag
No. 2   Omnibus full of wounded
No. 3   Waggon full of wounded
No. 4   Waggon full of wounded
No. 5   Dog cart with owner of horses (very sulky)

We were continually stopped by Prussian outposts and at last arrived at Meung about one third of the distance; the horses had to be reshod here and all the peasants rushed to greet the poor prisoners and bring them meat and wine. They ate as much as they wanted when suddenly we heard the booming of cannon and it appeared that a small engagement was going on about 4 miles off. The evening was fast closing and we had to pass through the French lines and neutral part first; we lit our lamps and started and had no interruption until suddenly a French cavalry soldier with a long white cloak, galloped up wheeled round and rode off as hard as he could. He evidently could not believe we were French. Soon after two more galloped up swords and pistols all ready, they were exceedingly cautious in approaching us and were not comforted until they had read our papers; all this happened when it was quite dark and in a drizzling rain. After that we were stopped at least 12 times. We rested when once in French lines at Mer; I saw that the wounded men were provided for and had my first initiation in dressing wounds. One man was evidently suffering so I asked him what was the matter. The poor fellow had no one to dress his wound, a ball had taken the half of his finger completely off at the second joint. I dressed and washed it and bandaged it up for him and he was so grateful. I went over several ambulances at Orleans and have given away all my tobacco, they had none to smoke and it soothes them so. I could not buy any as the Prussians had taken all.

We left our wounded in a loft in Mer and they arrived safely this morning. I with Touanne drove on to Blois where we arrived this morning at 10, having been 14 hours on the road. I never slept so soundly in my life. Got up this morning at 8.30 and have had a splendid breakfast! I am prefectly well and am glad to have accomplished my mission. I started off for Tours at 3 p.m. this afternoon and hope to receive letters from you and our committee. I shall write my plans from Tours. I hope to be sent on somewhere with goods etc. I carried back many messages from people shut up in Orleans to their friends – there being no means of communication by post.

There have been very severe acts of war about here: the town of Chateaudun was burnt by the Prussians and they burnt a village close by where I passed yesterday. I travel about without much trouble as my papers are all strictly *en règle* and being an Englishman is a great thing. Everyone is very kind and obliging if you are polite to them. It was a great compliment the Bishop paid me by asking me to stay with him; he is a very celebrated man in France being of the Liberal school in religion: he received the Protestant curé while I was present.

Touanne and I slept in a little 2 bedded room last night, I am writing from the same. The window is open and I am looking over the splendid old Chateau and what I think is a convent. The streets swarm with soldiers and every now and then bugle bands pass. Orderlies fly about with dispatches and here and there you see a little knot of men talking to one of our wounded prisoners. They are made heroes of and are followed by a troup of admiring gamins.

Hotel Frascati   Monday, 31st October 1870
Havre

My dearest Brackley,

I have not been in much danger, for you have always to take the greatest precaution everywhere as people are so suspicious near the evening; I was stopped in the street one night at Blois and had to give an exact account of myself, being cross-examined by a soldier! The Prefect at Blois also questioned me a great deal but as I gave direct replies and remained calm he was quite satisfied and thanked me for my mission. I never saw such a kind good old man as the Bishop of Orleans; He is, as you perhaps know, a very celebrated man, having opposed the Pope on the Infallibility question; he knew I came from Cambridge etc. and we talked about it and other interesting subjects. It is not a very pleasant sound hearing the soldiers put their guns at full cock when they say 'Qui Vive?', you have to answer very sharp. One man had his horse shot under him as he did not answer quickly enough. I saw plenty of Ulans [*sic*], the celebrated light horse of the Prussians. They scour about the country in every direction. The Franc Tireurs regularly stalk them and shoot them down when they get near enough. They always fire twice, one shot for the horse and no. 2 for the man, so I hear.

. The inhabitants of the villages occupied by the Germans are in a great state of fright as they have to be continually supplying food etc to the troops; the Germans make themselves quite at home and eat tremendously, with full rosy cheeks and good natured looking faces. There are, however, some who look ferocious especially as they have not shaved for a long time. The officers seem very careful about their toilet, their long cloaks and high boots look very picturesque . . .

The country about here is quite lovely and very rich. I have, of course, passed through nearly all the prettiest part of France between here and Tours. I was not far from Barentin – the place where our family came from and which Sir Jonah mentions in his sketches. They say that there is some chance of an armistice, but according to Gambetta's[3] last dispatch it does not look probable . . .

My dress is as in the drawing [see illustration]. I shall have the International Uniform buttons put on my coat as they are so well known and it saves questions being asked if you have them. I have to take care not to lose my papers or my brassard. Here I am flag and all: someone stole my flag with which I protected myself and my bales to Orleans. It was worked, I believe, by some ladies at Tours and I am in rather a rage! My papers are

Vincent's self-portrait, letter of
31 October 1870

getting rather shiny! I have pulled them out and shown them so often. The
sentries and outposts badger you so. I take an officers ticket wherever I go
and pay one quarter of the fare only – the bales are only charged one
quarter freight.

*Despite his expectation of being sent to Versailles, he in fact returned to
London via Dieppe on 4th November 1870.*

68 Rue St Denis   19th December 1870
Lagny

My dearest Ma,
I am writing from Lagny where I have to distribute some stores among the
French prisoners who pass through in thousands; we were at Meaux station

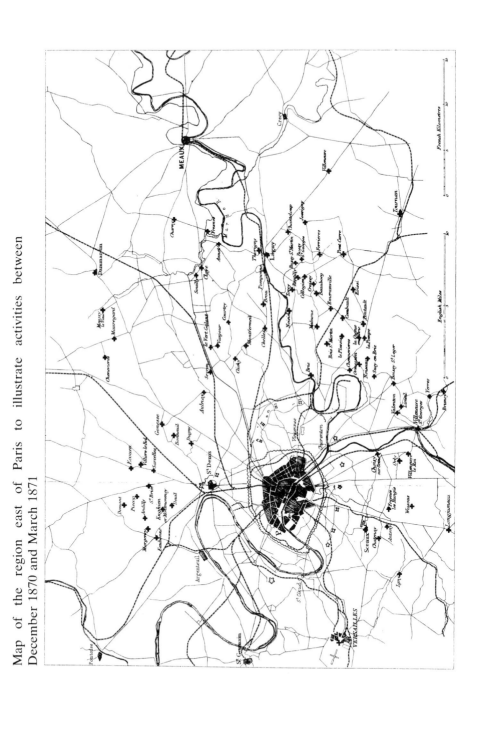

Map of the region east of Paris to illustrate activities between December 1870 and March 1871

the other day when a train with about 1,400 prisoners passed. It happened that there was no bread in Lagny to give them so the poor fellows had nothing to eat for two days. I never saw anything like their gratitude when we threw loaves into the trucks in which they were packed like sheep. It was not the fault of the Prussian authorities as it was really impossible to get bread for them at Lagny before arriving at Meaux.

Yesterday I got up at 6.30 a.m. and packed a waggon with meat in time for the prisoners. I then wrote my report on my last journey and after breakfast started off with the waggon for Lagny. The prisoners for that day had gone before I had time to make the distributions but we were expecting some every instant today. They will be put in the beautiful church here. I went through some wards of the Hospice St Jean today and distributed cigars.

I am now the guest of Dr Baar, a most delightful man, so kind hearted and good. He is attached to the Prussian Corps and can speak very fair French. I can speak French now almost as well as English and am beginning to pick up a little German. Dr Baar and three other officers have been fortunate enough to settle in this little bijou of a house in which I am staying today and tonight. The bedroom in which I sleep is most magnificently furnished; the walls are covered with thick velvet paper and gold and hung with pastel portraits and pictures in light gilt frames. The carpet is so soft that you cannot hear a footstep. There is a beautiful little garden, fountains and fish, and stable etc all complete. The owner of the house ran away in a great hurry and left everything behind. Luckily for her my friend Dr Baar and three officers took possession immediately and they have taken the greatest care of everything and the house will be left in as good order or better than the owner left it in. The china and desert service is beautiful – our living is substantial and good. I went this morning to the Mayor. Some 60 French wounded prisoners arrived last night and were distributed among the various ambulances. About 800 wounded Germans arrived last night at one ambulance – Madame Simon's. The night before 600, on Friday 1,600 and on Thursday I think 1,900 including 60 officers. Many of the wounded could not procure bread as there had been a dearth of it for a few days here but at Meaux, only a few hours from here, there is as yet plenty. The 1,200 prisoners whom I expected did not arrive yesterday so I sleep here tonight and expect them tomorrow morning.

Mr Sutherland, one of my fellow workers or 'camarades' as they call them here, arrived today from Meaux with a waggon full of bread for the prisoners. I have now 20 cases of preserved meat and these 200 loaves in my sole charge to distribute; I cannot tell you how the old Mayor thanked me in the name of the town for our help. I have been invited by Mme

Simon to take a seat in her carriage and accompany her on her official tour round the hospitals in the districts neighbouring. I am not certain whether I shall be able to accept her offer as I may have to take charge of another convoy immediately I return to Meaux. We have not had a day's holiday, except my day of 'thorough rest' for a long time. Madame Simon distinguished herself greatly in the Prusso-Austrian War and she has entire charge over the hospital and ambulance arrangements for the Saxon army and receives also wounded of the other German corps and French. She introduced me the other day to Prince Edward of Saxe Weimar with whom I had a long talk. He was extremely kind and polite and told me much about hospitals in the Southern districts of Paris.

I wrote my report yesterday for my chief. My greatest friends at Meaux are Capt. Nevill, our chief, and Sutherland, who was at Eton and whose brother was at Eton with me. He is one of the best fellows I ever met in my life. We all work capitally together, I never was in better health in my life. I smoke a good deal and do not fear in the slightest catching any disease as I am so well. I am going to sleep here this night and return to Meaux tomorrow. The huge stone bridge here has been blown to atoms and the supports of the iron bridge. . . . All the windows of the neighbouring houses are blown to pieces. All the large houses are turned into ambulances and hospitals. The Prussian doctors are much better than our doctors as they have, many of them, much private practice at home and only become army doctors during the war.

MERRY CHRISTMAS AND HAPPY NEW YEAR   V.B. Kennett
and send this on to Ma as soon as possible
English Depot
Place Henri IX
Meaux
Marne
France

Xmas Eve 1870

My dearest Arabella

I do not intend to forget you in my home letters; it is now Xmas Eve and we are all talking and thinking of home. I can picture you in your happy little circle with your four little ones.

The state of affairs round Paris is getting really terrible. There was a sortie two days ago. We went off first thing in the morning with four waggons full of things for the wounded. The Prussians said that all the wounded had been picked up and were very glad to receive our donation. From what some of the officers said however we are afraid that many killed and wounded are lying between the lines of Prussian and French outposts. These poor men who are too bad to walk must by this time be frozen to death.

We passed close by the field of battle but they were not firing when we were there. When there is any real danger the convoys are immediately stopped by the Prussian outposts as they might draw the enemy's fire.

We did not go further than Joues where we slept and came back the next day – yesterday. We slept there in a little wee room. I never had a better nights rest. I picked up a Prussian helmet smashed up a good deal which will make a good trophy. Tomorrow, unless something new turns up, we all dine together and shall make punch in the evening. I am so well – I can stand fatigue and exposure better than any of our staff. I systematically take an extra pair of boots and socks and have my mackintosh so that I am always more or less dry.

Meaux   4th January 1871

My dearest Ma,

I have not had any letters from you for ages. My last, as I told you, was Alfred's one announcing the birth of the little nephew. I am in happy ignorance even of his name.

We had a group of our staff, servants, horses etc outside of our stores taken yesterday. I shall reserve several copies for us at home. It makes a very pretty picture. In the middle of the group is the secretary of the Bishop. An old good natured priest who said that the group would not be perfect without him.

About my dress coat etc. I think that my old one which I have here will do well enough. I see an account of our Society doings at Meaux in *The Times* of December 24th. You will find an account of Sutherland arranging to feed the prisoners of Lagny. It was a mistake of the correspondent – it was myself and not Sutherland who did what you will read there but I did not see the correspondent so he did not know my name, and therefore, true to their character, he stuck in a name he knew as a shot. Nevill writes today to tell him of his mistake . . .

I have not much anxiety about you all as I know you would write me a registered letter if anything went wrong, but now and then I feel a little anxious as I get no news whatsoever.

One of our fellows engaged to be married did not receive a letter for five weeks and was in an awful state of mind, when his fears were allayed by receiving a registered letter.

If Augustus or Alfred or someone can call on Sutherland some morning he could ask him whether he has room for the new dress coat and if so give it to him, but it is not worth while risking sending it out under no ones special care. S. is very good natured.

Care of Mons Tyler   24th January 1871
English Ambulance
17 Rue Nexirue
Metz

My dearest Brother [Brackley],
I advised you to see the fighting part in the South if you could as it would be more interesting but of course come here, or whatever other place they may send you, as soon as possible. Capt. Burgess[4] perhaps thinks that you would not care about going anywhere else but here so tell him that you do not care where you are sent to.

I advise you to bring your uniform with you as it is so very useful in some cases – your undress uniform I mean – you can get on much better with the officers etc by wearing it occasionally.

I am sticking indoors today to get rid of a nasty cold which I caught from riding and getting hot in a canvas shirt when I was accustomed to wear a flannel one. I am better today and shall be all right in another day or two. Little things give you cold so much easier than the general exposure to which we are subject. I am much harder than I was this being the first cold I have caught. Nearly all the rest have been ill off and on except myself.

I had a good view of Paris from a hill which I passed on my last journey. I have been nearer Paris than Sceaux, and seen the forts firing away. They do not do much harm as the Prussian batteries are well made and masked. In the advance trenches they tell me that they set their watches by hearing the striking of Notre Dame. I was near the scene of the Versailles sortie last Thursday and heard the firing very distinctly; the other forts were also firing tremendously.

I am very anxious that you should come out; perhaps the siege of Paris is after all the most interesting thing, but we are so seldom near enough to see it. The hospitals lie all round Paris but you only now and then get a view of the forts.

We are at present cut off from our communications with England as far as stores go, as the Franc Tireurs have succeeded in blowing up a railway bridge not far from Frouard so we cannot get our stores from Saarbruck and Metz through which they all pass. Our depot is nearly empty in some things so it is a great pity. We shall have to wait several days I fear before the bridge can be mended. Major Lewis Jones, one of our Society, was in the last train which went over the bridge – in charge of waggons for our ambulance at Orleans etc. He had only passed the bridge about 10 minutes when he heard the explosion. The Germans must be in an awful rage. I fully expect that they will blow up or burn a few villages in the neighbour-hood by way of revenge. The French seem to be getting terribly thrashed in the North and South. I wonder what will be the end of this horrible war.

Bring with you two pairs of dog skin gloves from Grants, not lined, and size eight and a half if you come.

Tuesday, 24th January 1871

My dearest Arabella,

I have not forgotten you since I have been out although I must say our correspondence has been somewhat limited. I am now going to make up by writing you a good long letter – which please send the 'domestic round' and preserve as my letters form my diary. I am going to tell you about my last fortnights doings. On Sunday 8 January I left Meaux with Hinton and two four horsed vans with four servants – 3 English and 1 French. Our mission was to hunt out the hospitals formed for the bombardment [of Paris] and distribute our stores among them at our discretion. The day was bitterly cold when we started – many weeks of frost had iced up everything and made the roads like a sheet of ice. However, we managed to get along pretty well to Villeneuve le Compte where we found good stables and slept. The first thing we always have to do in arriving at a place for the night is to find stables. We can always make shift for ourselves, taking to our waggons as a last resource. I visited the fine old Church there which has lately been restored. We made our cuisine from meats preserved in tins etc there not being much to be bought in the village. Early the following morning we started for Tournan where we lunched in the open air. The passage through the woods was most difficult, the sleet falling from the trees had made the roads so slippery that the horses could not stand. We had not taken the proper tools for rough shoeing horses so we had to put in nails with an old knife, a hammer and pinchers. We took off the leaders and made the wheelers pull the vans along, which arrangement improved the going wonderfully. The horses tumbled down repeatedly. We reached Brie Compte Robert the same night and went to the Etappen Commandant [officer in charge of billetting and housing arrangements] for our billets etc. After hunting about for some time in the town, which was full of soldiers, we found stables and were ourselves asked to stay at the Mayor's – a rich distiller who lived in a first rate house built on the site of the old chateau of Compte Robert. We had beautiful rooms and cooked our dinner in the kitchen of the Mayor; greatly to the astonishment of the cook. After dinner the Mayor, a jolly old fellow, came in and discussed matters in general over some cigars and punch.

Early the following morning the horses were rough shod and we purchased some tools for shoeing etc, after which we drove to Corbeil and lunched there. We were delayed some time by a large column of troops which we could not pass owing to the narrowness of the road. We drove as far as Ris that afternoon where we found some stables and stayed for the night. Hinton and myself were billeted on an old 'Courier de Malles' [official who carried letters in the mail service] who had travelled all his life and told us long stories of his adventures as we sat over a good wood fire after dinner. We always pay for everything we have although our billet entitles us often to have food besides lodging. We only take the billets to protect us in case soldiers or officers want to turn us out. We have the same right to our quarters in that case as they have.

The following morning we were ready to start when two German Gendarmes came up and asked for our papers. I showed them but they were not satisfied as there was no pass for our servants. I insisted upon our right to protect our servants without any special permission. Arguments were of no avail so we had to follow the Gendarmes to the Commandant. We met an officer on the way who was very kind and civil; he took our papers to the Commandant who allowed us to leave the place but sent two mounted soldiers with us to see us out of it for six miles! We passed Savigny to Longjumeaux – at the former place we visited the beautiful hospital formed in the Chateau and gave some stores. We found stables at Longjumeaux and slept there that night. The following day we drove to

Sceaux and enquired about hospitals etc. We gave some stores where they were wanted but were informed that the large hospitals were more in the rear at Igny and Verrieres. We were offered stables and a room so we stayed at Sceaux the night. The room was in the hospital and formed at once our kitchen and the bedroom of Hinton, myself and the three English drivers, the Frenchman slept in one of the vans which were drawn up in the adjoining park. The guns made a tremendous row all night as there were two little sorties one at 1 a.m. and the other at 8.30 a.m. We could not get a good view of the forts as there was so much fog. It was very interesting, however, to be so near the scene of the bombardment and there was no practical danger.

The following morning after seeing all I could and making every enquiry about hospitals, we started off accompanied by a young medical officer of the Bavarian Corps to Igny. We found there a beautiful chateau fitted up as an ambulance. There were about 60 badly wounded men there, the slightly wounded had all been 'evacuated' which means sent to hospitals more in the rear or to Germany. Only the graver cases remained. I saw some frightful wounds. . . . I began in this scratched out part to describe one but it is not a pleasant idea so I have erased it.

I do not think the actual suffering is anything like in proportion to the lacerations of the wound. Some men suffer more from a small bullet wound in the hand than from the most fearful looking injuries. One gets hardened to these dreadful sights as far as ones nerves go, although I feel as much as ever for the poor victims. It is impossible to describe what a boon Chloroform is – without it I cannot understand how men can stand the pain of the operations.

To turn to more pleasant things – the scenery about Igny was lovely; often covered with rich woods and dotted here and there with villages and divided by a valley of the greenest pasture and a winding rivulet. The people left in the half deserted villages consist of old men, women and children. The large majority of the young men have joined the army so you may imagine how anxiously the parents watch every fight that takes place. In the departments near Paris the 'mobiles' have all gone inside Paris and are thus only a few miles off from their wives and families – who however cannot by any possibility hear from them except by the merest chance. Every train of prisoners and wounded is anxiously watched by those who have the opportunity. I have had a good deal to do with the prisoners in the way of giving them food etc, as I always like to assist them when possible. They are in such a miserable state.

We send off Sutherland tomorrow with some loaves and sausages for the prisoners who are expected to arrive from Le Mans. I hear that many thousands will come through. But 'Revenons a nos moutons' after leaving at Igny nearly all our stores, there being many more wounded expected there, we left for Longjumeaux. The roads were exceedingly slippery and our horses had a bad time of it. It was most extraordinary to see a convoy of about 40 waggons coming up a hill near Longjumeaux. I am sure that some of the horses fell down at *least* twenty times, and did not seem to hurt themselves much. A broken knee seems however to count for nothing. Nothing is more common than to see a dead horse by the road side or rather what part of it the crows have left. I often take shots at these wary birds with my revolver but although they let me approach quite close when I have nothing with me, yet directly I take my revolver they are exceedingly shy. They can smell gunpowder and are good judges of its effects by this time. We slept at Longjumeaux that night and started early next morning, Saturday 14, for Brie Compte Robert, where we slept the night at the hospitable Mayor's. I went over the ruins of the old chateau and visited the fine church in company with the curé. It has been turned into a barrack for the troops passing through and staying there the night. The next day we drove back to Meaux which we reached in the afternoon after an absence of the full week. I rested the next morning but in the afternoon was ordered to make the same journey again and start the following morning, so I had to make necessary commissariat arrangements and at 10 o'clock on Tuesday Jan 17th left Meaux for second weeks journey. The thaw had in the meantime set in and the roads were frightfully heavy. In some cases we stuck in the mud and it was with difficulty that the horses could drag us along. I returned again to Meaux on Saturday 21st. I picked up two wounded German officers in the wood near Fernieres; their horse had broken down and it was lucky for them that we happened to go by that way. There was a false alarm about the capitulation of Paris which was occasioned by some white flags being shown on Mont Rouge. There was an armistice to bury dead after the Versailles sorties. My second visit to Sceaux was still more interesting than my first. I must stop now so goodbye and love to all your chicks and Augustus – tell Ma I shall write tomorrow and show her this letter.

Vincent's diary shows that between 27 and 31 January he was engaged in convoying stores to hospitals in the vicinity of Paris before falling ill with jaundice at the end of the month.

Pantin – en route from Meaux to Paris   11th February 1871

I have perfectly recovered my health. Jaundice all gone.
My dearest Mother,
Here we are, stuck in the mud of red-tapism; we started this morning from
Meaux at 10 a.m. and arrive here without any mishaps of importance. This
is the last barricade before Paris and a new order has just come out not to
allow anything in the shape of eatables to pass into Paris by any of the roads,
all must enter by rail or river. They quite forgot to make an exception in the
case of ambulances so we are stuck here awaiting the order of the General
commanding the division. The Colonel has sent to him but he is out and I
have grave doubts as to whether we shall be able to enter Paris at all tonight.
We shall have to put up in some half ruined house and try our chance
tomorrow morning. It is now nearly six o'clock and the gates of Paris are
closed at six. However, we shall be accompanied by the officer commanding
at the barricade who will ensure our getting inside if we once pass here.

We have a most interesting drive today. We drove by Claye Vosjours
and Le Vert Gallant & Bondé – the latter place was the foremost position
of the French and is literally shelled to pieces. Nearly every house is utterly
destroyed and about every sixth one burnt. The French, however, seem to
have held it almost to the last. The Germans had raised huge barricades
across the roads and in any place which commanded an open space, we
passed these one after the other. We then drove along a long straight road
which was between the two lines and we then entered the French
barricades, which are most clumsy looking but quite as strong as the
German ones. It was curious to see the effect of the shells upon the houses;
some made quite a small hole on entering but blew the inside of the house
to pieces; others smashed the roof to pieces; others would set fire to the
house. Here and there a shell had fallen on the paved road, the effect of
this was to tear up 10 or 12 paving stones and make a hole as big as two
wheelbarrows in the ground, smashing all windows etc near. You can see
the marks of where the pieces of shell strike the walls etc. The houses
where the outposts have been are all loop-holed and any trees etc which
interfere in the slightest with the range of the guns are immediately cut
down. For miles round the forts trees and sometimes houses are pulled
down and the country looks like a desert. It is a scene of devestation which
I cannot describe.

The whole way from Meaux to here we passed people coming out of
Paris. They came some in cabs, others in carts, some walking and carrying
their little all on their backs and here and there you could see a touching
group; a husband supporting his poor wife almost fainting with exhaustion

and the little children following how they can. A great many however manage to get a lift somehow or other. The Prussian convoy soldiers are very kind to these refugees and take them up in their empty waggons. They seem to take special pity on the tired women and children. So many have their own homes and families in Germany and scenes like these touch their hearts.

I am so much better today. I ate a good dinner last night and am perfectly ravenous today. I ate a good luncheon, have been munching bread since and feel very much inclined to have a large dinner. I shall get some more Carlsbad salts in Paris. They are capital things for me I am sure. I do not dislike taking them nearly so much as I used.

Meaux   Saturday, 18th and Sunday, 19th February 1871

My dearest Mother,

I am so glad to hear that Brackley has started for Tours; please let me know all about his plans and orders. If I knew his direction I could send him a letter of introduction to the Bishop of Orleans, etc. As it is I shall send him a general letter of introduction which, if it reaches, he can show to any of my old friends in that region. I expect that he will go to Le Mans and work the district between that place and Orleans. I shall now write you a short diary of my proceedings during the last few weeks.

I gave you an account of my journey to Chateau Etiolles and Brie Comte Robert the last few weeks of January. On the 1st of February I did not feel well and lost my appetite, could not smoke etc as these symptoms had been coming on gradually I saw Dr Schmit, a very good Wartenburg [*sic* Württemberg] army doctor who was attending Jeune very successfully for typhus. He said I had a slight attack of a sort of jaundice which was very prevalent among the troops and gave me 10 days to get well, he gave me some calomel and rhubarb. I, of course, took care of myself so as not to catch cold etc. Schmit left Meaux on the 2nd and I then saw another Wartenburg doctor who gave me Carlsbad salts; the same as those prescribed by Quain. These agreed with me wonderfully and I gradually got better. On the 8th I drove to Thorigny, near Lagny, and slept at the hospital. The next morning Capt. Nevill rode over from Meaux and we then drove together to Fort Rosny. We were most kindly received by the officers commanding etc. The fort was not battered about nearly as much as I should have imagined. We drove back together that evening to Meaux.

72

This little outing quite cured me. The following day, 10th, I loaded up some waggons to go to Paris the next day.

In the afternoon [15 February] at about 3.30 we reached Paris and discharged the contents of our three waggons at the British Embassy. We stayed that night in Paris. I strolled about Boulevard and Palais Royal with Nevill; the great dining restaurants are open and you can have as recherché a dinner now in Paris as ever you could, of course you must *pay* for it. Prices have gone down with a tremendous run in the last few days owing to the enormous supplies of meat etc. continually flowing in. Our Mansion House Relief Committee ought to look sharp and distribute all their goods immediately as there will be no great want in a week or two. There will be plenty of work for the people repairing houses and manufactories in the environs. The elections seem to have taken place very quietly – the great masses seemed to care but little who was likely to be elected, all the interest in politics seems to be concentrated in a few place hunters.

On the following morning, Friday 17th February, we started from Paris. We stopped for about 20 minutes at the ruined village of Bandy and picked up a bucket full of pieces of shells. I have a really splendid collection of them now. I am not certain that I shall be able to bring back all the pieces to England as they are so heavy. We reached Meaux the same evening. I drove our four nearly all the way from Paris to Meaux and am getting quite an A1 four-in-hand driver!

On our arrival we found that Mr Hinton, who had been sent to London by Nevill to make inquiries about our future orders, had returned. Our orders from the committee are to proceed to Belfort – horses, waggons, men and stores. We are to have a special train to convey us there en masse. There is, I hear, a great deal of distress there and an immense number of wounded from Bourbaki[5] and Garibaldi's[6] three days fighting followed by the unsuccessful German assault on Belfort. It has now, as you know, capitulated so all the fighting is over. I am not certain when we shall start, in about three or four days I expect. Nevill will ride over to Versailles tomorrow to make arrangements about our special train. Direct all letters to *Metz* as usual, they will be forwarded from there to wherever I am. I have not heard from any of you for nearly three weeks or a fortnight.

Vincent's diary shows that he was sent on ahead of the main party to find a suitable base for its operations in the Belfort district, and it was at his suggestion that Vesoul was selected. Once established there at the end of

Map of the Besançon region of France to illustrate activities in March and April 1871

February he resumed the familiar task of convoying stores to the various hospitals in the district during the first ten days of March. He then went to Besançon on 9 March where he was taken ill again, this time with a bad throat condition.

13th March 1871 [14th deleted]

My dearest Ma,

I am writing this from Besançon where I arrived the day before yesterday with Hinton, De Velna and three waggons full of stores. There are about 15 hundred wounded here and another 1,000 in the environs. Besançon is throughly French, the Prussians surrounded it but never took it, they are therefore very proud of their town. It is well fortified by works on the heights round it but the town itself lies completely in a hollow and might be easily bombarded. The Prussians surrounded the place during the armistice which did not extend to this department. I am sorry to say that I caught a rather bad sore throat yesterday. It was a glorious day, the sun shining brightly and all the Besançonians promenading about and sitting down under the shade of the trees in the place. I had a little time to spare so walked down to the Cathedral and sat there for about three quarters of an hour listening to most lovely music. The interior of the Church was very damp and cold so hence my cold and sore throat.

I return to Vesoul tomorrow and shall be all right after a day or twos doctoring.

This is the 15th March and I am going to write to you a little account of my doings during the last two days.

Yesterday I visited the central committee room and saw the head man there, helped to arrange the stores which we were going to send to the villages around Besançon. At one place, 20 kilometres off, there are 400 sick and wounded, at another 200 and so on. There are a great many cases of frozen feet which were occasioned by Bourbaki's long march in the snow.

My sore throat is decidedly better, in fact getting quite well. I never felt such a difference as between yesterday and today. A German military doctor has given me a capital gargle and I was nursed last night and today by the people of this house who are kindness itself.

Three French soldiers slept here last night. They were a pleasant change to the masses of Germans who are often quartered here as I cannot talk to the Germans.

Had rather an adventure yesterday. Found in a village a way hence an old French officer superieur en retraite,[7] decore'd etc, great good old, and his daughter whom he had been looking for. She had bolted on approach of Prussians.

They had no means of getting to Vesoul, no horses to be got for love or money etc. Gave them a lift in my van with daughter's baggage and all (the former, i.e. the daughter, rather pretty). They were, as you may imagine, very thankful as they might have waited a week in Rioz without having a chance of being conveyed to Vesoul. Unfortunately I could not talk as my sore throat was so bad!! Rather an unromantic ending. I gave a lift to 12 poor French soldiers, most with feet which had been frozen. One had just recovered from scarlet fever. It is so satisfactory to assist the unfortunate French in these little matters. You have no idea of the privation and curious adventures which families in first rate positions have to go through.

Vesoul   15th March 1871
Haute Saone

Dearest Ma,

I must now tell you more about Besançon as my last letter was scribbled off at odd times in a great hurry. Besançon was never taken by the Prussians, they surrounded it completely but never approached nearer than 12 kilometres. They were within 10 kilometres of it in October but were beaten in a fight near Voray. There are still marks on the stones where the mitrailleuse rained as it were from the high cliffs above. It appears that there were a few companies of mobiles and Franc Tireurs with many mitrailleuses in a sort of natural fortress and the high road from Rioz to Besançon winds along the foot of the hill on the summit of which is this fortress. The French allowed the Germans to approach within 1,000 metres without firing a shot. The Germans did not know that there was anyone on the hill. Suddenly the French opened fire on the German line which was marching along quite ignorant that any enemies were near. They say that 1,200 were killed in that afternoon's fight as the Germans lost many hundreds in an unsuccessful attempt at taking the fortress by assault. The place I call a fortress is not anything but a long line of perpendicular rock on the top of a steep hill. It looks as if it had been built but is really a natural formation.

Besançon is a curious old town. It lies in a low valley and is surrounded entirely by high hills – most of which are strongly fortified. The French have been making many new fortifications round the town since the commencement of the war. The town is full of French soldiers of all descriptions imaginable – Cavalry, Infantry, Turcoes, Zouaves, Franc Tireurs, Mobiles, Garibaldines and nearly all other Franc Corps have their representation there it would seem. There were 2,000 sick and wounded in the town itself 10 days ago but the number is now reduced to 1,500 – they told me that they at one time buried at the rate of 300 a week – only counting hospitals. I do not think that the French hospitals are so well managed as the German. The former seem to depend so much on private charity. Bourbaki seems to have started on his march wholly unprovided with proper medical stores and ambulances, and it was lucky for his army that some international ambulances followed them during their frightful march of two months in the snow without proper food or clothing. Many died and many more have ruined constitutions. I saw some soldiers on wooden legs in Besançon, those who have suffered amputations are now beginning to walk. It was a disgraceful sight as the poor fellows were so young . . .

16th March

This morning there is quite a change in the weather, snow has fallen in the night and it has been snowing nearly all day. The view from my window has changed wonderfully. The hills are all white and the trees charged with snow. It seems as if winter has visited us again. The wounded and sick here are rapidly recovering now and trains full of convalescents are being continually despatched from the towns containing large hospitals. The road from here to Besançon is in some places almost crowded (for a country road) with mobiles and regular soldiers returning home to their parents and families. You see old men and boys, all weary and some hardly able to walk. I gave a lift to a boy not more than 17 years old carrying a heavy knapsack. I saw a band of Francs Tireurs par excellence at Besançon. They had seen much fighting and were all of a dusty brown complexion, clothes worn out and torn in woods, armed with rifles and revolvers, strong healthy . . . [The rest of the letter is missing.]

Entries in the diary for the period 14 March to 13 April reveal that Vincent's throat trouble recurred and he was again treated successfully by a German military doctor at Vesoul. He went, on recovering, to Metz to fetch money and stores for distribution in the Besançon district before returning to England by way of Metz, Saarbrucken and Sedan.

Charleville   5th April 1871

My dearest Ma,

I am quite well and have had a very interesting tour so far. I saw battlefield of Sedan yesterday and today, also the poor village of Bazeilles which was burnt to the ground by the Bavarians in cold blood several days after the battle.

I took diligence yesterday from Libramont to Sedan, slept at Sedan last night and drove over here this afternoon by diligence. Mézieres and Charleville are really almost the same town, only divided by a river. Mézieres held out for some time against the Germans and was bombarded for 24 hours most severely. All the houses round the Cathedral are completely destroyed to a distance of 150 to 200 yards. The Cathedral itself has been knocked about a great deal.

TWO

Letters from the Carlist Wars, 1874–6

CHRONOLOGY OF THE CARLIST WARS, 1872–6

1872

14 April	Don Carlos orders uprising to begin on 21 April.
2 May	Don Carlos arrives in Spain joining volunteers at Oroquieta. Lacking arms and equipment they are rapidly defeated by Government forces and Don Carlos returned to France.
November	General Dorregaray appointed commander-in-chief for Navarre and Basque Provinces and sets about creation of a trained Carlist army by sending officers and equipment from France. Between December 1872 and February 1873 the nucleus of a regular army is created in northern Spain.
May to December	Carlist operations in Catalonia, Navarre and Aragon and Castile are little more than uncoordinated guerilla attacks of frequent savagery, made by local bands.

1873

February	Abdication of King Amadeo and declaration of the Republic. Dorregaray arrives in Navarre from Spain to commence regular military operations.

May	Carlist victory at Eraul, near Estella.
July	Don Carlos returns to Spain.
August	Estella captured, followed by most of smaller towns of north-western Spain but not Bilbao, San Sebastian or Tolosa.
November	Carlists repulse attack on Estella at battle of Montejurra.
25 December	Don Carlos anointed King of Basque Provinces.
September to December	Carlist forces in Catalonia re-organized into a effective fighting force under Infante Alfonso, Don Carlos's brother.

1874

3 January	Military coup of General Pavia creates a conservative Government pointing to an early restoration of the monarchy.
February	Carlists begin siege of Bilbao, defeating Government forces sent to relieve city at first battle of Somorrostro.
28 February	Carlists capture Tolosa.
25–7 March	Second battle of Somorrostro where Government forces again defeated in attempt to raise siege of Bilbao.
April	Vincent arrives to work on Government side, probably via Santander. Helps in hospital work at Castro Urdiales, full of Government wounded after second battle of Somorrostro. Visits front and takes some wounded by sea to Santander, landing at Santoña.
2 May	Government troops enter Bilbao ending siege. Vincent goes to Santurce, held by Government troops, to arrange removal of Carlist wounded to Carlist territory via France on the *Somorrostro*, leaving on 13 May. Wounded reach Lesaca on 15 May via Socoa in France. Vincent arrives there on 18 May before returning to Santander via St Jean de Luz, sailing for England on 22 May.
25–7 June	Government attack on Estella repulsed by Carlists.
16 July	Don Carlos issues political statement in his Manifesto of Morentin.
July to August	Infante Alfonso launches attack toward Madrid from Catalonia, capturing Cuenca. Town sacked with much bloodshed and offensive stalled; Government forces rout Carlists in a counter-attack.

October   Infante Alfonso resigns and leaves Spain.
Vincent arrives at Irun on his second mission. After helping spectators of fighting at Behobia wounded by stray bullets while on French side of river Bidosoa he travels on 24 October via Hendaye through the battlelines to Pamplona besieged by Carlists who permit him to enter the town to deliver supplies to the hospital. Leaves Pamplona on 27 October, re-entering Carlist territory. Visits hospital at Puente la Reina and arrives at monastery of Yrache, near Estella, on 28 October, making this main Carlist hospital his base of operations.

November   On 23 Vincent takes nine Government wounded across the lines to Logroño, going by train to Haro and on to Miranda de Ebro on 28 November to visit the Red Cross Hospital there. Marches with Government column to Vitoria, there for three days, before returning with three wounded Carlists *en route* for Estella.

1 December   Alfonso, son of abdicated Queen Isabel, issues Sandhurst Manifesto stating his commitment to constitutional, hereditary monarchy as a preliminary to his restoration.
Vincent returns to Yrache by 4 December, leaving on 26 December with a party of eleven nuns whom he takes across enemy lines to Logroño. When there he visits the Government generals Serrano and Laserna.

1875

January   Military pronunciamento ends the Republic and proclaims Alfonso King. New ruler arrives in Spain on 14 January. Vincent is slandered by a Madrid journalist. He returns to Yrache. From there operates with an ambulance taking thirty-five wounded from Bargota to Yrache before travelling at the end of the month to St Jean de Luz. Arrives there 27 January and brings medicines for the hospitals at Yrache and Puente la Reina and secures money from Doña Margarita. Hasten back to Puente le Reina.

2 February   General Moriones defeats Carlists at Carrascal and raises siege of Pamplona. Vincent help remove Carlist wounded from Puente la Reina to Artazu in face of imminent attack.

3 February	Carlists win battle of Lácar.
	As Puente is captured by Government forces Vincent and wounded are caught on a dead-end road at Artazu by contending armies. On the night of 3 February they removes the wounded on stretchers to Guirguillano and eventually back to Yrache on mules. On 21 February Vincent rides to Artazu to rescue three ambulance carriages and take them to Estella. He is back at Yrache by 24 February.
March	On 2 March Vincent takes twenty-four Government wounded to Oteiza and hands them over, returning the same day. On 10 March he rides through the lines to Logroño on hospital business and between 22 and 25 March he travels to St Jean de Luz and Bayonne to buy medicines and from there to Pau to collect money for the hospitals from Doña Margarita.
Spring	Government forces systematically re-establish control over Catalonia.
April	Vincent travels back to Yrache via Lesaca, arriving on 6 April. On 13 April he starts for Biscay and visits hospitals at Durango.
May	Vincent spends the early part of the month near Hernani, San Sebastian and Tolosa before leaving for England later in the month.
Summer onward	Two Government armies under Quesada and Martínez launch sustained campaign against Carlist forces in Navarre and Basque provinces which lasts until the following year.
September to October	Vincent's third mission. He visits the Catalan and Aragonese Pyrenees to protect Carlist soldiers captured by Government forces, especially irregulars.
November to December	Vincent is at Yrache.

1876

January	By 21 January Vincent is at San Marcos, a Carlist outpost before San Sebastian, and on 22 January goes to Tolosa.
18–19 February	Last two battles of the war at Echalar and Peña Plata, with Government capture of Estella on 19 February.

28 February   Don Carlos leaves Spain.
                 During February Vincent is in charge of the hospital at
                 Lesaca and is caught between the lines with three hundred
                 wounded. On 28 February he went to Vera and Irun to
                 arrange evacuation of the wounded to Bayonne.

March   The evacuation of the wounded to France is carried out
                 and Vincent goes to Madrid to secure possession of
                 hospital stores and remains there during April before
                 leaving Spain in May.

Map of north-western Spain to illustrate activities during the Carlist Wars, 1872–6

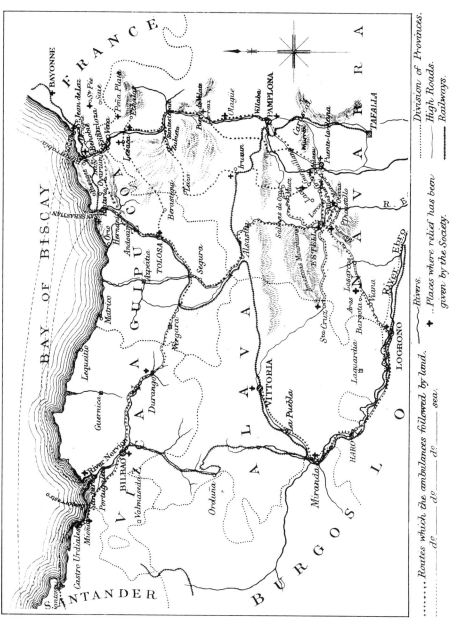

········ Routes which the ambulances followed by land.
——— do. do. sea.
.... Division of Provinces.
——— High Roads.
━━━━━ Railways.
——— Rivers.
+ . . Places where relief has been given by the Society.

. . . On arriving at camp we went first into the Church of Somorrostro. The altars were beautifully decorated with gold and richly painted. Church was headquarters of commisariat dept. and full of biscuits, cartridges, etc. Soldiers were eating their breakfast off the altar of the Lady chapel. We then walked on to the ruined village of Murrieta, and saw the place which the G[overnment's] Troops lost 1500 men in storming. We walked on to the extreme outpost within 150 yards of the Carlists. A Carlist soldier came down and spoke with a G[overnment] soldier near me; we hear them also shouting 'aqua' meaning that they were coming down to fetch water. We afterwards had lunch in the 'covered way' which was the only shady place. We paid a visit to the correspondents quarter and then returned home in the diligence. All came to tea in my room. I sprained my ankle slightly during the day. Took little sketch of the view from the Battery facing San Pedro Abanto.

Sunday, 26th April

Rested. Bathed at 9 am with M[urrieta?] and Gilward. Visited hospitals of Carmel and Church during the middle of the day. Found everything well arranged and no want at all. There were 60 wounded in Carmel and only 18 in Church. There are five hospitals at Castro in all. March came in the afternoon and told me about his Carlist experiences. Heard that Serrano had 12 brigades, each brigade = 4 battalions of average 500 men, 8 companies in battalion; also 2 brigades in Castro. Concha has 23 battalions averaging 600 each. Seven battalions of Carlists had gone out to meet him. My ankle not quite well. In evening wrote to Ma.

Monday, 27th April

Was taken very ill in night and sent for Murrieta in morning; I had been poisoned by something which I had eaten, I believe by some shell fish which I partook of yesterday. Tulloch, Austen and Gilward came to see me. Tulloch gave me 15 drops of Chlorodyne which sent me to sleep for the day and quite cured me by the next.

3rd May

Not hearing from C[ristóbal] M[urrieta] I visited the hospitals of Santurce; they are four in number, namely,

	Her. Carl [Carlist Cavalry]	Do Lib. [Liberal Cavalry]	Enf. Carl. [Carlist Infantry]	Do Lib. [Liberal Infantry]
La Fonda	4	1	109	3
Lazcano	15	1	1	0
La Torre	21	1	4	7
La Cruz	74	2	0	6
Total	114	5	114	16

I met Mr Bourgade of the Soc. Fr. and Caridad; he was manager of these four hospitals.

The Societe [*sic*] de la Caridad is a large relief Society under the immediate patronage of the Duchess of Madrid[8] and other distinguished persons. Their funds are very large and are subscribed from all parts of the world; I saw a bag of gold which had been sent from the Empress of Austria's committee. The following is a list of their hospitals.

Provincia de Navarra:	Yrache	300 beds
	Leiza	100 beds
	Lesaca	100 beds
Guipuzcoa:	Berástegui	60 beds
Prov. de Biscaya:	Santurce	350 beds
	Portugalete	200 beds

and also a great camp ambulance.

I never saw anything so beautifully arranged as the hospitals of Santurce. It was curious to see how much brotherly love seemed to exist between the Carlists; they thoroughly believe that they are fighting for a good and noble cause, the cause of God and their King, but they do not hesitate to admit that they are also fighting for their liberties and fueros which the rest of Spain do not feel disposed to allow them. They all seemed to endure their sufferings with ever cheerful patience and resignation. The good sisters of La Cruz nursed the wounded in these hospitals and well did their hard task: by night and day they worked and seemed never weary in fulfilling their mission of Charity, relieving alike both friend and foe.

As usual, he kept up a steady correspondence:

Castro Urdiales   26th April 1874
Provincia de Santander

My dearest Ma,
It is Sunday, and we are going to have a day of rest unless anything unusual goes on in camp. It is so funny that we have quite a compact little set of Englishmen here, all good friends, we meet every night for tea before dinner, and generally spend the day together more or less. The special correspondent of *The Times* arrived yesterday and I took him to the camp . . .
    We found all quite quiet and a sort of armistice going on between the two sides; it is not an armistice *actually*, as there is some fighting, we hear, going on in a South West direction where Concha's column is moving but the news is not certain.
    . . . We went to the ruined village of Murrieta, the storming of which cost the government troops 1,500 men. The Carlist lines were on the hillside not far off and the Carlist soldiers came down to talk with the government soldiers where we were and to fetch water; it was such a curious sight to see the soldiers such good friends and talking about past and future events; discussing their respective rations, wine etc. and each trying to make the other desert. The Officers are extremely polite and explained everything to us.
    There is a lull happily in the ambulance work, I have been the round of

some of the hospitals, and there is not now any great want, the Societies and the Government having come in aid.

After the battle of Somorrostro the privations of the wounded must have been awful as no provision had been made for such a large number as 3,000. We have now everything ready in case a battle does come off. Our steam ship, the *Somorrostro* is lying off the harbour full of stores . . . [The rest of the letter is missing.]

A full yet succinct account of his work was sent to the Society in London:

To the Secretary of the English Society   20th May 1874
for the Relief of the Sick and Wounded
of the Spanish War
Hotel de France
Saint Jean de Luz

Dear Sir,
I have the honour to report to the Committee of the Society the following particulars relating to the transport of wounded and convalescent Carlists from Santurce to Socoa en route for Lesaca. The numbers were as follows:

Wounded and convalescent	242
Staff of four hospitals, including 4 doctors, 7 assistants, 41 infirmiers 1 Chaplain etc. and 6 ladies	68
TOTAL	300 [*sic*]

The materiel consisted of complete hospital stores, beds, mattresses etc. for 250 patients, also a carriage and four horses.

Marshall Concha had given permission to allow the transport, but difficulties arose as to whether the order referred to *all* the materiel of the four hospitals of the Society of la Caridad at Santurce. This caused considerable delay.

On May 12th the *Somorrostro* steamed down the river from Bilbao to Santurce and anchored about 1½ miles from the shore owing to the shallow water nearer in. The embarkation of the stores began at 2 p.m. and was finished by 8 p.m. The embarkation of the patients and staff then began and being continued through the night was finished by 6 a.m. the following morning.

When all were on board I went to Portugalete and to the Alcalde of Santurce to get a bill of health and other papers, and at 2 p.m. we weighed anchor. We arrived off Socoa at 10 a.m. the following morning May 14th. Two doctors were sent on board to inspect the ship and we were kept waiting until 12 o'clock that we received permission to land. Carriages on shore were ready to receive the wounded by 3.30 p.m. and then the disembarkation began. It was completed with the exception of a few infirmiers and stores by 8 p.m.

Lesaca, the destination of the wounded is about 22 kilometres from Socoa, the road passes over the frontier near Irun by the bridge of Behobie, the Spanish side of which is held by the Government troops. These refused to allow the wounded to pass in the Carlist country until 10.30 p.m. when M. Bourgade, the director of the ambulances of Santurce and myself drove to the frontier. We showed the order of Marshall Concha again, and after some explanation the 35 or 40 carriages containing the wounded were allowed to pass in batches of 5 or 6. We waited until 11.30 when the last passed safely into the Carlist lines.

The carriages had to be ferried across the Bidasoa river about three kilometres beyond Behobie near the village of Endarlaza, as the bridge had been blown up by Santa Cruz many months ago. This was effected by means of a raft constructed by fastening planks across two flat bottomed boats; two horses fell into the river during the transit but were not hurt. All arrived safely at Lesaca early the following morning May 15th.

About 30 of the most serious cases were not conveyed direct to Lesaca, but have since been taken on by easy stages. There has only been one death during the whole journey, which was very satisfactory; the poor man died after being landed, he had been placed in a cottage on the road to Lesaca, as it was not considered that he was strong enough to stand the journey.

I drove to Lesaca with Mr Bourgade and Mr Allen Young on the 18th, and visited the hospitals to which the wounded had been taken; I found all most comfortable and well arranged, and the patients doing very well.

On the 16th May I saw the Duchess of Madrid who expressed her sincere thanks to the Society for the service which it had rendered in the transport.

Sixty Carlist wounded are still lying at Santurce, they not having been in a fit state to be moved on the 14th May. Mr Bourgade is very anxious to have them transported to Lesaca in about 8 days and has asked me if there was any chance of our Society helping them. I sent a telegram to the Society on this subject.

Please send an answer by telegram or letter to Mr W. Bourgade, Hotel de France, Saint Jean de Luz.

I ordered the Capt'n of the *Somorrostro* to sail to Portugalete late on May 16th and immediately communicate with Mr Batters's agents at Bilbao and Santander. I have left 14 mattresses on board in case of any further transports, but these will be returned to the Society.

The ship was thoroughly fumigated and cleaned out the day after the wounded were landed.

Mr Allen Young joined the ship at Santurce and accompanied it to Socoa; he has been of the greatest use and assistance in our somewhat difficult task. He wishes me to say that he has landed the stores which he brought out at Santander under the arrangement which Mr C. Murrieta made; they are in the hands of the Military Authorities and at the disposition of the Society. Mr A. Young will bring home the receipt unless it is required at Santander.

Mr Allen Young and myself go to Santander tomorrow, and sail the following day for England in the yacht *Dream*. I hope to have the pleasure of calling at Messrs Murrieta's office soon after arriving home and shall bring with me receipts and my account of the money placed at my disposition by Mr C. Murrieta.

I gave most of the stores which were left in my charge on board the *Somorrostro* to the care of Mons Mardnin, the servant of Mr Ybarra under an arrangement which I had made with Señor Don Carlos de Larrea, who was to convey them to Madame de Los Heros. I gave some to the Military Hospital of Bilbao, and others to the Sociedad del Estella Benefica [*sic*] and the Sociedad de la Caridad. I have the honour to be,

Yours very truly,

B.K.

Between October 1874 and May 1875 Vincent carried out a second expedition to the conflict:

Hotel Legarralde   22nd October 1874
Hendaye
France

My Dearest Ma,

I wrote a long, long letter to you yesterday, and by some chance it has been lost. I told you all about the battle which took place near Behobia, it was one of the most extraordinary things I ever saw in my life. The enemies were only a few yards off, throwing sometimes even stones at each other. There were a great many present at the fight, they came flocking in from Bayonne, Biaritz etc. even ladies and young girls! It was a curious sight to see these, with thoroughly French costumes, sitting on a hill within 50 yards of the combatants.

I had something in the way of ambulancing to do as there was no doctor at the place. I attended and dressed the wound of a young Frenchman who was shot in the ankle, and while with him was called to help a young girl only 18 years old who had both wrists broken by a bullet. She showed immense courage though in great pain. I went to see this young girl afterwards in the hospital of St Jean de Luz where she was taken to, she is getting on very well and I believe that they will save both her hands.

You will read accounts of this fight in the papers so I will not tell you about it here. I wrote a letter to *The Times* and sent two sketches to the *Graphic* also to the *Monde Illustré* of Paris. I expect that they will come out *if* put in *next Saturday*.

Pamplona   26th October 1874

One line to say that I have safely crossed the lines, I hired a mule and a boy and leaving the Carlist lines at 4 arrived at 4.45 in this beautiful and strong town of Pamplona. To my great delight I found Landa, who was the Government Inspector of Voluntary Societies at Somorrostro and whom I saw in French War. He introduced me to the Governor today who was very kind etc. I have brought in two cases of Liebig with me which will be very acceptable to the ambulance. My name has been sent in for a medal.

Ambulancia de la Caridad   29th October 1874
Yrache

My dearest Ma,

I am sure that this letter will at last reach you. I have been very anxious about you as I fear many of the short letters which I have casually packed off may never have arrived. I have completed my ambulance mission to Pamplona, and got in and out of the besieged city without any danger or difficulty to speak of. I have written a letter by this messenger to *The Times* describing my journey there, which I expect they will put in if there is no more exciting news. It is dated from Pamplona Oct 27th.

I am here in the middle of friends, most comfortably located in a convent, the guest, or rather co-worker, of my friends Señors Bourgade and Barrena, . . . They are very kind and have given me a room and lent me a horse, and asked me to work with them from here. As there may be a battle about 10 miles off I think I can do most good by co-operating with them. Do not therefore be in the least anxious about my safety.

I had a talk with the King for one hour tonight. I was presented to him yesterday. He has a most agreeable manner and received me most kindly . . .

31st October 1874

. . . I shall write you a long letter of news tomorrow, but am tired tonight.

Beaumont and Havilland are still here.[9] It makes it very pleasant for me. They have very grand uniforms as Knights of Malta and I feel rather small at times trotting beside them in my shooting coat, however there is, perhaps, something distingué in being the only civilian when all around are soldiers.

I was very well received by the King when I saw him the day before yesterday, or rather night, for I only went there at 10.30 and it was 11 p.m. before he invited me to come into his private room and we had a long talk for nearly an hour.

I like Beaumont very much and Havilland too. We have been out riding every day I have been here.

We are located in an old convent – high cloisters etc. The long galleries are well fitted up for a hospital. Fancy the place was deserted only 6 months ago and was fast becoming a ruin, when Bourgade and Barrena's enterprise turned it into a hospital for 400 men!

I am of course the only Protestant in the place and they have many a sly allusion to it, but in the best humour possible, of course, I have my hit too now and then.

Yrache   20th November 1874
Address same as before as I return here

My dearest Ma,

I am now perfectly well again and to restore myself perfectly spent yesterday and today riding, morning and afternoon, so you see I cannot be very bad. The vaccination marks are drying up completely, it has taken enough to be efficient. I begin to think the sun is shining upon me again. My voice has come back as strong as ever, I have not had any return of the cough and the Austrian doctor says that I *must* be perfectly cured of my bronchitis or it would have returned when I took that chill.

Now for the future and my plans.

There are some wounded Republican soldiers lying in this hospital, and they want me to take them back to the Republican lines; then go to Vitoria and fetch a wounded Carlist, someone of an influential family and who is lying wounded in hospital there. They give me a couple of mules and a coche, a sort of covered carriage, and I have decided to do this little business. I shall most probably cross into the other lines in about 2 days and return here in 5.

I shall distribute my money or rather the Society's while in the Republican lines and shall then be free to return home. There will be no danger I am sure. I shall be as well known among the Repubs. as here, and remember I have the excellent passport signed at the Spanish Embassy in London, and also the still better passport of several wounded Republicans – Do not be nervous.

Fonda de Cristo   24th November 1874
Logroño

Please address any letter to Hotel de France, St Jean de Luz.

Dear de Murrieta,
I yesterday arrived here safely in the charge of nine Republican wounded who had been treated, ever since the battle of Abarzuza, in the Carlist ambulance of La Caridad established in the Monastery of Yrache. The Republicans received a most friendly reception from the Carlists at Los Arcos, where we stopped for lunch; they drank each others healths, and seemed to part on excellent terms. I had no difficulty in passing the lines, being well supplied with the necessary papers.

Immediately on arriving at Logroño, I gave over the wounded to the Chief Medical Officer of the Military Hospital 'el Seminario', together with the hospital reports on each case. He expressed his thanks most warmly for our Society having undertaken the evacuation of these men.

I shall be at Miranda tomorrow or the day after, and shall write to you about the hospital of the Cruz Roja which I hear has been established there.

An extract from Vincent's unpublished report to the Society:

On the 28th Nov. I left Haro and arrived at Miranda on the Ebro, where the Red Cross Society of Madrid had formed a permanent hospital of about 60 or 70 beds. These were nearly all occupied by sick soldiers, the wounded being treated in the Military hospitals. They were in want of some blankets and tobacco which I brought back for them from Vitoria. I also gave Don Juan D. Gulado, their medical director a donation of £40 out of our Society's funds. The Red Cross Society of Madrid had for some time discontinued sending any ambulances to accompany the armies in the field, and confined itself to keeping up the permanent hospital at Miranda to which I have alluded.

Hearing that a column under General Loma was going to march to Vitoria I arranged to accompany it. The Carlist, who held the village of La Puebla between Miranda and Vitoria, retired on the approach of the column so we passed without any fighting. I remained at Vitoria three days and visited all the hospitals but did not find that any pecuniary assistance was wanted. I then purchased the things required for the Red Cross Society and, obtaining the wounded Carlist soldier, returned to Miranda. We met a Government column half way, and the Carlists having again retired from La Puebla at its approach, we passed without any difficulty. I left Logroño on the 4th of December and passed safely into Carlist lines. I had great difficulty in persuading anybody to give me a conveyance, owing to the danger of passing the lines being so greatly exaggerated.

Before leaving Logroño I asked the Inspector of the Military Hospital if he was in want of anything which I could supply. He told me that the Military Hospitals were not in want of any assistance. He was, at the same time, very anxious that I should bring back to Logroño any other Government wounded whom I might find in the Carlist lines.

Part of letter to his mother. The date is not known but it was probably written in late December 1874 from Yrache:

I ascertained that no priests ever went near the prison to instruct or console. I then visited the civil prison and spoke to a boy of 16 who, three years ago, killed a woman with a knife; the woman was attacking his mother, and this young boy of 13 took up the knife to defend his mother. No priest had ever given the boy any instruction and he seemed of a good though passionate character. I pitched into the priests right and left, saying that I as a Protestant was astonished to find that in a country which prided itself on its religion, which was actually carrying on a religious war, that not a single of the multitude of priests thought it worth while to say a kind word of comfort, or give religious instruction to the wretched inhabitants of the prison. They were utterly ashamed of themselves and I was informed by one of their heads that they were going to give instruction immediately but the truth was that everyone had forgotten about the prisoners. They were in all about 250 in number.

The priests even were pleased with me for having spoken out so openly my mind; I am sure that this is the best way down here. They trust me to any amount. Do not think of publishing any of this letter as I do not wish to expose their faults after they have corrected them.

I am (from today) making a reform in the stables. I am going to buy cloths to put under the saddles of the horses and mules who are always getting sore backs. The Spaniards are most cruel to animals and I am trying to teach them a little humanity. I have seized and *hidden* most of the curb chains which I can get hold of, as they always ride on the curb with very severe bits, to the agony of the poor beasts.

Convento de Yrache   23rd January 1874 [*sic* 1875]
Near Estella
Spain

My dear Fleetwood,

I promised to let you know something of my ambulance work, and I am going to fulfil my promise, though rather late. I have made this place my headquarters for nearly three months as I find I can be of more use here than on the Alphonsist side where there are no voluntary Societies in the field. I have occasionally passed the lines into Logroño and Vitoria on ambulance missions, but this is very dangerous work and I hope never to have to do it again. I got into difficulties last time and had to resort to a very hazardous way of getting out of them.

I had been asked to pass some hospital Sisters of Charity into Logroño (as they had to go to Madrid) and to buy some medicines and other things for our hospitals here, also to treat about some Carlist wounded who were in the then Republican lines. We all started from here together and in about five hours reached Viana, where Carlist outposts are generally placed. There had been a Republican raid on Viana two days before and in consequence both sides were very 'savage'. The commandant of the 'partidas', Carlist Irregulars, who were in occupation of Viana told me that it was impossible for me to pass into Logroño, would very probably be shot and at the least lose my horse.

After this warning I rode on by myself through the deserted four miles between the lines until I reached Logroño Bridge. I had almost arrived at the guard house when out jumped a soldier and, pointing gun at me, told me to halt. I did not object to this, but I did to his continuing to point a gun at me until the guard turned out, a period of about five minutes which seemed to me quite half an hour. I was then kept waiting half an hour until they received a communication from the Governor of the Town, and was then allowed to pass. I saw General Laserna the next morning and obtained from him permission to pass the Sisters; so I rode back to the Carlists and returned with the Sisters who had to walk as the owner of the diligence which brought them to Viana had taken fright and driven back to Estella.

It so happened that I arrived the day before the pronunciamiento of the army, or rather of its officers for Prince Alphonso.[10] This was unfortunate for me, as it looked very much as if I had gone to Logroño on purpose to find out what was the effect. Who suspected me I do not know, it could not have been Laserna as he knew me; however a rascally Spanish correspondent was writing all manner of absurd things against the Carlists, and wishing to give some extra authority for his statements, quietly wrote my name as an authority for the nonsense! I found myself in a very difficult position; I could get no redress from anyone. The correspondent had left the place, luckily for him before I received the newspaper, I knew that the Carlists would receive the Madrid newspaper and if they believed the statement about me would shoot me immediately on my return. I was told by an officer that this was an old trick, they try to get some innocent person shot in order to create bad feelings. I can hardly believe such a thing possible, but there are some atrocious scoundrels in the world. As this was a matter of honour as far as I was concerned and which implicated my ambulance friends at Yrache I determined at once to give the best answer possible to the statement namely to ride straight back into the Carlist lines with the Madrid newspaper in my pocket. The Alphonsist officers seemed astounded when I asked for the order to pass the bridge and return to the Carlists, several warned me of the fate of a poor Alcalde (Mayor) who was shot by the Carlists under precisely the same conditions, but I stuck to my own opinion, and felt sure that on my presenting myself to the Carlist authorities with the paragraph in my pocket, they would believe me rather than the paper. I accordingly rode back through the deserted four miles; my only misgiving was as to the state in which the Carlists were; how had they stood the pronunciamiento – was it true as the Alphonsist papers said, that they were all fighting among themselves? To my great relief on reaching Viana I heard that all was quiet so I pushed on to Yrache and Estella, and had a telegram sent to the Carlist Minister of War to say that I had returned to Estella with the newspaper in my pocket, or rather the paragraph out of it. This at once set matters right; they laugh now over the matter at the hospital but are utterly surprised at my having so coolly cut the Gordian knot by returning at once from Logroño. How foolish the Spanish correspondent must have looked when he heard that I had returned to Estella! I was told he had written it on purpose to prevent my returning to the Carlists, he was a Republican and might have had some notion that I was plotting with the Carlists and Alphonsists on the subject of putting down Serrano and arranging the 'pronunciamiento'.

I passed another time into Logroño to take back nine wounded Republican soldiers who had been lying in this hospital for over four months, and who had become at last so far convalescent as to be able to travel. This was a most interesting journey – the Carlist soldiers at Los Arcos, a halfway village where we had dinner, were very kind to their enemies' wounded; they gave them wine, cigars etc. and all shook hands heartily as they separated. The Republicans were very grateful to me for this work.

A civil war is a terrible thing indeed, brother against brother and father against son, and I am afraid that the war is likely to last a long long time, even if the Alphonsists are successful in forcing their way to Estella and Pamplona.

I paid a Christmas visit to the Republican prisoners in the prison of Estella, and gave them some blankets, shoes and cigars, the poor fellows were so thankful.

They were all anxious to be exchanged, as their position is not altogether a safe one. At any moment they may be shot in retaliation for some act of the other side. A few days ago four Carlists were taken by Moriones' soldiers near Tafalla, and said to be shot in cold blood; General Mendiry, the Carlist Commander-in-chief accordingly ordered eight Republican prisoners to be shot the same night, their names to be chosen by lot.

There are rumours that the war is now going to be carried on without quarter; if so our position here at Yrache is a bad one. We are at the foot of a splendid mountain called Monte Jurra; on the other side are the celebrated Carlist trenches which the Republicans could not take in November 1873, and which are now stronger than ever. If, however, they take them in the attack which is sure to come off soon, they will of course come along the high road to Estella, and this Monastery with our 300 wounded and sick is the first large building which they will come across. I must stay by the wounded to protect them and shall share their fate. I earnestly hope that quarter will be given, in spite of the occasional atrocities perpetrated. The greater part of the inhabitants of the monastery have all made up their minds that they will be massacred if ever the Alphonsists arrive here. I hope to be able to protect them more than any Spaniard could; as an Englishman, they dare not touch me *openly*, and I know some of the Alphonsist officers who were with me when I was working on the other side and who would assist me in protecting the wounded.

And now that I have talked a great deal about the Carlists you must not think that I take any party spirit in the war. I do not really sympathise with either side, but I pity sincerely the soldiers whose hard fate it is to live in a country where they must either fight or be a disgrace to their families and villages. When a man is once wounded it is too late to inquire whether or not he was justified in fighting. I have just been paying a visit to some of my 'favourite' wounded. I must tell you that some, who belong to families living on the other side of the Ebro, are completely cut off from all communication with their homes, and they generally belong to the Castile battalions who receive little or no pay: They are therefore very poor. I give them tobacco and cigarettes etc. I saw a strange scene in one of the wards. Two poor young fellows both very severely wounded, were lying side by side, being tended by their mothers who had travelled here on foot from their villages when they heard that their sons were wounded, I fear very much that one at least will die of his wounds.

I have lately returned from near Viana; there was an attack by three Carlist battalions on six Alphonsist battalions with cavalry and artillery which had entrenched themselves in a village called Aras near Viana. After resisting for three hours the Alphonsists gave way, leaving their dead in the hands of the Carlists. The morning on which I arrived was very foggy, and not having found a bed the night before I was very sleepy; I was accompanied by a doctor, an assistant, and an infirmier. We none of us knew the road and in consequence rode by accident quite close to the Alphonsist lines; had the fog lifted we might easily have been taken prisoner, as it was we found out our mistake in time, and cut across by a mountain path to our destination. We brought back the wounded the same night but they did not reach Yrache until the following morning owing to one of the ambulance waggons having broken down.

All is in profound quiet here now, it is the calm before the storm. We know that Prince Alphonso is at Tafalla and they say that the Alphonsist troops are massing there to attack the centre of the Carlist lines. Don Carlos is expected here shortly, so in all probability the rival claimants will be personally engaged on either side in the great battle that is expected.

The Carlist soldiers are extremely confident of success, and seem in the best of spirits. They have most of them fought at Abarzuza or Monte Jurra, and rely upon their trenches and bayonet charges at the critical moment to secure their success. It is a pity to think that so many of these fine young fellows are distined to be 'food for cannon' especially in a civil war.

I am living here completely among Catholics, and of course they have often tried to convert me, but never will. In this hospital there are 14 Sisters of Charity, about 12 Monks of a medico-religious order, some of them are celebrated doctors, others assistants etc. The men who do the secretary work are for the most part ex-students of the Seminario of Pamplona, which is a great training college for Priests. One of the directors of the ambulance is a professor of Theology and Moral Science of Pamplona University, the other an enthusiastic French Legitimist, among the Brothers of the religious order are one Greek and two Austrians, thus, counting myself, there are representatives of five nations at work here. I get on very well with all of them, we speak all manner of languages, on one occasion at dinner ten different languages were spoken in the course of conversation.

By way of contrast the following account of the same incident, written to his mother, is of interest:

The following is a short account of my last journey which I took *to protect 11 Sisters of Charity passing the lines.* Starting from Yrache at 9 on the day after Christmas Day we arrived at Los Arcos at 12. The nine Sisters with two 'Superioras' were in a diligence drawn by four mules and I was accompanying them, like an equerry, on horseback. We had a hearty reception and good lunch at the convent of Los Arcos, and started off on our way at 1.15, reaching Viana by 3. Here were the Carlist outposts, who were in a very savage mood. It appeared that the Republican volunteers had made, two days previously, a raid into Viana, and carried off 40 mules laden with booty, (the mules have been since returned). In consequence of this and of the day beginning to draw to a close, it was not considered advisable for the Sisters to enter the Republican lines that night, so I left my charges in the hands of the 'Superiora' and nuns of the Convent at Viana, and jumped on my horse, cantered off in the twilight to the Republicans. The last word of the Carlist outpost was 'Ride hard as it is dangerous to approach Logroño after dark'. I arrived within 50 yards of the bridge without meeting a soul, when suddenly out popped a soldier, who raising his rifle ordered me to stop. I can tell you that I stopped before I was told! A few minutes afterwards the whole guard turned out, and I was ordered to advance. A few minutes conversation with the officer commanding the post made matters all right. I was allowed to pass into the town tremendously to the astonishment of everybody: I myself knew it would be all right. I saw General Laserna that night and obtained from him the necessary pass for the Sisters of Charity; I rode back to Viana alone the following morning, passing on my way a large pool of blood where I was told a poor peasant had been killed by the Republican volunteers. I believe it was the blue blood of a Castilian mule, but I kept my opinion to myself, as it is no good contradicting a Spaniard.

On arriving again at Viana I found myself again with the Carlists, and, to my astonishment, heard that the coach and mules had 'retired gracefully' to Estella, leaving my Sisters at the Convent of Viana. Nothing was to be done but to walk to Logroño, so all the country girls stuffed themselves with a good lunch, and an extra supply of cakes and chocolates, and bravely set out on a four mile walk. We strapped their little luggage on the backs of two donkeys, which followed us. My horse having cast a shoe, I was obliged to walk too, which, considering that the greater part of the distance I was conversing with a peach-cheeked black-eyed novice of Navarre, was by no means a disagreeable occupation. I called my Sisters my 'Pollitas' (little chickens)! – at which they were greatly amused. Having previously made all necessary arrangements at the Republican outposts, I had no difficulty in passing my charges but unfortunately they all missed the train which was to take them from Logroño to Madrid, owing to the obstinacy or incapability of one of the donkeys who would lie down or kick off the boxes of the good nuns, containing, no doubt, many a holy relic!

However we were none the worse for missing the train as the Logroño Sisters have a large wing of their splendid hospital, and here the novices were housed for the night – the following day I saw them all off by the train, and wished them goodbye amid a chorus of melodious voices answering 'Adios Don Vicente'! Of course I am a good deal 'twitted' about the little Knight Errant trip, but I can defend myself well. I have had a longish talk with Marshall Serrano, and shall see this evening General Laserna after which I decide future plans.

An extract from Vincent's unpublished report to the Society:

During the last fortnight in January great preparations were being made to resist the advance of the Government troops on Pampeluna, the condition of which was becoming most critical. As there was a want of medicines and money in the ambulances at Estella and Puente La Reina I rode back by Salinas de Oro, Leiza and the Ezcurra pass to St Jean de Luz where I arrived on the 27th January. I supplied myself with money at Bayonne, bought the required medicines and then went to Pau to receive about £300 in gold which Doña Margarita wished me to take back to the Estella and

A Carlist ox-drawn ambulance

Puente ambulances, as quickly as I could. I had hardly recrossed the Spanish frontier when I heard the long expected movement had really begun. This was late on the evening of the 31st. The following morning I started on horseback from Lesaca and riding all day arrived the same evening at the Venta de Arraiz about 18 miles North of Pampeluna. I heard here a very confused account of what had happened, one thing only was certain and that was that I should have to ride hard the next day to reach Puente la Reina, and so it turned out. Starting an hour before day break the following morning I passed four miles to the north of Pampeluna, almost at the very time that Moriones[11] column was making its triumphal entry into that town, I then cut across country to Ororbia and thence followed the high road to Puente. I subsequently fell in with some Carlist regiments returning in disgust from Carrascal and entered Puente with these at about eight p.m.

Here I found everything in great confusion; the news of the entry of Moriones into Pampeluna had been rapidly followed by that of the advance of Primo de Rivera's[12] column across the high road between Puente and Estella. The latter movement completely cut off the retreat of the greater part of the Carlist Artillery which had been withdrawn from the trenches commanding the Carrascal pass, and the fortress of San Guillermo overlooking Puente and in addition placed more than half the Carlist forces in a most critical position.

Orders were given for a general retreat in the direction of Estella, and as a night attack on Puente was considered possible we were requested to remove at once all the sick and wounded to Artazu a village on the other side of the river, about a mile from and overlooking the town. The inmates of the hospital, about 50 in number, many of whom were in a very bad state of smallpox, were hurried out of their comfortable wards and, after being taken over the bridge, were laid down in rows by the side of the road, while waggons went back to fetch the large and valuable materiel of the hospital. The night was exceedingly dark and it was morning before we had finished our work and placed the sick and wounded in the cottages provided for them in the village. We little thought then that we should have to retreat under still more difficult circumstances!

The next day, February 3rd, was one of great suspense. While in our front General Moriones was advancing from Pampeluna, to occupy Puente la Reina, in our rear, at Lacar, the head of Gen. Primo de Rivera's column was beginning to entrench itself, and some picked regiments of Carlists were manoeuvring round it, preparing for the afternoon attack.

It seemed like a race, whether the Carlists would assault before Moriones came up.

All this was taking place in open daylight, with a bright sun shining overhead, it was difficult to believe that a terrible crisis was so near at hand. We found ourselves blocked up in a cul-de-sac at Artazu; the only road leading out of the village was the road to Puente; in our rear was nothing but the roughest mountain paths, difficult even for mules and perfectly impassable for carts or waggons of any description. It seemed certain that we must be taken prisoner, as we could not desert the wounded and sick. Under these circumstances, I volunteered to take charge of the ambulances and was allowed to choose a doctor and an assistant and a few infirmiers to stay with me. The rest of the personnel, including Don Manuel Barrena the indefatigable Director, by making a detour in the mountains, retired safely to Yrache, whence they immediately fetched other waggons and materiel and returned to Lacar to attend to the wounded who had fallen in the afternoon attack. These latter were all safely taken to Yrache, and consisted of about 50 of the Government forces and 250 Carlists. Some idea may be formed of the ferocity of that struggle when I state that over 950 of the Government soldiers were buried during the two following days, and the great mass of these had been killed with the bayonet. Of the poor fellows who were taken to Yrache, some had received over eight bayonet thrusts, and nearly all had more than one wound. The fighting which had provoked these terrible results, had taken place hand to hand and from house to house. I spent £20 of the Society's funds in aid of the Government wounded who fell into the Carlist hands on this occasion.

To return to Artazu, the battle of Lacar was not over when Marione's column appeared on the opposite side of the river. After occupying Puente where it met with no resistance, the head of the column crossed the bridge and advanced to within a few hundred yards of us.

A few Carlist companies had entrenched themselves on the sloping sides of the Santa Barbara hill close by and these offered a determined resistance, which resulted in the Government troops retiring to the head of the bridge, where they proceeded to throw up some earth works. Half an hour afterwards a battery of horse artillery emerged from Puente and taking up a position about 1,500 yards off proceeded to bombard us. I hoisted some red cross flags over the cottages where the sick and wounded were lying, which had not at first the desired effect of stopping the fire.

The Carlists, who had no artillery at Artazu did not return the fire, and the Government batteries subsequently retired to Puente but only to return the following day and send some more shells into the village.

I had not had a good night's rest since I left France, so I was utterly tired out but owing to an attack on the village being hourly expected I did not go to bed. The night was exceedingly dark and three times before midnight the outposts reported that the Government troops were in movement; I advanced each time with a red cross flag in order to make arrangements for the protection of the sick and wounded in my charge. After the frightful massacre at Lacar in the afternoon I knew that little quarter would be given in the event of the village being attacked with the bayonet. At about 2 a.m. five more companies of Carlists occupied the village, and I was given orders to take away the sick and wounded to a safer place before daybreak the following morning.

I then began my second night retreat. I had only been left three horses and a mule, the soldiers had more work than they could do, and we could expect but little help from the panic-stricken peasants. However by making all of the sick and wounded who could walk or ride do so and carrying the rest by detachments in stretchers they were all removed without any accident to Guirguillano, a little mountain village about a mile and a half from Artazu. We were supplied with beds and bedding by the hospitable inhabitants and in a few hours the invalids were all in comfortable quarters though dreadfully fatigued by their two nights journeys.

During the next few days I borrowed some mules at Guirguillano and returning to Artazu with Don Felipe Barrena, succeeded in removing out of danger the most valuable part of the materiel which we had been obliged to abandon in our hasty retreat. The unfortunate village was in the mean time being subjected to a bombardment by fits and starts. One shell only fell into the ambulance but fortunately it did no harm . . .

During the latter part of February negotiations were carried on with General Quesda about the wounded government soldiers who had been taken to the Yrache ambulance after the battle of Lacar. These negotiations resulted in the two directors of the Society of La Caridad, Don M. Barrena and Monsr. Bourgade together with myself taking over to the Government lines at Oteiza a convoy of about 30 of these wounded. Nearly all of them had been supplied at Yrache with new hospital suits owing to their own uniforms having been torn to pieces or lost at Lacar.

Extract from a letter to his brother-in-law, Alfred, from Yrache, 3 March 1875:

How sad are the consequences of a battle. Many of the poor young fellows whom our ambulance brought in from Lacar are dying off from their wounds. The rather overcrowded state of the hospital has made the air impure, and we cannot save more than one or two in six of the amputated.

Yesterday I accompanied 24 wounded Alphonsists to Oteiza, which is now occupied by the Government. They are nearly always firing between the outposts there, but yesterday afternoon let us go by unmolested. There was great excitement among the Alphonsist soldiers to see whom we had brought. I am sorry to say that in the heat of the fight many of the wounded were bereft of their clothes, being thought dead, so we had to re-dress the wounded in Caridad uniforms. The Alphonsist general was extremely grateful for our attention to the poor fellows. We returned to Yrache the same evening without any adventure, except that, in jumping a high bank, my horse fell and myself with it; I could not disengage myself from the saddle in time owing to my having those horrid Spanish stirrups like this and my foot stuck. I was not hurt and was soon in the saddle again, jumping other banks, much to the surprise of my Spanish companions, who, like most Spaniards, are shockingly bad and timid horsemen. The cruelty of these people to animals is something revolting. I am in charge of the stables, and try in vain to check it. They laugh at the idea of humanity towards beasts, and beat and torment them to their hearts' delight. I had a tussle with a man the other day who beat a mule on the *nose* and *head* with a big stick until it fell to the ground: I seized *by force* the stick from the brute's hand; and held it over his head with my finest Spanish oath that I would kill him if he touched the animal again. He became subdued and still more so when I had fined him a fortnight's pay for his brutality! The Spaniards themselves cannot manage Spaniards except by force of bullying, and they are accustomed to it. The only difficulty is that all Navarrese carry huge knives in their belt, and now and then use them when they completely lose their temper. However they are invariably *afraid* of an Englishman.

Vincent's third and final expedition to the Carlist Wars was made between September 1875 and May 1876. On this occasion he does not seem to have written home much, but he did write to Mrs Schuster, a benefactor of the Society and friend. On his return he also gave a lecture to the Order of St John:

During the last two battles of the war, namely those of Peña Plata and Echalar, fought on the French frontier in February 1876, the neutral position held by our Society was of great service. I had undertaken the charge of a hospital and field-ambulance at Lesaca, in the Carlist lines, a few miles from the point at which the Carlists had determined, with terrible odds against them, to make a last stand. We were engaged with our ambulance section both days, and on the second were exposed to a very heavy fire, owing to the rapid advance of the Government troops. The Town Hall, the School, the Tower (for smallpox), and the chaplain's house, which four buildings formed our hospital, were full to overcrowding; besides, there were numbers of wounded in the neighbouring cottages under our care. After having been driven from the heights of Echalar, the Carlist troops were thrown back on Lesaca, where we were subjected to a short bombardment from the Alphonsist mountain artillery cresting the hills on the further side of the Bidasoa. The Carlists then evacuated Lesaca, when we found ourselves between the lines with our 300 wounded, including General Larumbe, the commander of the Carlist forces engaged in the two battles. As we had no adequate provision for so many wounded, and scarcely any one dared venture out of the village for fear of being caught and treated as a spy by either Alphonsists or Carlists, we decided to treat with the Government General, Martínez Campos, with the view of securing protection. I approached the Alphonsist lines near Vera under cover of a white flag, taking with me four of the Government wounded who had fallen into our hands, and whom I handed over to the medical authorities on my arrival at Vera. I had no trouble in passing the lines, being well received by the Brigadier Navascues, in command at Vera. Not so, however, at Irun, farther on, where I was arrested by the civil police, and had great difficulty in bringing the fact to the knowledge of the Commandant. He immediately put me at liberty, and censured the police for their officious interference. . . .

Lesaca was, as I have mentioned, overcrowded with wounded; and small-pox of a virulent type and broken out in the village. In consequence I made arrangements with the French Government authorities at Bayonne for the evacuation of 80 of the worst cases of wounded who could stand the fatigue of a journey, to the civil and military hospitals of that town. They were sent from Lesaca by our ambulance mules and country carts to the Bidasoa. The bridge had been destroyed, and as the ford across the river was too rocky and deep to allow a cart to pass, we took the wounded over in boats, and also in 'cacolets' on mules. On the farther side of the river we placed them in omnibuses and conveyed them through Vera as far as Endarlaza, where another bridge over the Bidasoa had been blown up. The omnibuses were here ferried across in large flat-bottomed boats. We followed a good road to Beobia, where we crossed the Bidasoa for the third time, and entered French territory. Another half-hour's drive brought us to Hendaye railway station, where refreshments were provided, and whence the wounded were sent by train to Bayonne. I had some luggage-waggons fitted up with thick layers of hay to make the railway journey as comfortable as possible. At Bayonne omnibuses were sent down to meet the wounded, and they were at once conveyed to two of the best hospitals in the South of France. The Inspector of the French Military Hospital of Bayonne gave us every assistance, and was unremitting in his labours to promote the comfort of the wounded placed under his charge.

So great was the panic and excitement at the termination of the war that it would hardly have been possible to carry out these operations without the intervention of a Society acting in a neutral capacity, and trusted by both sides.

Vincent's letters convey something of the urgency and chaos of the times:

Ambulancia de Lesaca   7th February 1876
Navarre

My dear Fleetwood,

I have been out here since the early autumn on my ambulance work and have had a more or less hard time of it, now and then taking a delightful holiday at Biarritz where I have met many old friends. I hope that this will find you and all at home well, the cold winter must have been very trying to Mrs Sandeman but I hope the frost has now passed for good.

I left England in August and after spending a few pleasant weeks in the French Pyrennees with Brackley, I crossed into Catalonia and Aragon, where the Carlists were retiring and then passed to my old quarters in Navarre.

I found the ambulances much poorer than when I left them in May last year, partly owing to the large subscriptions which had been given to the sufferers from the French inundations, and partly owing to the dissensions among the Carlist sympathisers after the defeat of Dorregaray in Valencia and Saballs in Catalonia. I was on my way home when I stopped at this hospital which I found extremely badly off for funds, so much so that I took over the whole responsibility of providing for it for six weeks or two months, in fact until the present series of operations are over. We have here in this, which I almost call my, hospital sixty sick and wounded, some very seriously ill, as today the chaplain gave the sacrament to one who is dying of his wounds and another who will fall a victim to typhus.

We are in addition threatened with a battle about three hours off to our left, and to our right 13 Carlist battalions are concentrated to attack the huge column of Martinez Campos. We are told to expect two hundred wounded more!

At present the only paid 'personnel' consist of the doctor, an assistant, a chemist and some infirmiers; these are all paid a merely nominal salary, as you can imagine when I tell you that the whole hospital expenses do not come to £30 to £35 a month, including the occasional purchase of blankets! You must remember that the ordinary *rations* are provided gratis; these provide for the great part of the 'eating', but of course there are many things which we must buy.

Several of my friends at Biarritz paid little flying visits here to see the hospital, and sent in contributions which were quite sufficient to keep it going, but now we shall have much greater expenses I fear, owing to the certainty of a great battle taking place on one or other side of us. If the Carlists are again obliged to give way we shall all be taken prisoner, as we all have decided not to leave the wounded and it will be impossible to take them away. Another point is that we should have nowhere to take them to!

I do not, as you know, take any personal interest in the success of either side beyond admiring immensely the courage and high principles of the regular Carlist soldiers who have left their homes, their wives, their all, to fight for a cause which they regard as sacred. I pity intensely these brave peasants, and still more so when they fall and there is no one to help them. If you only knew the horrors of the death of a poor wounded man when his wounds are unattended to, you would not require anything more to make you sympathise with him as much as I do. Say even that these fanatical uneducated peasants ought to know better, that they are the greatest enemies to *our* faith, granted all this, I appeal to the words of our Saviour, who taught us by the parable of the Good Samaritan to assist even our bitterest enemies in their moments of agony and distress.

8th February

My letter was interrupted last night by the disagreeable news that a white Andalusian horse which I had, had been taken ill. I rushed off to get a 'veterinario' who lives in the village and we did all we could, but the poor horse died in an hour and a half . . .

Yesterday morning the Carlists tried to advance from Echalar to attack the Alphonsist column which is now entrenching itself in the conquered positions, but they had to come back owing to there being over three feet of snow in the Peña Plata over which they had to pass. This weather tells very much against the Carlists, who ought at once to dislodge the huge column of Martinez Campos which, by a splendidly executed movement, took by surprise the important Elizondo frontier. From every side except St Sebastian bad news for Don Carlos seems to come. I wonder what will be the end of it all!

Smallpox has I am sorry to say broken out here, two bad cases, (soldiers) have been placed in a little hospital which we have arranged expressly for those suffering from the disease; I hope that it will not spread. One case began in the hospital which looks bad.

As I dare say you may have read in the papers there is a prospect of the rations running short, in this case we shall be put to infinitely greater expense.

If you or your brothers would like to assist in what I conscientiously think is a good human work, I can assure you that your little contributions will go farther to relieve actual physical suffering than you can imagine. A very little goes a long way here, especially when everything is done in the most economical way possible as in the ambulance of Lesaca. I ought to have told you that the Chaplain-Director, the three Sisters of Charity, and two administrators give their service for nothing. We shall have to send for more Sisters.

In case of your wishing to help, pay any little sum to my account at my bankers, Messrs Cocks Biddulph & Co., 43 Charing Cross, SW2 and I need not tell you that I shall thank you in the name of the wounded. You are too old a friend that I should apologise to you for writing a begging letter but I will tell you that I prefer being in a dozen battles to writing one such . . .

Ambulancia de Lesaca   15th February 1876

Dear Mrs Schuster,

Here I am back again at my old quarters; there was some skirmishing in the Echalar direction today but nothing more, neither side seemed inclined to do anything decisive. For two days we have heard a heavy cannonade behind us in the direction of the San Sebastian lines and today there was a sharp fight at Mendisorrotz, some gloomy reports are coming in about the Carlists having abandoned that position; but nothing is known for certain yet.

The bad luck attending the Carlists seems to have followed them in the battle last Sunday near Vergara and Elorrio. They drove back the Alphonsists with great loss at first, but the latter sent round a reserve column which took the Carlists in flank and forced them to retire with 200 killed and wounded. The loss of the Liberals is reckoned at 2,000! How many lives are being sacrificed in this unfortunate struggle. We are gradually getting pinched up in a corner and there the decisive battle will take place.

I have just received news from Estella in which it is said that some large Liberal columns are concentrating in the neighbourhood and that an attack is hourly expected. They seem to be determined to force through the

Carlist lines in all directions before the arrival of King Alphonso, who is to be the 'matador' and give the 'coup de grace'. There is something rather revolting in this project – I do not know why they have not attacked Vera before now, as the Carlists have recommenced work at the shell manufactory.

7 a.m., 16th February

We have had a noisy night. A Navarrese battalion has been sent up in haste from near Santesteban and they arrived here at 11 p.m. last night. The poor fellows were not allowed much rest as before 12 the 'llamada' (assembly) sounded and in another quarter of an hour they were toiling up the steep slopes leading to the mountain position of Echeruleque.

The 'correo' is waiting – so goodbye with kindest regards to all. Tell Miss Schuster, please, that I have not lost the stick which I so ungallantly borrowed for my use.

Yours sincerely,

V. Barrington Kennett

Echalar   Friday
Navarre

Dear Mrs Schuster,

The fight is going on near Echalar and we are sending the wounded as hard as we can to Lesaca. There are a great many. Tell please Jeringham to tell Capt. Chapman to be ready tomorrow at St Jean de Luz, Hotel de France. Perhaps we may send some wounded over the frontier. We are very much in want of a doctor and are sending for one from France.

Eleven years later Vincent had the opportunity briefly to revisit Spain and to meet again some of his friends and co-workers. In his role as travelling representative of the Melbourne Exhibition he went to Spain as well as to other countries to enlist interest and solicit exhibits. By then he had married Alice. He wrote regularly:

Fonda de Roma   17th October 1887
Madrid

My own dear Alice,

I have only written to you such scrubby cards that I feel quite ashamed of myself and though tired to death am determined to write a few lines before sweet sleep carries me back to you and the chicks. I have had a very busy time of it. As usual things drag on in Spain. The fatal Mañana, tomorrow, is the day for doing everything that can possibly be put off, and here I am, not much more advanced than a week ago.

I hear good news from Austria in *The Times* of October 14th and there is also some mention of me in the same paper as regards Spain. Alas, I shall be doomed, not to disappointment, but to failure here I fear. But I can have the pleasure of saying 'I told you so'. I advised against my coming here, but it has resulted in my receiving a very high honour!

A special meeting of the Executive Central Supreme etc. etc. Council of the Spanish Red Cross Society was held last night to give me a reception! The President, who is Major Domo of the Palace first made a pretty speech, followed by a very eloquent one from the 'Advisory Council' of the Red Cross, one Pando y Valle[13] then followed the President again who proposed that the Grand Silver Star of the Red Cross of Spain be conferred upon me. Then was my turn – I really believe I made a good speech in Spanish! and was not in the least nervous though very hungry as I had had no dinner!

I began by quoting the Spanish proverb,
Muertos e idos no tienen amigos
The dead and the absent have no friends
and said that though this was a Spanish proverb yet it was not true as regards Spain. In no country are cherished with deeper veneration the valiant deeds and good works of its illustrious ancestors than in Spain. Cervantes, Palafox, etc. are dead but a thousand friends revere their memory.

As regards the absent I said that I had been 12 years away, and this re-union, this honour bestowed upon me showed that as one of the idos (absent) the proverb was not true 'as I found I have yet amigos en España'.

After, recounting what I saw of their ambulancemen in Somorrostro and the battle of Muñecas and relief of Bilbao, I alluded to the ladies of Madrid and the duchess of Medina Celi, their president who sent so many gifts to the wounded soldiers of the Navarre and Biscay. I spoke of Concha's noble conduct in letting me take away the wounded Carlists to their homes and told them how the Carlists returned the compliment by sending me with a mule load of Liebig into besieged Pamplona. I told them how I saw the Carlist wounded leaving their beds to make way for the more seriously wounded enemies and how those who had been enemies in the field became friends in the hospital and many a tear was shed by those sensitive good hearted peasant soldiers when the enemy of yesterday, the brother of today, had to return cured to join his regiment.

I then said that our Association must not take all the credit. Civilisation, education and progress among people had prepared the ground for the Geneva Convention of which the Red Cross was the flag and symbol for Military as well as for voluntary ambulances.

I wound up by saying that without forgetting what a country owes to its brave soldiers and victorious generals, we looked upon our banner as being that of Peace in War. The banner of chivalry rising in the midst of the worst passions of men, the symbol of the fraternity of all nations and of all classes of Society (which, by the way, someone said was rather Socialistic!) . . .

By the way I hear that in the new book in Spanish on Military Law and Custom they quote my going into Pamplona during the Siege with relief to the wounded as a new precedent for future action. Rather a curious fashion to set!

Fonda de Roma, Madrid   20th October 1887

My own dear Alice,

I called upon the charming widow, the Excelentísima Señora la Duquesa de Medinaceli and Tarifa. She expressed a wish to see the individual whom she had recommended for the Cross of Isabella the Catholic 12 years ago! She was *the* hard worker in the Red Cross. I was charmed with her frank and honest face and manners, and we had a long and most interesting conversation which resulted in her asking me to come in quietly and have dinner with her in her splendid palace tomorrow evening – which I accepted. She must be 40 but I think she looks about 30 and is rather like you! This is why I like her so much.

After further work I went home and found a deputation of the Red Cross Society awaiting my return with a large document and beautiful star, 'Placa de la Cruz Roja' the highest distinction which can be bestowed for ambulance services. They presented it to me and I duly made a nice little speech and accepted it. Also I obtained a medal for Cashel Hoey who was the Hon. Sec. of our Spanish Aid Society for so long and who always put off publishing the beautiful little book of reports which I wrote.

Sir Andrew [Clarke][14] may accompany me through the Carlist country as far as Bordeaux or even Paris and as he has a 'valet courier' I shall probably persuade him to accompany me; but of course I really like Sir Andrew's company. He is a marvellously well read and experienced man. He has filled the highest posts, etc.

Among other people I was introduced to the Marquis Concha, Marquis de la Habana,[15] the brother of the good and brave general who was killed soon after I was with him at the battle of Muñeca. At Muñeca he got a bullet through his sleeve. The brother who is a great gun here, President of the Senate and one of the four 'Capitan Generals' or Marshalls, was much affected when I repeated to him the words his dead brother used when I asked leave to take away the wounded Carlists to their own lines. He said 'Don Vicente, I am a soldier, and I cannot bear to see brave men suffering. If you have the means, I for my part give you leave to transport *all* the wounded Carlists to their homes. May they go with God's blessing!'

I quoted this in my speech last Monday and told him so.

I gave my speech to the interesting Duchess of Medinaceli to read as she was so much interested in all my works and apparently words.

Lesaca   27th October 1887

My dearest Alice,

The Parson of Lesaca, my old friend, Don Hypolito in whose house I am staying won't let me go today and so one more day will elapse before I am fairly on my way to home sweet home.

I left Madrid Tuesday night and arrived at Irun on the Spanish side of the frontier at 11.30 a.m. on Wednesday (yesterday). I at once gobbled down some lunch (oil and garlic predominating) and, hiring a couple of ponies, started off along my old tracks to Lesaca. I felt quite affected as I rode by the houses and bridges and recognised the turnings and pools of the lovely Bidasoa all of which I remember so well, and many recollections and associations of the past rushed into my brain. I remembered my old ideas, my enthusiasm for the work on which I was engaged, and how I longed for the day to be 48 hours long that I might carry out more of it!

It is so satisfactory (is it vanity?) to be received here with honest welcome and gratitude. They tell me that had it not been for the subscriptions and help I brought from Biarritz and my sticking to the wounded when we were surrounded etc. . . . & thereby giving confidence to our employees and preventing them from bolting, the wounded would have been left in a very bad way. Their gratitude I really value intrinsically more than all the crosses and plaques put together. Last night I was sitting round a 'brasero' or brass dish full of smouldering charcoal, my companions being the village priest Don Hypolito, the village doctor Don Nicolas, who had just returned from shooting in the mountains, the old woman who makes the 'bolados' a whipped sugar which one takes with chocolate, and her married son and grandchildren. We were in the sugar shop and for two hours they were recounting to me forgotten stories about myself and I was reminding them of a thousand incidents. At 8 p.m. we adjourned to eat supper with the parson, his old father and mother and two little nieces who were staying with him, and who left today for Irun. Today we, the parson doctor and I, ride to Echalar to see the site of the last battle where I was so nearly shot and to get permission to pass over the mountains into France tomorrow morning.

Hotel de France   31st October 1887
Bordeaux

My own dear Alice,

Well, I must tell you about my mountain journey. I spent Wednesday and Thursday nights at Lesaca 'en casa del cura'. On Thursday Don Nicolas, the village doctor, and Don Hypolito, the priest, and I got on our steeds and rode to Echalar in the mountains close by where the last three days fighting of the Carlist War took place. It was *so* deeply interesting to me. We used to ride together during the war. How many forgotten incidents cropped up! A big stone here, a turn in the road there, a tumble-down cottage on one side or a glimpse at some familiar profile of the glorious peaks on the other, spoke in eloquent terms of a thousand old memories of what was perhaps the most useful and eventful portion of my varied life. I saw the spot where Don Manuel and self and our little ambulance party were caught by the Corpe Partidarios and so nearly lost our lives. I saw the spot whence I wrote a letter to Biarritz to say that we would be surrounded in half an hour and that the war was over. I saw the spot where the last shell fired during the war fell while I was in the next field. – Somewhat tired and a little 'bruised' I returned to Lesaca with the Cura, dined at the 'medico' and met his wife and three chubby children.

The next day, Friday, I rode by the old mountain pass to France, used almost exclusively by contrabandistas, and astonished the Carabineros (Customs Officer) by my intimate knowledge of the locality. I then followed the frontier ridge, and returned to the Endarlaza valley by the silver mines, arriving at Irun about an hour after sunset under a bright moon.

THREE

Letters from the Turco-Servian War, activities in Bulgaria, 1876–7, and at Constantinople, February–April 1878

CHRONOLOGY OF THE TURCO-SERVIAN AND RUSSO-TURKISH WARS, 1876–8

1876

February	First reports of Servian war preparations at Belgrade.
May	Abortive uprising in 'Bulgaria' followed by campaign of Bashi-bazuks with wholesale lootings, murder and burnings. Street demonstrations in Constantinople against Sultan Abd ul-Aziz, leading to his deposition on 30 May and the succession of Murad V.
18 June	Servian declaration of war and attack on Ottoman forces at Babina Glava.
July	Ottoman counter-offensive, advancing into eastern Servia and occupying Knjazevac. Front line stabilized around Aleksinac and Deligrad.
24 July	Prince Milan suggests to Servian Cabinet that international mediation be sought.
7–12 August	Battle of Aleksinac and Turkish offensive checked.

21 August	Servians abandon Adrovac.
31 August	Sultan Murad V deposed. Succeeded by Sultan Abd ul-Hamid II.
3–12 September	Unofficial truce.
3 September	Milan declared King by Servian army but refuses title.
16–18 September	Servian attack at Krevet followed by heavy fighting.
29 September	Vincent arrives at Belgrade.
October	Skirmishes along River Morava.
9 October	Ottoman forces break through Servian fortifications on river.
11 October	Unsuccessful Ottoman attack on Djunis.
17 October	Renewed attack on Djunis with complete defeat of Servian forces and collapse of their resistance.
18 October	Russian ultimatum to the Ottomans demanding an armistice which was immediately granted.
November	Six Russian army corps mobilized in area nearest to Moldavia.
December	Powers' representatives gather at Constantinople to agree settlement of Balkan troubles.
26 December	Vincent arrives at Sofia.

1877

January	Conference breaks up without result and war preparations in both Russia and Ottomann Empire are stepped up.
February	Vincent tours with Lady Strangford before returning to Gt. Britain.
March	First meeting of the new Ottoman Parliament.
24 April	Russian declaration of war.
Late May	Russian troops concentrated on the northern bank of the Danube between Nikopolis and Silistria.
22 June	Crossing of Danube begins against ineffective and spasmodic opposition.
3 July	Crossing completed.
July	Vincent goes to Constantinople for Stafford House Committee.
July and August	Russian cavalry under Gurko seize Shipka Pass and cross Balkan mountains by 19 July. Then move southward, taking Eski-Zagra and raiding the Philippopolis railway.

Confronted by hastily assembled Ottoman forces withdrawn from the Montenegrin front and threatened in the rear by the advance of Osman Pasha's army from Widdin to Plevna they withdraw north of the Balkans, surrendering Eski-Zagra but retaining Shipka Pass, control of which is never regained by the Turks.

20 July	First unsuccessful Russian attack on Plevna.
30 July	Second unsuccessful Russian attack on Plevna.
3 August	Further Russian mobilization of troops to reinforce Balkan armies.
August to December	Stalemate, with Russian forces pinned down around Plevna and a series of Ottoman attempts to recover the Shipka Pass which start on 21 August and last for four months of bloody and unsuccessful fighting.
11 September	Third unsuccessful Russian attack on Plevna followed by start of siege.
24 October	Russian siege of Plevna completed.
10 December	Osman Pasha's attempt to break out of Plevna fails and he and his entire force are captured. Russian forces immediately launch attack southward despite severe winter weather.

1878

January	Vincent returns to Gt. Britain and marries on 19 January.
4 January	Russian forces occupy Sofia.
9 January	Ottoman army at Shipka Pass surrenders at Kazanlik.
15 January	Battle of Philippopolis with further defeat for Ottoman army.
22 January	Adrianople occupied by the Russians.
31 January	Armistice signed with Russian forces at Tchorlu outside Constantinople.
February	Continuing threats of war likely to involve Gt. Britain.
16 February	Vincent arrives back at Constantinople.
March	Peace concluded between Russia and Ottoman Empire but tension between Britain and Russia grows.
30 May	Anglo-Russian agreement to submit terms to an international conference.
June and July	Conference at Berlin. Vincent and Alice leave Constantinople.
13 July	Treaty of Berlin signed.

Map of the Balkans to illustrate activities during the Turco-Servian and Russo-Turkish Wars in 1876 and 1878

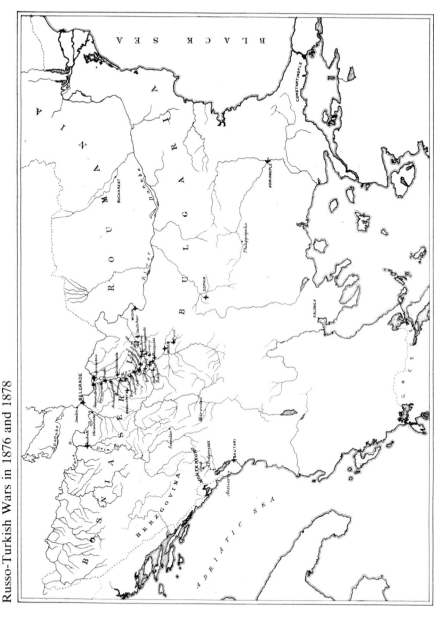

Belgrade   29th September 1876

Dear Burgess,
I was acting in conformity with Col. Loyd-Lindsay's wishes in reporting direct home. As the wounded will always in future be brought by river from Semendria to Belgrade (that is as long as there is money to pay for this transport) I and the waggons will but seldom be in Belgrade. Any stores which I may be required to distribute will in future be sent by river to Semendria and then taken by road to the front by me.

The wounded are taken back along the road from Delegrad and the front . . . and by a second road which leads to the Danube further east.

I am afraid that a letter which I wrote to you explaining why we wanted to buy horses never reached. I will therefore explain the whole matter again . . .

Col. Loyd-Lindsay on leaving Belgrade settled that three of our six ambulance waggons (Evans–Mundy system) which were lying idle in the barracks should be at once handed over to us. Two more were at the same time ordered by Col. Loyd-Lindsay to be sent from Vienna. Baron Mundy undertook to arrange with the Government that the latter should supply the necessary horses for these five waggons and also for the omnibus bought by Dr Laseron in Vienna.

Col. Loyd-Lindsay thus made most satisfactory arrangements and credited me with one hundred and fifty pounds in Mr White's [the British Consul-General's] hands for the transport expenses, which was quite enough had the Government carried out the arrangement. But unfortunately Col. Loyd-Lindsay had hardly gone when a telegram from Baron Mundy informed us that he could not obtain the horses and a day or two afterwards General Tchernaieff[16] took over *all the six waggons* on his own account and horsed them with the horses destined for the artillery. The authorities here expressed their regret but at the same time could not interfere with the direct order of the Commander in Chief. We were thus left without either waggons or horses. I do not see how anyone in the Society can be blamed for this. Some people, I am aware, blamed the Society for not having bought waggons and horses at once but if we could have got the use of them for nothing as Col. Loyd-Lindsay was promised it would have been an unwise thing to do, to purchase them.

Under the above circumstances Mr White, McKellar and myself decided that we ought to buy horses and at the same time, as the necessity of a stronger transport service was so apparent, we thought it desirable that one or two more waggons should be bought and horses. This decision was followed by the telegrams for five hundred pounds which you received.

I may state here that strong horses cost from twenty pounds to twenty five pounds each, the waggons (Mundy system) seventy five pounds each (including carriage), harness (double set) about six pounds the set.

I have engaged two assistants for the transport service and distribution of stores at the front. They can both speak French and Servian and will be most useful to the Society. One is a Servian the other a Bulgarian. Their salaries come to about five pounds a month with food etc.

When the war is over, or the Society's work suspended the horses, harness and waggons can be sold without much loss except for the latter, which would have to be converted into ordinary omnibuses.

Philippopolis   28th October 1876

Dear Mr B Kennett,

This is not a letter – I never had time to write to you after you left me in the lurch and I have not one moment now. I was fairly overwhelmed in London and I had to get help as best I could. The last week I had about 4 secretaries ever at work and sat up myself. I could not get to bed until 3 or 4 a.m. any night for the last three weeks. The journey out rested me and restored me. I was sorry not to go to Belgrade but it would have been a great blunder to go there and I gave it up. Now let me tell you: I know pretty well what your work is, its labour, difficulty, hardships and I can tell you truly its Hyde Park Luxury compared to ours.

The peoples distress and misery has never been in any way described. It is awful, overwhelming, appalling and I am working nearly alone no [illegible] no one who can *understand*, *organise or work* anything. My best help is a missionary and that good young fellow Dr George Stoker. Him I have engaged as my own chief doctor – for I am devoting three quarters of my energies to village rough hospitals. He will serve me for any number of months that I will use him – I pay all expenses . . .

But now do you help me if you can. For heavens sake send me some nurses, experienced and willing to make the best of it with rough and hard lives – no comforts and no anything except all I can give – interpreters and all else I can manage. We are getting up five hospitals – one is done but we have no nurses as yet. I will pay all their expenses of course and anything else that is necessary. But they must be rough, hardy, willing women accustomed to fever and dysentry. There is nothing else. Don't send me either Miss McLaughlin or Miss Pearson[17] for I won't have either of them but for pity's sake spare me some others and send them quick.

If Mr White would pay their journey I will pay at once, only help me. I have sent to England only help from there takes long to come.

The cold is bitter, snow everywhere on the mountains and no shelter for any of these thousands of poor creatures. Write to me if you have time. British Embassy Constantinople. Remember me kindly to Mr and Mrs White and believe me,

Yours ever truly,

E. Strangford[18]

Belgrade   1st December 1876

My dear Fleetwood,

I came out towards the end of August and have been more or less actively employed ever since at my old work transporting the wounded. I never saw transport so much wanted as out here. The Servians seem to have forgotten that they could not fight without losing some wounded, and in consequence made no provision for their transport. I have two large ambulance waggons of the best design, an ambulance omnibus and carriage; besides convoys of country carts at my disposal when necessary with these I used to convey the wounded to the rear as far as Semandria, a town on the Danube. Thence I took them to Belgrade in a floating hospital. I had this constructed by the Government engineer; it consists of a barrack built on an ordinary Danube barge, with kitchen attached. The barrack is fitted up with good beds and stretchers are slung from the rafters of the roof. Below there are arranged beds and benches for the less gravely wounded. When I had a sufficient number of wounded to convey, I had the barge towed to Belgrade or higher up the Sava by the first Austrian steamer which happened to pass. The even motion of the barge was not even felt by the poor fellows inside, who required rest after a weeks torment of being jolted in country carts and waggons. While on board we provided them with good dinners, suppers, and all they wanted, while an English surgeon was always ready to attend to their wounds. I have taken as many as 80 wounded at a time in

Servian ambulance drawn by oxen in the Balkans

this barge, besides attendants and materiel. They are so glad when they at last find themselves comfortably in bed in one of the good Belgrade hospitals.

The road work was much harder than the river, especially during the abominable weather which we have had here in the middle of October. I was then asked to accompany the expedition which attacked Saitschen and was driven back. The mountain roads were almost impassable; we often had to put four oxen to draw an ambulance waggon. At times we had to chase the peasants who refused to lend their oxen for this purpose, thinking they would never get them back.

Of course we had accidents – I was tumbled over cart and all on the incline of a mountain, but luckily the two horses were of a stoical temperament and remained still so we did not roll on. We had missed the track owing to the darkness in a wood and by some mischance had left our lamps behind us. A few days after I had a great smash with a vicious horse which bolted over a ditch and fell on its head in a steep road on the other side, rolling completely over me. I was a little hurt but am all right again.

I am thankful that I have been but little in Belgrade, I scarcely ever return there without hearing of some disagreeables about the Society and attacks in the press on the judgement of Loyd-Lindsay. A general idea seems to have spread that he was very Turkish in his sympathies and this accounted for some very sharp criticisms on everything he arranged and did. Some of these were most unfair and no doubt gave him great annoyance. I fortunately was left in charge of the transport service from the front and was quite independent of the hospital and its rows.

The last journey which the waggons took was the worst of all. They were caught in a snowstorm in the mountains betwen Kragnievatz and Oube. The snow was over the axles. The night came on and no village near, when all at once the horses reared and snorted, and tried to bolt. It was quite dark but the coachman knew that nothing but wolves could frighten the horses so much. When the lights were lit they immediately saw six wolves within a few paces. These ran away from the light but continued to hover about for nearly half an hour. No one had any firearms so had the wolves been hungry they might have had a good dinner without paying for it! On another occasion one of the horses fell through, or rather into a hole in a broken bridge, but was luckily supported by the harness and pulled out. The huge ambulance omnibus was upset about the same time on a steep road near Deligrad.

The Society has finished its work today. I have just returned from the Ministry of War where I have formally handed over as a present from our Society to the Medical Dept. of the Government, all the transport materiel, including horses, waggons, tents, barge hospital, blankets, stretchers etc. I was so sorry to part with the horses which know me now after so much knocking about together.

The administrator of the hospital, Dr Laseron, with seven Sisters of Charity left us yesterday morning by the early boat. Their places have been supplied by Servian Sisters but their absence leaves a great blank. The wounded were most affected when they wished goodbye to those who had been tending them so carefully. General Tchernaieff the Commander in Chief left by the same boat. A guard of honour of Russian infantry, one of Cossacks and the Servian Bodyguard of King Milan were drawn up on the bank to wish them goodbye, and gave a lusty cheer as the defeated general left. They say he is now to be appointed Commander in Chief by the Czar, instead of by the Prince Milan. I am not surprised as the Russians are in reality in occupation of Servia. They no longer go through the farce of putting on Servian uniform, but wear regular Russian uniform, officers and all. A Russian is governor of the fortress, another head of the Police, and the most important places on the staff of the Army are also held by them.

I shall tell you plenty of anecdotes of the war when I return, but I am afraid that all at home must be tired out of Servia. The poor refugees are in worse condition than ever. Many hundreds of women and children are literally starving and dying from cold and exposure near the frontier. I have just seen Dr Ziemann who is most active in distributing the funds which the good people of Manchester send to him so liberally. He returned today from the frontier district.

I have been writing this letter all about myself while my thoughts have been about you and those around you. Write me a little wee line to the British Embassy in Constantinople, and tell me how you all are, and any news. I am going to bring home some Servian knives which look somewhat terrible; I think that one added to your sister Alice's Circassian dress would look well, the Circassians on the frontier wear them.

I am going on a somewhat difficult mission in a day or two. I start from here with a doctor and an assistant to pass through the lines and enquire for Servian wounded among the Turks. I then go on to Philippopolis to join Lady Strangford, who has written and telegraphed to me and the Consul. I was working with her in London to get her fund up before coming out here. I am afraid that should England disappoint Turkey in resisting Russia, the position of Lady Strangford and her nurses will be a dangerous one.

Sofia   26th December 1876
Turkey

My dear Fleetwood,
With agony, misery and starvation all around me my Xmas brings me little other cheer than an excuse for forgetting for a while my work and myself, and thinking of brighter, happier friends at home.

I suppose you are all in London, and that you have been doing the part of a good brother and chaperoning your sister Alice to all those little informal festivities which I used to like so much and which exist in London only at this season of the year. You must write and tell me some home news, and direct your letter to my Club, the Oxford and Cambridge.

I have had a long and somewhat adventurous journey from Belgrade here, having driven the whole way in the caleche which I invested in when I first came out, and which, with the exception of a wheel coming off occasionally, has borne me well during many a long night and over many a mauvais pas.

I must tell you that I undertook a mission to try and find out the whereabouts of the Servian wounded prisoners in the Turkish lines and for that purpose started off from the Servian outposts on 17th December. A half hours drive brought us to the Turkish outposts who at once challenged us; on our explaining the nature of our mission they treated us very courteously, and we were soon drinking coffee with them round a large camp fire – Our Servian escort of two cavalry soldiers; armed to the teeth (for one has to be prepared in this Country), three or four Turkish cavalry, an English Doctor, and my transport assistant Ivanoff, formed the party. I must not forget a tall handsome Circassian who, I hope, did not take part in the atrocities generally put down to his fellow countrymen. After nearly three hours waiting for permission to proceed on our journey, during which time night had overtaken us, the necessary order was sent, and by 9 p.m. we found ourselves at Alexinatz in the presence of the dreaded Hafiz Pacha,[19] the *Lion* of the Turks. To my surprise he was exceedingly kind and quite entered into the spirit of our mission. He did not know where we should find the wounded. The following day we began our journey across the Nisch swamp to that detestably dirty town. I have heard of a lake of Crystal, I have seen a 'mer de glace' but it was reserved until a memorable 19th December that I should stand on the shores of a sea of mud, which I have christened *La* Mer de Boue.

A short account of our little accidents across the swamp will amuse you. Halfway between Alexinatz and Nisch is the Turkish frontier line. Up to this point there is a road, but unfortunately the Servians in their hasty retreat had time to cut it to pieces for the benefit of the Turkish artillery which was following them up. Driving over this was not worse than what I should imagine would be passing in a London cab up and down the steps of the Mansion House Railway station. Then came the tug of war. The road stopped short, and we saw before us a wide desolate plain. Before a couple of hundred yards were accomplished we were fairly in a bog. One horse in its struggles smashed the harness and broke away, but only to fall over on its side utterly exhausted a few feet further on. By the time we were in motion again night came on, a thick dark night. Luckily we had secured the services of a good Turkish driver and his cart, he knew the way by day but occasionally lost it that night, when we had to get out and hunt with lanterns for the track of his particular cart. We passed safely two deep streams and three rotten bridges, in one of which we had to plank over a hole into which the horses most assuredly would have slipped. We were congratulating ourselves on our success when we heard the sound of running water and soon after the track led us to the bank of a swift stream. We found what was, before the rains, a practicable ford. The country cart was just going across when our horses took fright and, before the coachman could stop them, tumbled carriage and all a distance of four feet or more into as many feet of water. The bed of the stream being shingle and mud, they could not keep their feet and had to struggle hard to keep their heads above water. I naturally went in after them and found myself up to my shoulders nearly in the river. After several unsuccessful efforts Galton and myself managed to turn their heads downstream and guide them half swimming, half sinking, into shallower water. How the horses were not drowned is a miracle.

We had to remain in our wet clothes for another three hours when we arrived at Nisch, but too late for our comfort. Every house was closed and it was not until an hour had elapsed that worn out with cold and thoroughly out of temper with the world in general we fairly broke into a low inn and kicked, I am sorry to say, the rascally garçon until he lit a fire and administered the necessary comforts to us, which he had positively refused to do.

We found nearly 100 prisoners of whom some had been wounded. The names of all these we took down to let their families know of their existence. How many poor wives and children will be put out of their agony of suspense when that list arrives!

We did what we could to comfort the poor fellows and Medjib Pacha, the Head of Staff, promised his support to the proposition for general exchange of these prisoners with those in the Servian hands. I was the bearer of this proposition having been in communication with the Servian Government and the Demarcation Commission on the subject. You have no idea how grateful some of the prisoners were when they saw me. I only hope that the exchange can be successfully carried out.

I am much disappointed to find no wounded to speak of in the towns south of Nisch, sorry because I can draw but one terrible conclusion as to the fate of the many wounded which were left behind at Djuinn and on the Morava after the last fight. One hundred and thirty alone were left at the little temporary ambulance at Djuinn on the approach of the Turkish cavalry. What has become of these? I have enquired everywhere for them and cannot find a trace of them!

I have not slept in a bed for nearly a week as we have been continually on the move, and resting at night anywhere where we happen to be; every room being crowded with soldiers we have always considered ourselves lucky when we found space to roll ourselves up in blankets either on the ground or on a bench.

My hands are so cold that I can scarcely write any more.

Diary kept while touring with Lady Strangford, 1877:

Sophia to Carlova

. . . We met two of the Soc. Doctors who were returning from Nisch. Galton gave me an overdose of morphia which had the effect of making me sick a dozen times the following day and of contracting the pupils of my eyes – God preserve me from the doctors out here. A few days after Stoker gives me an overdose of belladonna and dilates the poor pupils so much that I have been blind partially ever since.

The drive over the pass disappointed me but when we arrived at the other side I was delighted at the grand view over the plain of Philippopolis. It lay stretched out like a map at our feet while the whole horizon was bound with the never ending chains of the Balkans. On descending we passed through two burnt villages. Cold reception by a boor of French doctor, Long's lot.[20] He was mightily sold when he saw me as Long's guest at dinner afterwards. Arrived at Tartar Perhazik in dusk and decided to stay the night there. Called on Long and dined with him. Extraordinary cuss. Very cold at sound of Lady Strangford's name. Told me all about his work. Seems to be doing well in building for poor and in buying land for himself. Cunning old boy.

8th January.

My drive to Carlova. Started riding with Stoker. We had a glorious day. I rode one of Lady S. ponies which went very well. Stopped about three quarters of way to lunch. Excellent fare. View of Balkans glorious; the snow laying on the crest of the mountains, while a rich red glow was shed over the lower parts where forests of young oaks and underwood abounded.

We arrived at Carlova after 8 hours ride. My headache was well at end. Ali came up with carriage and horses soon after us. I was fool enough to have my eyes doctored by S.[Stoker] who has partially blinded me. God knows when I shall get my sight back.

9th

CARLOVA Glorious day. But the sun has lost its attractions for me who am so fond of it! My eye was very painful and I could not read a line scarcely. Spent very fidgity day in consequence and enjoyed nothing. Awfully slow evening at a Carlova shopkeepers. Swear I shall never go to another if I can help it. We sat round a large round table, ate apples and drank *sour red wine*. Glorious harmony of colour and taste displayed by their Bulgarian belles of fashion. The beggars and refugees were more pleasing to behold than those whose feeble attempts to imitate the clothing of civilised people made them the greatest guys it ever shocked my nerves to behold. Went to bed thoroughly bored.

10th

CARLOVA Misty day. In morning sat quietly at home, bandaged horses legs etc. In afternoon went out for a ride to Sopot. Visited Monastry of the Ascension and was received most kindly by monks. Bulgarians – order anonymous. Told us the Bashi Bashuks had bagged up to 20,000 piastres of property during their little visit during the recent disturbances. We then visited the convent and inspected the cloth manufactory established there. Most interesting to see the hand-looms etc. Had to buy some cloth like flannel. Rode back at dusk through mist. Clouds lifted in middle day and disclosed mass of mountains almost touching the village.

By the way, yesterday we went out for a drive and visited the Sulphur baths. S. and Ali had a bath but I have given up playing tricks on myself. Saw the 'peoples bath' where men, women and children were all bathing together! Frogs and geese being dabbling about at the same time.

PHILIPPOPOLIS Following day drove to Filibe. Called on Lady S. [Strangford] She was away. Called on consul who offered to put me up. We however stayed at the Headquarters of Lady S. and telegraphed to her. I had had headaches from the effects of the morphia so they said and I doubted. S. duly appeared one fine morning. He was the same man as I met on the steam boat on the Danube. Funny chance! Uproarious spirits etc. Regular Irishman. D– him he has blinded me I believe. Correspondence with Lady S.

Filibe is most picturesquely situated on a rock which rises like an island in the middle of the surrounding plain. The streets are very steep, some quite impossible for carriages. Consul Calvert was very kind indeed and formed a great contrast to old White at Belgrade who always behaved so much like a wild boar.

Somakoff   Sunday, 17th February 1877

My dearest Ma,
I write you a few lines from this outlandish little town, nestled at the foot of the grandest mountains in Turkey, and forming the centre of the iron industry of the Country.

Vincent with Lady Strangford and her party

Lady Strangford and myself, with her maid and a dragoman, started off from Philippopolis Thursday afternoon by train; we were joined at Tartar Bazarjik by Mr Clark, a well known American Missionary whose head-quarters are in Somakoff. We went on by train the same night to Salem Bey, where we rested for the night at the Station Master's house. The carriage and pair with three ponies had been sent ahead to meet us and the following morning we took to the road. Lady S. and maid in one carriage, luggage behind in a country cart called Britscha, and Clark, self, dragoman and groom riding with an escort of four mounted police called zaptiehs accompanying us.

The roads were frozen over in the morning but the midday sun thawed the ice and deep sank the wheels in the clay soil adjoining the Balkans.

We had many minor difficulties which resulted in our passing the second night to Banja where we put up at the Turkish Khan (inn). There were

131

The Strangford party

sulphur baths there and I took one which resulted somewhat naturally in my catching a cold (slight).

The following morning we started at daybreak and arrived at Somakoff before midday after a lovely drive across the Balkans. The view was splendid, not a cloud in the blue sky and the sun shone in all its glory on the countless peaks of the snow mountains round us. On every side there was some beautiful effect of snow and ice. One mill in particular attracted our attention. The water had been frozen while falling and the frozen spray had coated all the woodwork of the wheel and timber so that the effect was of a crystal mill with flowing crystals instead of water.

We are the guests of the worthy missionaries here and most comfortable they make us. Lady S. is put up at Mr Clarks and I am lodged here at a Mr

Lockes. Today I gave two little addresses to the students on the Red Cross work in general. Some understood English but for the benefit of those who could not it was translated by Mr Clark.

Tomorrow we start for Sofia. All the dignitaries of the town called on Lady S. yesterday. The Authorities of Sofia have made preparations for her reception.

By the way I had rather a squeak the other day. I was riding back from Permshtitza to Philippopolis accompanied by a peasant, as I started late I knew that we should be caught by a dark night on the road, I took a gun with me slung across my shoulder. Lucky I did, for on cresting the hill on a desolate part of the country we were accosted by one of a band of robbers, armed to the teeth. I slipped off my gun and put it at full cock. My peasant guide, unarmed, got into a fright but had the good sense to tell the Turk that he did not care a d— for him as he had an armed Englishman at his side. This satisfied the Turk who pretended to slink off but we were not such fools as he thought. He wanted us to follow our original road which led through a ravine in which many robberies have taken place. Instead of this we struck out into the open plain and rode along cautiously for over half an hour, I with my gun cocked and ready. Well, nothing happened. But two days afterwards the neighbouring villages were full of police. It appeared that three robberies had been committeed by that man and others on that very spot the same day and within a few hours of when I passed. The gang were 15 in number, I saw only 1, but I have no doubt the others were hidden about and were frightened to attack an armed Britisher!

They did not know that I had only dust shot for killing larks in my gun and that the chances were 2 to 1 against it going off at all.

And now good night and goodbye – I shall write you another letter from Sofia.

Philippopolis   1st April 1877

My dearest Ma,

I started on Monday last riding with Lady S. We had sent on Miss Barclay and nurse in the caleche. We arrived at Pemshtitza towards evening and slept there in the wooden huts. The evening was lovely. A glorious moon was shining over the mountains at the foot of which Pemshtitza lies and a balmy warm breeze blew from the South over the Bazardyik plains. I found at Permshtitza the Servian nurse Petrovitch whom I sent for from Belgrade. Poor thing she has been attacked by that dreadful fever which is so prevalent here.

Well the next morning Lady S. and I started off, riding. We were accompanied by a mounted Zaptiéh (guard), one dragoman and a pair of pack horses for luggage, provisions, blankets etc, for we carry all our bedding with us; this is necessary as sometimes we sleep in some cottage, where all that the poor people can offer is empty clean (or unclean) rooms with mud floors! About 2 p.m. we reached Radilovo and soon after began to difficult ascent of the Batak mountain gorge. The melting of the snow had turned the mountain stream which flows down it into a torrent across which we had to cross seven times. It was very dangerous at times as the water reached up to the bodies of the ponies which could only just keep their legs on the rocky bottom in a rushing stream. We did not reach the top of the gorge until dusk owning to a delay occasioned by my horse casting a shoe. Betak was reached an hour afterwards and we were glad to rest our weary selves at the hospital which Lady S. founded some few months ago.

Betak has been partially re-built but its aspect, even now, is enough to bring tears to the eyes of a harder hearted man than myself. On every side the village once so flourishing and pretty, has been turned into a heap of stone. The old watch dogs lie among the ruins of their former homes while here and there efforts have been made to re-build what has been so ruthlessly destroyed. The Church floor is still red with the blood of 1,200 people cut to pieces within its walls when the carcasses lay four feet deep, and the wounded were mingled in one hideous confusion with the dead.

The stories which eye witnesses tell, and unhappily confirmed by good authority, are too horrible and revolting to repeat.

We were happy to quit these terrible scenes and turn towards the mountains in the fresh mountain air the following morning. We reached the woodcutters village of Assecoria about noon and after lunching in the open air, inspecting some saw mills which were recently erected by our fund and also doing other business, we returned to Batak where we rested for the night.

The following day we descended by another route to Rachilovo and put up at the Strangford Hospital there. I slept in the ward, there being no other place, and found myself in uncomfortable proximity to a poor man dying of Typhoid fever. He did not quite die that night but is quite given over.

Lady S. found herself here completely knocked up so we had to stop our journey and send for a carriage, in which we returned the following day to Philippopolis.

Our man whom we sent in to Bazardji to get the carriage returned shortly afterwards in great excitement. He had been fired at by some Turks between Radibuo and Bazardji. However these little affairs are trifles out here, especially when it is only a Bulgarian who is the target.

Lady S. is far from well. She has kept to her bed since we returned. Nurse Petrovitch has fever and is very weak. Miss Barclay is also laid up with a violent cold. We have 'hard lines' indeed with regard to our staff. Coachman Ali much better.

Vincent returned to Constantinople after his marriage to Alice.

Pera   Afternoon, 16th February 1878

My own darling Alice,

Once more I find myself in my office writing at the same table from which I have so often before penned my hurried notes to you. Thoughts of all the past are floating before me and after them come a long string of resolutions for the future. Dear good girl, how thoughtful it was of you sending me a telegram announcing your arrival at Mentone. You have no idea what pleasure it gave me both on account of the news and of your thoughtfulness.

I have begun work at once, no sooner had I landed than all the S.H. staff in Constantinople called upon me. When we neared the port I saw a boat with a Stafford House flag approach and at once recognised some familiar faces on it. From that moment until now I have been continually shaking hands and receiving congratulations on account of you and of my return. I had lunch on arriving and then drove down to Dalma Butschi Palace and attended a large séance of the Red Crescent Committee. I had to give them a sound rating on account of their having mentioned my name in one of their published Procés Verbeaux and said a thing which was not true. In consequence the secretary will call on me tomorrow morning to receive whatever correction I wish to be published . . .

There is no panic here at all at present. Everything is unusually quiet and dull. The Mosques in Stamboul are crowded with refugees but none come to Pera. The hotels are not crowded at all and everything is exactly what I thought it would be. However, I am not quite satisfied as to the sanitary state of the town. Dr Sarell, the leading Doctor here, tells me that Pera is quite 'healthy' and that there is no fever.

One very sad thing has happened. Mr Gay, the correspondent of the *Daily Telegraph*, sent for his wife from England. She arrived in blooming health and was quite well here. When the Russians were advancing on Constantinople Gay sent away his wife to Athens for safety. Fancy what bad luck; she caught fever at Athens and today we received news of her death! . . . there is no reason for you to run into danger and I wish, dearest, to keep my promise and if I feel in any doubts always to decide on the safe side for you. It softens the 'hard lines' of our separation when I think that it is for your good. Never be anxious about me, darling Alice, for I am an old hand and know how to look after myself. I am thoroughly seasoned to all this sort of work. I shall write a bye bye note soon – until then goodbye.

Feb 17 – night. Goodnight my own good Alice. I miss you terribly and long for Friday to come when I shall hear some of your news.

I have been at work all day. In the afternoon I went to the station and saw several hundred refugees. One never sees a *single one* in Pera. You would never know that anything was going on. The Turks seem utterly bewildered and know not what the morrow may bring forth. It appears that orders had actually been given to fire on the British Fleet but that these were countermanded by a subsequent order. Hobart Pacha[21] thinks that had the first order been carried out we should have lost *at least* one of our ships if not more. So we ran a great risk!

I cannot make out what is going to be done by the Turkish Authorities about their wounded in the Russian lines and so cannot decide about the destination of our Doctors. They are having a little rest meanwhile which is very necessary for them.

18th February

My darling Alice,
I shall see Layard today and hear more news. The attachés thought affairs looked warlike last night. Today the new post with Odessa goes, and to that I shall confide this letter although I feel some misgivings as to the safety of this route.

The Russians send in to Constantinople for all manner of delicacies such as champagne and other wines. They pay any amount for these delicacies and are being well robbed like the Philistines!

Owing to the jealousy between foreign surgeons and our own we have had to give up Varna Hospital, but we are going to form a barrack hospital here and a soup kitchen with some other systems of relief for the wounded soldiers returning from the Russian lines.

Goodbye dear Alice. You are never out of my thoughts. The more I see of this world the more convinced I am that I could not be happy without you. It is such a pleasure to me to think how our short married life has endeared you to me. How you far excel all that my fond imagination painted . . .

Pera   19th February

Goodnight my own dear Alice. I have been dining with Bartlett who is superintending the relief of the poor refugees here and have just returned to my sanctum. I had a long chat today with Lady Kemball,[22] who regretted your not coming out but I fancy she was disappointed for her own sake as she would have like to have had you for a companion . . .

The refugees are being shipped away as fast as they can be loaded on board the Government transports. These are Turkish refugees from Bulgaria and Roumelia which makes me think that the Government has made up its mind to yield to the Russian demand that all Turks should be expelled from those provinces. What a terrible thing it is. Misery and starvation seem staring these poor people in the face and God knows who will help them.

Pera   20th February 1878

My dear little Alice,

I am writing you a goodbye letter and hope that the little volumes will arrive at their destination safely. I send you some more dresses which you can give away to friends or keep yourself. I prefer the latter if you would like them. The hood is intended for you. Do you like it? It is a little theatrical but will do well for the opera etc.

I am giving away a quantity of our stores to the hospitals here which are in immense want. The difficulty is how to get the things to the wounded.

The poor fellows are dying for want of proper food and the Government is too poor to buy it. I am contracting for a large amount of milk to be supplied to the hospitals as *none* is allowed by Government.

There are many difficulties in our way. The Turkish head surgeons are so poor that they have to sell their rations in order to provide themselves with pocket money. Others are not to be trusted and we have to deliver the stores actually into the wards of the hospitals themselves to prevent peculation. Then everyone is tired and weary of the war and there is no *go* left in anybody.

Afternoon, 22nd February

Dearest Alice.

I have just time to write you a few lines to tell you that I am well and anxiously expecting your letter which has not yet arrived. I never was so anxious for a letter in my life.

Darling girl I love you more and more. Last night I slept with some violets under my head and your dear likeness. I send you the violets after kissing them for you.

Pera   Night, 22nd February

With this letter he enclosed the ribbon of the newly issued Ottoman war decoration, commenting:

This is ribbon of War Medal folly and vanity!! Good for grandchildren.

My dear good Alice,

I have just returned from the Club where we have had a pleasant evening. Some of the doctors who were returning invited me for a farewell dinner. Baron Mundy, of course, was present; after dinner there were of course toasts and speeches and Baron Mundy proposed your health which I need hardly tell you was responded to most cordially. He, at the same time, sent me two bonbons for you, of which I send the rosettes.

This for good luck etc.

I am so utterly disappointed at not having received a letter today. The post is not yet in but the letter will arrive tomorrow for certain. I look forward so intensely to news from you that all the stirring events happening around me seem of secondary importance.

Darling goodnight and may God make your slumber sweet and let you know how I love you.

Pera   Evening, 23rd February 1878

My dear good little Alice,
I must now tell you the real reason you had better not come out – a great deal of smallpox had broken out among the refugees who are crowded together in the mosques and as very few are vaccinated the disease may spread alarmingly. I have put on four surgeons to vaccinate right and left, and may perhaps by providing vaccine induce the Government to order all Turkish surgeons to be placed under our orders and assist so as to vaccinate the whole set in time. There is, of course, a certain amount of danger in consequence of the prevalence of smallpox but I hope soon that it will abate. Shiploads of refugees leave almost every day for the Asiatic coast and others are returning to their homes, so affairs will soon right themselves.

I was received today by the Minister of War and presented together with Drs Sandwith, McQueen and Busby with the war medal. This reminds me of writing to [*sic* from] Spain. Goodbye for an hour or two I am off to dinner.

Pera   23rd February 1878

Goodnight my own dear Alice, I have been spending the evening with Bartlett and we have been concocting plans to stop the spread of smallpox. We have practically the whole thing on our hands! It seems absurd that the stopping of such a pest among 80,000 refugees should not have been taken seriously in hand before. It was not however until I sent four Stafford House doctors to vaccinate people that anything was done.

Tomorrow I shall be vaccinated too so do not be in any fright about me. I shall not catch it. I had plenty of chances in Spain when smallpox broke out among our wounded and others – I do not think I am liable to catch it.

Map to illustrate activities with the Stafford House Committee at
Constantinople between February and April 1878

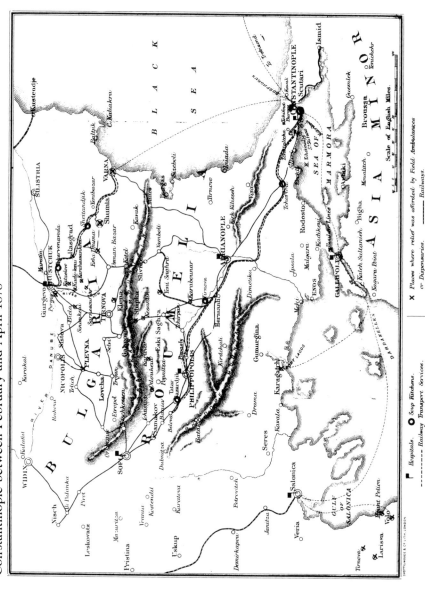

I am so pleased with your letters and love my affectionate little wife dearly and tenderly. Every moment darling I feel that there is something wrong and that is your absence. Exactly as you describe of yourself so I feel. I do not like anything so much as I did before as that short experience of a heaven upon earth has spoilt me for ordinary everyday life under other conditions! . . .

Just received news of advance of Russians to St Stephano. Am off to meet the rascals and see what they have done with our ambulance near St Stephano.

Pera   Night, 25th February

My darling Alice,

. . . I returned today from the Russian lines. After doing all my business satisfactorily. Our ambulance at Kutchuk Tchechmedje was duly taken by the Russians, who however treated our surgeons well and allowed them to depart with all their stores and horses. I rode out to see what had become of them and found them safe at Makrikeui, where we chose a house and at once started an ambulance.

I rode into the Russian lines at St Stephano and found them very civil and polite. They seem to look upon Stafford House men as almost belligerents, but treat them with great respect. Perhaps on that account! Nothing could have been more courteous than their behaviour to me. Today I was riding between the brigades of Nedjib Pacha and Yayah Pacha when I found myself in the midst of a party of Cossacks. They let me pass without saying a word!

Last night the Turks did some damage to the village of Nijorski where I arrived this morning and they succeeded in burning a house or two. However, on the whole both sides behave well and do as little harm as possible.

I have today engaged a whole dairy for our hospitals. Tomorrow I shall engage another or buy some cows. One is very apt to be cheated if one purchases by these rascally Greeks and I believe that the subject of milk is a most difficult one.

I was at a reception at the Embassy tonight and saw Raouf Pacha, the War Minister.[23] He is very pleased as I have arranged to bury all the hundreds of dead horses, mules, donkeys and oxen which are lying along the paths leading to the Turkish lines. The soldiers have too much to do and I have arranged to pay 200 refugee Turks to do this disagreeable work. It is most necessary as all manner of fevers are contracted by these carcasses remaining unburied. I have a report from a doctor today that the smallpox in Stamboul is *not* a bad sort. However, what between that and typhoid the mortality among old people and children is very great indeed. The poor people have nothing to eat but bread and *not* much of that by any means. I gave 30 shillings on your account to the fund to feed some and 30 shillings on my own. Do you object? I have also ordered some milk to be given every day to some of the youngest children to keep the poor little things alive. There are not many of them left and the mothers of these are trembling for their lives.

Pera   Night, 26th February

I know full well how trying it must have been for you to have been left behind in that strange place [Menton], it gave me a little pang to leave you there. Often and often I thought of your last look at me as you left and over and over again did I go through the pain of our goodbye.

Dearest we have curious news tonight and I fear that what you will read in tomorrows paper will make you anxious. God forbid that the terrible war should recommence. We must however face possibilities and I am making all necessary preparations for the worst. Should it recommence over the Bosphorous we go with most of our stores etc. and as for the sick and wounded, we shall leave a few surgeons to look after them. Of course I shall do whatever I think my duty but promise not to expose myself in any way uselessly for your sake. I again remind you that I am an old soldier and take every precaution. Of the men under my charge in this war there are many good and trusty fellows and we all stick together. This prevents the necessity of any useless exposure as our men do not need encouraging. Rest assured Darling and trust that God who brought us together in so marvellous a manner will not turn away from us now. We shall meet again before long I feel quite confident and happy about that.

Pera   27th February 1878

My dear good Alice,
I have had my patience tried all day long and am now writing to you a little
line before going to dinner. These Turks are completely demoralized as far
as helping themselves go. They seem quite exhausted and powerless. It is
indeed very uphill work what we are now doing, but I hope that matters
will mend soon. The hospitals are crowded to excess with wounded and
sick and many of the doctors report to me that they have no medicines or
even bandages. At the same time one cannot trust the rascals so much as to
give them the things they ask for. Quinine and instruments are in great
request because they are so easily sold!! And once that I part with the
things what power have I? I cannot supply doctors for all the hospitals and
must trust therefore to the honesty of some, or let the wounded go without
proper medicines.
    I have wasted half the day at the War Office where all is utter confusion.
It is quite ridiculous to see the disorganisation and chaos into which
everything has fallen.
    I am so glad there is still prospect of peace owing to Russia not claiming
to alter the status-quo of the Dardenelles.
    But I am afraid that Russia will still keep her eyes on that point and carry
on its intrigues in the new Principality of Bulgaria.
    The latter will never pay its tribute regularly and then what redress will
the Turks have. It is true that until the Russian indemnity is paid off it will
be Russia's interest to keep Bulgaria a tributory state as the indemnity is
secured on the tribute. Turkey is utterly ruined as European power.
    My dear good girl goodbye for the time. I wish I were with you. And
now as to your joining me. I do not fear at all anything but the outbreak of
smallpox and typhoid. Poor Mrs de Winton, wife of one of the military
attachés at our Embassy has been attacked with the latter and Dr Attwood,
one of our doctors at Philippopolis, is also dangerously ill. I am too fond of
my darling to see her exposed to such evils and must reconcile myself to
being separated for a little while longer. I shall finish my letter after dinner.

Night, 27th February

Goodnight dear girl, your own Barrington is thinking of you and longing to
be with you again. Sometimes I rebel in my mind against all this cruel

separation, but dearest, the object is a good one and God may bless us through it in some way in which we little think. How little could I have imagined that when we were separated for so many years the very separation was all tending to develop and mature our affection. 'God works in a mysterious way' and indeed he has with us. I saw de Winton this afternoon but he could not give me better news of his wife. He is so fond of her and looks dreadfully anxious and pulled down. However he goes on pluckily with his work among the refugees. He is a Military Attaché at the Embassy, but manages to spend all his time assisting in the distribution of bread etc. to the poor starving creatures in the mosques.

Pera   28th February

Just one line sweet Alice to say goodmorning. I am quite well and refreshed with a good long sleep. I eat plenty and take great care of myself according to your special request! . . .

Goodnight my little Alice – I have just returned from a long ride in the dark on a most detestable road. Poor Mrs de Winton is worse and her husband was in a great state of mind as they cannot find any trained nurse who can speak English in Constantinople and Mr and Mrs de W. cannot speak any other language. By a lucky accident I heard of the difficulty and happened to know of a Baroness de Rosen, a very skilled nurse, who told me she was returning to Germany tomorrow. I could not find out where she lived until this afternoon late, and then discovered it was at Bebek a long way down the Bosphorus. There was no help for it but to ride out and find her. This I did, taking with me young Harvey, who knows the country, and a carriage to bring her back in. We found Madame de Rosen and I brought here back to the Embassy where Mrs de Winton is lying in a rather precarious state of typhoid fever. Poor de Winton was so pleased and I only hope that Mme de Rosen will be of much good.

Pera   Night, 2nd March

Goodnight dearest Alice – I was riding out into the lines this afternoon and paid a visit to Muchtar Pacha[24] who used to be the great hero in Asia. He seemed very low spirited about affairs in general, but expressed great thanks to Stafford House for all that its section had done in aiding the wounded.

I afterwards rode round to our section established at Makrikeui and found one of our men laid up very ill, otherwise all was going on well and the hospital half full.

I have just received a telegram from Dr Eccles head of our section there. He describes the want as terrible and adds that typhus fever is raging. This is bad news.

I am glad to give you good news from Erzeroum. Yesterday we received our reports from there. Typhus is on the decrease and our two hospitals getting on famously. Though I deeply regret when I hear of scenes of suffering and want, yet it is a consolation to know that wherever there is such, we have a body of true and skilful men on the spot.

Our Doctor Lake found 8 fresh cases of smallpox in the St Sofia mosque today. The Turkish women hide their children under their blankets etc. when they have the smallpox as they are afraid of the doctor taking them away. Our Doctors complain of the Turkish authorities sending back to the mosque cases of smallpox in their early stages of convalescence; when contagion is most dangerous! Fancy in one of the hospitals there was a ward full of women who were well but lying in the same beds with their children who had smallpox! I cannot imagine how it is that there is not more disease. I am employing refugees to bury the hundreds of dead oxens, horses, donkeys etc., which abound round Constantinople and especially near the encampments of troops. The Turks seem quite ignorant of the simplest sanitary precautions; they are like babies on these subjects . . .

You will be delighted to hear that Mrs de Winton passed her crisis last night and is decidedly better today. When I called at the Embassy to see de Winton he thanked me over and over again for having brought Madam de Rosen, and said that she had been a God-send to his poor wife. She arrived at the most critical moment and nursed her through the crisis.

Afternoon, 4th March

What can be the matter darling? I have not heard from you for over a week. No letter by Friday's boat nor by Saturday's boat, and today a mail arrived and no letter from you. I have received other letters so the post is all right. I hope very much that nothing has gone wrong – I cannot help feeling anxious. If you were ill I should rush off at once to my own Alice. I expect that you have written and that by some mistake the letter has not been posted. I must now wait until next Friday or Saturday. I never was so long without hearing from you. I am determined to make myself think that you have written.

Today I have been at our new hospital and have also had to smooth down some bitter rows which were beginning between some of our doctors. I saw Dr Stephenson who is Lady Strangford's ambulance doctor and he told me of sundry rows down at Sofia which escaped my observation before. However on the whole we are at peace with all around us. I have no time to meddle with the business of other Societies and there is such an appalling amount of distress and misery all round I let all quarrels 'slide'.

I feel very lonely tonight and rather unhappy at not hearing from you. I am sure I shall not be able to live much longer without you; at times I get very impatient about our separation and have to call in plain common sense to the rescue.

You have no idea how difficult it is settling up such a large affair as ours here. There are so many vultures all round wanting to devour the spoil that one has to be doubly circumspect, especially as ones employees are rather tired out and inclined to be apathetic. I had to give such a blowing up last Sunday as I found our depot closed and also no one working at the new barracks. Since my absence in England it appeared that Sunday had gradually crept in as a holiday. I was amazed as, in consequence of the men not working, 300 wounded who arrived the same afternoon had to be crowded in an empty room and sleep on stretchers or on the ground.

Night, 4th March

My own dear Alice – I am so happy to have received your letter dated from 17th to 22nd –I was really getting very anxious indeed, and should have telegraphed most probably in a day or two. I am so glad to see from your letter that you are quite well again; but you must take care of sitting in the shade while painting as the weather is always treacherous in the South, warm in the sun and cold in the shade.

Dearest girl I cannot conscientiously telegraph for you just yet, as there are too many refugees etc. in Stamboul, where I must go every now and then and in fact very often. I should always be in a fright of bringing back smallpox or some such horror in my clothes. I do not believe I am liable to catch these things but I am not so sure about you by any means. Should the refugees be sent back to their homes then by all means you will come to me.

However I have another little plot. Should the weather turn out fine and the spring come early, I propose that you should go to Therapia or Princes Island, a lovely island near Constantinople quite free from all disease. I could go backwards and forward every day from there to here. I shall run over there in a day or two to inspect the place. It is a favourite and 'fashionable' resort in summer, but now very few families live there.

Darling goodnight – I am much happier tonight than last night: you have no idea what pleasure your letters give me. Once more my own darling goodnight and may God bless and protect you and bring us together again soon.

Pera   Evening, 6th March 1878

My dear good little wife,

I have just sent off some letters for you and also a packet of [blank in original]. When you eat it you must think of me and imagine yourself here! Dearest I seem to be leading a double existence now, one with you, my real solid existence and the other a sort of reflection of my former life. You are never absent from my thoughts and every day I prize more and more the treasure I have won.

I am sorry to say that all the administration of the Bulgarian provinces seems to be falling into the hands of the Russians. If England had followed a bolder and I think wiser policy it might have been in ours, for I am sure that the Bulgarians like the English a great deal more than they do the Russians. . . .

We have just received a telegram from Salonica announcing that poor Dr Beresford is down again with fever. He had a severe illness before. I am sending off another doctor to Salonica to help our section.

We had news today from Erzeroum. All is going well in our hospitals except that one of the rascally Turkish surgeons and several Turkish dressers have abandoned their posts and bolted on the approach of the Russians who are going to occupy the place in a day or two, if they have not already done so. Can you imagine such curs as these deserters, leaving their own fellow-countrymen wounded. I am writing to press Dr Ryan to try and find out these rascally curs and have them hanged or shot. I prefer the former for choice. I have just had a long chat with Dr Stephenson, Lady Strangford's doctor. He gives me woeful account of the work of the Red Crescent Society. I am really ashamed of that badge, although not now connected in any way with them. I cut off all connection with them long long ago. I am very sore on the point of ever having had anything to do with them. But I did all I could to help them.

Pera   Night, 6th March

Goodnight dear Alice – I have just returned from the Club, and have had a long talk with two men, old friends, who have been all the war with the Russians. It was rather interesting as I knew them in the Servian campaign and of course they considered me somewhat of a deserter going to the Turks! I am quite well, dear Alice, and obey all your injunctions as to 'feeding' very regularly.

I have tumbled into my regular routine of work and one day passes very much like another. We have finished our new barrack hospital and are all ready to receive more wounded. They will come in fast enough, poor fellows, from the hospitals of Philippopolis, Sofia and Plevna. I think myself that it would be better – far better – to leave them where they are instead of bringing them into the overcrowded hospitals here, but the Government thinks otherwise, or is co-erced by the Russians.

I hear that the Grand Duke Constantine[25] is to make a triumphal entry into Constantinople with a large escort tomorrow to pay a visit to the Sultan! What absurd buffoonery is all this pomp and show, and the glittering tawdry uniforms etc., all at the expense of the poor masses, who bear the burdens and pains of war. It makes one feel very republican or democratic, or some such thing, when one sees these things and especially when one can peep behind the scenes.

Pera   Night, 8th March

There is a biggish fire in Stamboul, a somewhat common incident, I hope that it will be put out soon as these poor people can ill afford to build new houses now.

Today has been a busy day with me.

Got up at 7.30 a.m. Breakfast at 8 a.m.

Received four or five Government doctors and settled about supply of stores at 9 a.m. Then gave instructions to doctors leaving for Salonica, Gallipoli and Philippopolis. Wrote report to Stafford House Committee. In afternoon saw ambulance sections off by steamer to Gallipoli and Salonica. Took Dr [illegible] of the Blues over our stores and went through some of our books, then took him over some hospitals and the sanitary train. Afterwards dined on board the *Enchantress* and finally I am doing the pleasantest part of my days occupation in writing to little Alice; this is my real rest.

I have received a telegram from Philippopolis about Dr Attwood. He is still very ill. We have sent our best surgeon Dr Neylan to him and made arrangements for his transport to Constantinople. I have today also received a telegram from Trebizond giving us good news of our Erzeroum hospitals. All going well.

I am so pleased with the idea of having you at Therapia, I have talked to plenty of people about it and eveyone says that there can be no objection. Therapia is a lovely place in the early spring. It is about 10 miles up the Bosphorus, close to the entrance to the Black Sea and is perfectly free from any illnesses. There is always a fresh sea breeze blowing down from the Black Sea. We can go out in caiques, ride, walk etc. etc. etc. . . . As soon as I can secure a house I shall write to you so be prepared to start about the end of this month!

I cannot tell you how pleased I am at the prospect. Are you the same dearest?

Afternoon, 9th March

I have just received your looked for letter dated from February 24 to 27. I can see that you are not happy, the whole tone of your letter is sad. How hard is our fate to be thus separated when we love each other so much. Thanks darling for all your affection, thanks for the very sadness, however much I deplore it.

I am quite decided now in principle about Therapia. I have made a further enquiry about it and think that there can be no possible objection to it. There is one first class hotel there called Petulas which is always crowded in the summer but which will not be full in April. We shall go there first and then migrate somewhere else afterwards. I do not intend to allow you to come to Constantinople at all! I shall meet you on board the steamer in a caique and take you off bag, baggage and maid to Therapia. . . . I did not know that it would be pleasant at Therapia during April or I should have written to you before. They say that affairs look somewhat bellicose now but I do not believe in a European war. I am rather in a fright about what you say about the Militia[26] and shall write by next post and send in my resignation; I shall have to serve for at least three months this year. Two at a School of Instruction and one with the Regiment. Now whatever happens I do not see any possible advantage in the Militia. It leads to nothing at all, and seems a mere waste of time. Supposing there is a war our Regiment may be embodied and we shall have to serve at Cork or some such unearthly place perhaps for a year or so.

I rather wish I had resigned before I left England. If I were a Colonel or a Major it would be a different thing but the promotion is absurdly slow in our regiment and owing to my never having been in the Army I am not likely ever to get the Regiment.

Another thing is that I do not much care for the majority of fellows in my regiment and shall not therefore miss much enjoyment of their society! There are a few good fellows whom I can always see at other times. I am so happy darling with your affection that all these men friendships seem so much less strong than they used to be.

I am going to spend tomorrow in making enquiries about Therapia accommodation etc. It is now March 9 – supposing you started on March 23 by the Messageries from Marseilles you would be here on let us say March 30th (Not April 1st)! April is a pleasant month at Therapia, but rather inclined to be cold owing to the sea breeze from the Black Sea. It will be colder than Mentone but you will enjoy the bracing air and be able to ride every day that I get away. I shall get a Zaptieh attached to us and then you could ride every morning part of the way here with me and return with the guard. One is quite sufficient if you take Ali my faithful groom.

Pera   Night, 10th March 1878

My own dear wife,
I am not at all happy tonight. I cannot stand our separation any longer. I have put the best face on it so far and could have borne it longer had you written as if you were enjoying yourself. But I see that you are not quite

happy and, good affectionate girl that you are, wish to return to your old boy.

I have had a long talk with Mrs Whitaker and Mrs Henicker, two residents here, and both say that the only possible fault of Therapia is that it may be rather cold and that it will be very slow for you as so few people live there just now. Madame Petula at the hotel will make you quite comfortable and I shall return there every evening. Darling I shall be dining with Mrs Layard tomorrow evening and shall then settle finally. I cannot tell you how I long for you to be with me. I cannot take interest in anybody's society, and feel in my intervals of work lonely, very lonely . . .

No one has been ill lately in Pera and even in Stamboul the sickness is diminishing. The smallpox is now entirely confined to children and I have withdrawn our doctors from the mosques, so now I never come into contact with any of those 'heathen' diseases. I no longer have the faintest apprehension for your safety so you will come out and join me, my own Alice.

Tonight is the last day of the Carnival and the foolish people are running about the street with masques on. What a strange mockery all this seems when only a mile or two off hundreds of poor wretches are almost starving!

Pera and Stamboul are quite different towns and might be hundreds of miles away from each other, so utterly different are all the customs and people.

I had a basket of my things sent back from the laundress stolen from my quarters today. It is rather provoking as I cannot replace here some of the things stolen! I have had arrested an individual on suspicion but only suspicion. I hope I have not made a mistake.

I am told that I am not looking well and should take more recreation so I am going to begin having a ride every day and get myself strong and well to receive my Alice! The second union of the streams, darling, will be far happier than the first. We shall not have that horrible ceremony to go through! I feel as if I were going to be married again sometimes; I look forward to my meeting you again more intensely than I did to my wedding day.

Pera   Night, 11th March

Darling little Alice,

I received your welcome letter of March 1 to 2nd. Poor dear Alice. I think I have caused you some anxiety and pain; this separation is too unnatural. I have quite decided about your coming. Let me now calculate when you should leave Marseilles. Either Saturday March 23rd or the following Saturday, March 30th by the Marseilles boat. Perhaps the latter date would be best as every day in April the weather gets warmer at Therapia. I must see that you do not suffer by coming to a colder climate too rapidly.

You must bring warm clothes, your habit, saddle etc. – I think that you might bring your other luggage, as there may be a good deal of entertaining going on and people dress a good deal. Do whatever you like about your maid and the 1st or 2nd class ticket for her. You are quite right in saying that it will be inconvenient having her with you.

Dearest girl, I am only too glad when I hear of your enjoying walks etc., and do not think that I want you only to speak to old gentlemen or relations. We love and trust each other completely dearest, and if I was separated from you for years and years, never would the green-eyed monster put in an appearance. I look upon you as simply everything in the world to me, God grant that I may make you happy – you best and most loving of wives.

Goodnight and meet me dearest in dreamland.

Pera   13th March 1878

I have just had a great discussion with old Mundy and Mr Young. The latter is rather a jealous fellow and it is with great difficulty that I now and then keep my temper when I hear some of his remarks. The National Society do not like Stafford House having done so much more than themselves, as of course the Nat. Soc. ought to be the representative Society of England. They have, I believe, spent almost the same amount as we have, but the expenses of their special ship[27] swallowed up a terrible sum and after all was of little use. I used to have all our stores and men taken free by the steamers of Austrian Lloyds and the Messageries.

It is rather fun having an argument. Especially when the old Baron takes part in it.

Pera   15th March 1878

All our ambulance sections are getting along famously. There is far more work to do than Stafford House can afford. It is heartrending however to see how little these Turks will do to help themselves! Actually in the large hospital of Silminia, just the other side of the Bosphorous, there are many wounded dying of starvation because they cannot eat the coarse food supplied by Government. One of the chief surgeons has just been this instant to tell me of the fact. I keep up three wards in that hospital with S.H. stores, but then these wards are under doctors on whom I can depend. I am afraid to give anything to the general depot of the hospital as it would never reach the wounded.

All this is most trying but one must bear with it and do ones best. One cannot uproot the vicious system which prevails in all the Government Administration.

I have just received news that all the Turkish wounded left in Plevna are dead, and no wonder if they were treated like those left at Kezanlyk. I have just received an account of the latter, and a terrible account it is . . .

I fear that there are not 903 remaining alive now, more than half must have died. I at once ordered provisions and medical stores to be sent from Philippopolis and Adrianople to the poor fellows. The Red Crescent Society undertook to look after the wounded at Plevna, Kezanlyk and Sofia, but they have done nothing. They sent a special Vice-President down with seven hundred pounds in his pocket and a great flourish of trumpets calling him attaché to the Plenipotentiaries, etc. etc., but he remained eating and drinking with grand dukes and princes at Adrianople, while his wretched fellow-countrymen were starving only a few days journey off. I am so angry about it that I have sent off help there without asking anybodys permission, and shall make no small row if they stop me. They dare not. I cannot say all I want about certain people high in authority in this rotten government, but as it is I am very free in giving them large 'pieces of my mind'. And these poor Turkish soldiers are so patient, and long-suffering, they die quite resigned to their fate and without a murmur of discontent on their lips. I often think that there must be some punishment awaiting those whose apathy and greed have brought these disasters on the people.

I am beginning to become very republican and really if there was a revolution to put down the authorities that be I should feel half inclined to lead it! I certainly would if I was a Turk! But then would any Turks be fit to rule?

They seem to spoil immediately they have power. They are destined to be a subject race now and will prosper far more as such.

Evening, 17th March

Rather an amusing thing has happened about our ambulance at Philippopolis. The Red Crescent had a large sanitary train which was got up at great expense, however the Red Crescent do not 'hit it off' with the Railway Company and there is always some difficulty about the train working. The Russians have got so bored with the Red Crescent that they have made an impromptu sanitary train of their own and, putting our Surgeon Dr Neylan in charge, have sent off the 300 Turkish wounded remaining at Philippopolis under him. We expect them here in a day or two. I am afraid that the Red Crescent will be very angry indeed. It is so unfortunate that they cannot do anything well. They have gone dreadful 'muckers' in Asia, in Roumelia and on the Danube. The real truth is, I fear, that there are too many on the Committee who think of their own selfish ends and vain glory. Another thing is that they do not like parting with their money.

I am on very good terms with them as I can do no good by censuring them, only harm, and I have to consider the good of the wounded above all things. You see in how difficult a position one is placed!

Evening, 18th March

My own darling Alice,

I telegraphed a reply to Fleetwood yesterday asking you to come out by the steamer leaving Marseilles on Saturday March 30th. This corresponds to the date about which you tell me most people begin to leave Mentone. I wonder if Mrs Hanson leaves about that time, if so you might leave with her – she would I am sure be delighted with the company of a dear good girl like you. Otherwise come alone (maid of course) and take 1st or 2nd class ticket for her as you find it most convenient for your dear little self.

Night, 18th March

Goodnight my little Alice. I am so intensely pleased at the news that peace has been ratified between Russia and Turkey. This is one step towards the general peace which we all long for so much.

Night, 19th March

Goodnight dearest Alice, I have just returned from the Club where I have been having a long argument about my favourite subject, humanity in war. There were some people there who hold the now exploded notion that the more terrible you make wars the less we should have of them; as if anything could be more cruel, more terrible, than the sufferings of the wounded in even the most merciful of wars. Extending them to women and children, and taking away unnecessarily lives of innocent harmless people is in my estimation a barbarous aggravation of the sufferings a nation must go through. This is not quite logical but I shall not re-write the phrase, as you know what I mean . . .

I was today for three hours at the Seraskerat [Turkish Ministry of War], fighting with three pachas about a new barrack in which I wish to place the wounded. I have got partially my own way but not all . . .

Poor Dr Attwood remains in a most critical condition; no better. Madame Von Rosen is nursing him, while Baron Mundy and Dr Hume are treating him. It is very hard lines on poor Attwood having passed through the whole campaign, and being laid up at the last moment.

20th March

Dear Alice,
No time to write more than a hurried line. Bring with you one or two good dresses as you will be obliged perhaps to go out a little at Therapia if we stay through May, which we shall do for certain! If you can cut down to one box all the better. Could you not leave it at Mentone, and then send for it if we require it? Mind bring your jewellery and those diamonds with you as people often wear these things and you can easily place them in safety.

Pera   Night, 20th March

My dear little wife,
I wrote off my last letter to you today in a very great hurry, I had a long report to write home to the S.H. Committee, and a great many other

affairs to settle. I am so happy at the prospect of seeing you here on April 6th. I shall meet you in a caique and take you at once to your new abode where I shall put you at work, as soon as you have rested, in all manner of useful ways! I was telling several people today that you would be coming out soon; in fact I am so pleased that I cannot help telling my friends so . . .

There was an interesting ceremony at Galeta the other day. Four young Jewesses, who had been outraged by the Bulgarians on their occupation of Eski-Zaara, were married at the same time at the Synagogue with a sort of High Service, music etc. It appears that the young men had been engaged to these girls before the Eski-Zaara affair and when they heard of the misfortune which befell their affiances, had refused to marry them! Magnanimous individuals! However Baron Hirsch, the rich owner of the railway, and a very great philanthropist,[28] bribed these unfaithful Israelites into carrying out their contracts by giving every girl a good dowry. After a great deal of bargaining the dowry was made high enough and the bridegrooms duly landed at the altar. Mrs Layard and many other ladies attended, I fear from curiosity. The whole matter disgusts me in the extreme. I cannot imagine marriages being happy with such brutes of husbands who first refuse to marry the girls to whom they were engaged because they had met with a terrible misfortune and secondly who accepted bribes to marry them. I wonder if these people have the faintest idea as to what true love is!

Afternoon, 22nd March

Dearest little wife,

I am going to see Lady Kemball off and am sending her a huge bouquet of violets, very dreadful!! However dearest, I am sending them for your sake because she was so kind in talking to me about you and seeing about a house etc. I like people who like my little Alice.

No time for more. Do not bother yourself in taking too much luggage but bring one good evening dress and your diamonds. Goodbye. God bless you and give you fair wind and weather to bring you to me.

I was much amused today at seeing a grand announcement in the local papers that the municipality was about to inaugurate a new work, viz the burying of the hundreds of dead oxen etc. in the neighbourhood of the town and the lines. It was announced with a great flourish of trumpets. The good people quite ignore that we have had 100 men at work nearly a fortnight on the disagreeable job and will have finished long before they begin! The people here are indeed aggravating in the extreme.

Tomorrow I am going to visit Prince Hassan.[29] I was told that unless I left that letter of introduction I should be looked upon as very rude. Leveson Gower, a relation of our President, [Lord Blantyre, President of the Stafford House Committee] is going with me as he was a personal friend of Prince Hassan at Oxford. Goodnight my dear. I wish you all peace and pleasant thoughts during the coming night. You are determined not to dream so there is no good wishing you pleasant dreams. You dear good girl. I wish so much that you were by my side.

Pera   Night, 22nd March

My own dearest Alice,
Today I received a telegram from Green [Secretary to the Stafford House Committee] to say that I had better 'begin the end' of our work. I am deeply sorry for the poor wounded who have been under our care.

I feel a sort of fatherly love for these poor helpless fellows – How terrible an end to some happy prosperous family once living in a smiling cottage among the cornfields or vineyards of Bulgaria. The husband a cripple in a fever-stricken hospital, the wife and children outcasts and refugees! May God in his Mercy pity these poor people, and sweeten the cup of bitterness which he has prepared for them. The Societies are working hard and well but what is to become of the people after they cease their work.

I do not like to dwell on these sad things especially when I think of my own happiness. I cannot help however feeling a tinge of sadness at leaving these people in their hour of distress. However it must be done.

On board Fraissinet Steamer going to Gallipoli,
off St Stefano [en route to inspect the Stafford House hospital at Gallipoli].

                                                     Night, 30th March

My darling Alice,
I am utterly miserable tonight, I feel as if some evil fate hung over our once bright future. I could no longer stand our separation, dearest Alice, when I sent for you. I had waited week after week, but at last could stand it no

157

longer. Just as we seemed on the point of meeting, another separation seems inevitable. Darling girl, I shall endeavour to use all my interest to be in some place where I can have you by my side, in case war breaks out between Russia and England, but you know I belong to the Militia, and may be called out, very probably will be called out. I hear that our regiment will do garrison duty at Shereness, in that case you will be with me, but all this is extremely uncertain. I shall try to get leave to be attached specially for ambulance work with Stafford House or the National Society and in this case shall have you darling always by my side.

I could not sleep last night and I feel quite ill today. The sun seems darkness to me and all the horrors of a new separation haunt me like demons. I firmly believe that I could not stand it. I do not know what I should do. I have tried to put the best appearance on matters and be bright and apparently happy, but I have had a dead weight on my heart ever since we parted. I have felt that parting was unnatural and cruel. I know it was in one way the right thing to do and I loyally kept my promise to Fleetwood and your family but, dear Alice, do you not know the pang it gave me, a pang which stings me now and will torment me until once more I press you to my heart. Nothing in the world will ever make me leave you again if I am not positively obliged to do so. I cannot write to you more on the subject. It pains me so much. I feel terrible pricks of conscience about having left you behind and now you darling good girl you are coming out to meet me just as war may be beginning.

Alice travelled out to join Vincent in early April, escorted part of the way by her brother, Fleetwood. Her steamer arrived at the Dardanelles at 5 a.m. on 5 April and Vincent immediately went aboard and surprised her. From there they travelled straight to Therapia, avoiding Constantinople. Her reactions to her new surroundings are captured in her letters home, from one of which to her sister Emily, dated 10 April 1878, the following extracts are taken:

We are getting on very well here and are now drifting into a regular routine which will enable Barrington to do his work and amuse me alternately. He will go in about three days a week to Constantinople. He gets to his office in about one and a half hours from here, starting at 8.30 and coming back in time for 7 o'clock dinner. It makes rather a long day for me by myself but then I always can find plenty to do and as the weather gets warmer I shall be able to sketch. At present it is a little too cold to attempt it. The sun is warm in the middle of the day but in the evenings we are glad of a fire, or rather the native substitute for one, a tinfull of hot charcoal brought

Alice at Constantinople

in on a copper stand. There are no fireplaces in the rooms and I don't think this method of heating is very wholesome, it makes the air of the rooms so dreadfully dry.

This is one of B. business days so I shall spend part of it in writing to you.

I think I told Fleetwood about the dear little Arab I have got to ride. It carries me beautifully and is quieter with me than it has been with other people who were treated to a bolt every now and then, my bit suits it perfectly and it scarcely pulls with me at all.

Barrington has a poor old ambulance horse to ride. One that was bought from the Russians and has been all through the campaign. You can count all his ribs and his coat is all rough and shaggy, however he goes pretty safely which is the chief thing.

Our groom is a perfect picture, a tall good-looking young Turk dressed in bright blue garments braided with black. He can't understand a word of English so it is a little difficult to make him understand what we want for B. does not know much Turkish. He is very intelligent and it is rather fun explaining things in dumb show. We had a splendid ride yesterday into Pera, the country we passed through was very like the wildest parts of Hampshire about Liphook a gravelly soil and lots of heather. I could scarcely realize that we were scampering over Turkish soil, it makes one feel so much at home riding in a foreign place, especially when I have my own bridle, saddle etc. and am so comfortably mounted.

The country is fearfully wild, and very solemn looking. The hills are high but so regular that when you are on top of them you fancy you are looking over a vast monotonous plain. Coming home last evening the sun was setting behind clouds and some of the views looked wild and dreary enough for Doré to choose in illustrating the most awful parts of Dantes Inferno.

At present the number of Turkish camps perched on all the hills brighten up the country immensely and make it very safe too. Last year B. says he could not have ridden the way we did yesterday without a pistol in his pocket. We passed several of the camps, the poor soldiers looked dreadfully travel-stained and miserable. It is sad to see some of them toiling up the hills perhaps with no stockings on and boots literally falling off their feet. I believe they get no pay and very little food. One of our horses had a loose shoe so we stopped at a battery of artillery and asked if someone could put it on. Yes it could be done but there wasn't a single nail to be had. The horses look very miserable and are used until their shoes drop off, then of course they go lame. What horrid lazy people these Turks are!

I was disappointed with Pera, the principal street is not a bit Eastern looking, you might fancy yourself in the slums of London if you did not see all the bright and varied dresses.

I had a peep at Stamboul from the Pera side of the Golden Horn. It is very picturesque but not a bit what I expected. Fancy a number of mangy Swiss cottages crowded together with an occasional mosque and minaret springing out of them. The wood of which the houses are built is not painted, gets dark with time and looks very sombre. Why did no one say that Stamboul was built of wood. I think Fleetwood might have mentioned it casually to prevent one from being so grievously disappointed!! I am disappointed with the East, I had looked forward to a perfect feast of colour and now I only find it in the dresses of the natives.

I wish I could draw figures, on every side one has the most fascinating groups, I suppose the bright, smiling Italian look of Mentone spoils me for other places.

It was no joke riding through Pera, the paving so awful and the crowds of pack animals one meets who prefer rubbing up against one if they can. Then the carriages dash by one and there is no rule of the road, you must steer your own course as best you may. It was quite bewildering to me for I wanted to take in everything we passed, besides wishing to know how the little Arab looked in the shop windows! We spent an hour or two in B.'s office, and a number of people dropped in to see us. Among them the grim Queen's Messenger, Mr Woodford, who still persists things look very black though the news has been getting more pacific every day . . .

Lady Strangford came to see us last Sunday and spent a long time here. I was prepared to dislike her but after all found her very pleasant. It was most interesting to hear all her experiences at Sofia when the Russians took possession of it. They seem to have treated her abominably, but then she sets herself up as a Turcophile in a very obtrusive way. The first Rusky's that came into her hospital brushed by her, knocked off her cap and dashed into the wards. She thought they meant to murder all the wounded men. She says she defended these herself and defied the Russians to touch them. Afterwards she went out and harangued General Gourko[30] as soon as he arrived and complained of the treatment she had received. The sentinels used habitually to spit in her face and when she complained to the officers about it they punished and turned away the offenders, but the next would do exactly the same. What wretches they must be!

Constantinople is full of Russian officers but we did not notice them much yesterday as they are only allowed to appear in their plain clothes, they made themselves very objectionable before by swaggering about with their swords dragging on the road . . .

11th April

We have just come in from a ride along the coast beyond Buyukdere, there we discovered that a quantity of forage was being landed for the Russians, actually supplied by an English contractor. Is it not too bad when we want them to be as short as possible of provisions. It is supposed that the Russians are determined to embark at Buyukdere if possible and like to have everything ready for their arrival! I hope you have looked at the map to see the positions of the places I mention.

Yesterday I went to see some Greek people living here, old Mrs Hanson having given me an introduction to them. I found them very friendly and pleasant. They took me out for a walk on the hills and we found some lovely wild flowers. The weather has become suddenly warm so I hope to be able to do some sketching, it is a horrid bore not being able to go about comfortably where one likes, people say the country is not very safe. I shall take Ali, our groom, whenever I go out and if he has some weapon of defence it will be all right. This place agrees with me very well, my appetite is too fearful, Barrington can't get over my having 4 courses at breakfast this morning! But as we had this meal at 10.30 and dine at 7 I don't think it was out of the way! We are capitally fed here and Mrs Petula certainly makes us most comfortable. I am getting quite reconciled to living in heathen lands and seem to feel at home anywhere.

FOUR

Letters from Egypt, March–June 1885

CHRONOLOGY OF THE SUAKIN CAMPAIGN, 1885

1885

17 February	British Government contract with Lucas and Aird for construction of a railway from Suakin to Berber.
20 February	Sir Gerald Graham appointed to command Suakin Field Force.
13 March	Railway construction begun.
19–22 March	Skirmishes with Osman Digna at Hashin and Tamai.
24 March	Vincent arrives at Suakin.
3 April	Occupation and destruction of Tamai.
15 April	Suspension of railway work announced.
16 April	Otao occupied.
19 April	Tambuk occupied.
21 April	Decision to evacuate Sudan announced in London.
30 April	Railway reaches Otao where work stopped.
2 May	Wolseley arrives at Suakin to determine size and composition of future permanent garrison there.
17 May	Withdrawal begins with departure of Brigade of Guards and Australian troops.
19 May	Wolseley and Sir Gerald Graham leave.
20–1 May	Rest of British troops leave.
June	Vincent winds up NAS affairs.

Brindisi   9th March 1885

My dear good Alice,
I write to you a last line from Europe. We are nearing Brindisi, and
embark during the small hours of the morning. The old, old story will again
come round. I shall listen to the thud, thud of the screw and think how far
happier I shall be when each thud is bringing me nearer to you than when it
is taking me away. However I am happy in feeling that I am carrying out
my mission in life and I know you, dear girl have some feeling of
satisfaction at that too.

The bitterness of our parting we neither of us gave way to, altho',
dearest, I felt it very very much. All that hurry and scurry was a good thing
in its way and diverted thoughts from their natural channel of the sorrow of
parting.

You may depend upon my keeping you well informed of my whereabouts and my work, and you on your side dearest will not I feel sure miss a
post. I am perfectly well and so rested with my voyage so far!

This seems absurd but it is true – We have got into hot weather and I
have a ravenous appetite – Have not smoked a cigarette since being on this
side of the channel.

Mind send my light Norwegian home-spun suit, the quite new one by Sir
Allen Young's yacht if he will take it with my gun and some cartridges, also
my cartridge case. N.B. better still ask Mr Vokes, our sec.

I have thought of a still better way, Burton is going to accompany Dr
Newby on *Oceano* which sails about 14th to 16th March – Please pack up
my new light grey Norwegian home spun suit which I left on top of the
Eton cupboard, coat, trousers and waistcoat, pack it up in brown paper,
and give it to Burton to take out with him in the *Oceano*.

As to the gun and cartridges I should rather they go by Sir Allen Young's
yacht. You might send me for my own use in case of illness 2 bottles of that
old brandy which you have at H.P. Gardens, Fleetwood can get the Lane
to replace, also any other little thing that you can think of. I may telegraph
you as to any wants, but I left nothing behind at all.

This bold assertion was to be negated by his subsequent correspondence.

Alexandria   11th March 1885

My own dear wife,
We are nearing Alexandria and expect to arrive there tomorrow morning
about daybreak. Our passage has been like a summer cruise under the lee
of some high mountains so smooth is the sea and balmy the air. As I near
the scene of my future work I feel a little of my old spirit returning and feel
inclined to throw myself body and soul into the business which I have in
hand. I know that you, dear, are not unsympathetic as to its objects and
this is one of my chief consolations in a separation so painful to both of us.
And now dearest I must tell you something of my fellow passengers.

We arrived at Brindisi on the 9th, soon after midnight and routed up the
unfortunate 'through' passengers of the *Lombardy* in their first sleep. The
good ship had brought them from Venice and was waiting at Brindisi for us
and the mails. I was singularly unfortunate about my berth as Cook and
Son through whom I bought my ticket omitted to requisition one for me.
However I was placed in a cabin with 2 other men, good fellows, and
though we make hay in the cabin every morning, a worthy steward
disintegrates our belongings and divides them off before nightfall . . .

How you would enjoy this lovely voyage; just enough breeze to temper
the warmish sun, just enough ripple to make that sweet sea music as the
ship glides swiftly between the blue seas. We had a concert last night but I
was not 'found out' and kept myself quiet in the tent fitted up on deck,
enjoying the lovely night and a pipe of peace. All this sounds very
enjoyable but it is a mar to it all that you are not here to share it.

Now I do not like to trouble you but would you carry out the commission
which I have put on the accompanying page. I find that I have not quite the
underclothing required in the hot regions where I am going. In fact I did
not go to the right people.

For you   Private
Would you please go to Cocks Biddulph & Co. and ask them to show
you the young man who wished to go out with me. Please take down his
name, age and Christian names and send them to Mr Vokes in case he or
Sir A. Young wants someone to look after stores etc., also send me out the
same particulars as I may want him.

Explain to him that the uncertainty of the military operation makes it
impossible for me to decide as to what our staff will ultimately consist of.
He might be wanted or he might not.

And now dearest girl, you and the darling boy [his son, Guy] are
constantly in my thoughts; I feel that he would be a companion to me if I
were alone and still more so will be one to you. The memory of mother and

165

child is one that makes me feel sad, but there is on the other hand the intense feeling of confidence and love in knowing that I am nearest and dearest to them in affection.

Shepherds Hotel   16th March 1885
Cairo

My own dear Alice,

What a huge amount of preliminaries are necessary in the polyglot, polytheistic, polyblood country. I have been driving about incessantly all day for three days with the following results. Perhaps I had better begin from our arrival at Alexandria.

We arrived at daybreak on March 12th. I found a boat of Capt. Bloomfields, the port police inspector, (to whom I had a letter of introduction from Lady Brassey) waiting for another man. So in I jumped after the other had been dealt with, and spent all day making an inspection of sanitary conditions, looking over two vessels for hospital ships, tele-graphing all over the country as to where the *Ganges* was and finally sat down to a good dinner rather done. The next morning at 8.30 we were on our (rail) way for Cairo where we arrived at 3.30 p.m. I met Col. Lennox, an old Turco-Russian war friend, in a compartment reservé (he was with Chermside then as military attaché). He kindly asked me to share his carriage and we had a pleasant chat in which he told me about his duties as Governor of Alexandria. Of course he was grumbling like all Englishmen at not being sent to the front as he had been selected (almost) for the post which Maj. Gen. Ewart R.E. now had. I lost no time in changing my clothes and washing, for in about half an hour I was driving on my way to official visits to Sir Ev. Baring and General Stephenson the commander of the Forces. The latter is a most polished gentleman, so genial and kind, he has assisted me in every possible way. I found Walter Barings letter of introduction to his brother waiting my arrival which gave me a welcome there. The next morning I had a letter from one of the English Attachés also an old commissioner friend, Elliot, to say that Sir E. Baring would present me to the Khedive[31] next day.

At 10.15 a.m. I called on Sir E.B. and found a carriage and pair waiting in which he and I drove to the Palace, escorted, or rather preceded by, two 'runners' in gorgeous liveries and carrying two long rods. We were first received by Zulfikar Pasha, the chief Pacha at the Palace, and then conducted to the Khedive. I had a long conversation after my presentation by Sir E.B. in French, and I found the Khedive a very well-informed and pleasant companion. After discussing the ambulance matters we had quite a good laugh over some amusing episodes of the last year or two. I then devoted myself to buying a horse and found horse-dealers were as almighty rascals here as elsewhere. Every screw in the place followed me about, and I was continually interrupted by messages that a horse was at the door! Such a motley crowd, Europeans of various colours, Arab, broken-down English grooms all vied with one another in their endeavours to stick me. I had some rides gratis and bought O. The next day however I was suited in the purchase of a strong black pony. Four times in the course of the day a certain Bey from the Palace tried to catch me in! At last he succeeded, bearing two letters signed by the Khedive ordering the Red Sea authorities to give me every help, very thoughtful of him. At 3 p.m. I heard that a battery of mule artillery was to start the same evening for Suakin. I luckily caught Dr Squire in time and got him off at 6 p.m. with a free ticket for Suakin. A splendid transport, the *Mareotis*, was waiting for the special train bearing the mule battery, so Dr Squire will travel to the front as comfortably as mortal man could wish. Moreover being attached to the spendid mule battery will be a great beginning for him. I went to dinner rather tired out especially with the dust and confusion of 'training' the mules. They were shoved into open trucks, closely packed – so closely that they could not kick or bite. . . . The scene in putting them in baffles description. Mules kicking, plunging, snorting, squealing, biting; men seizing them bodily, shuffling them in like cards, hauling at their ears and tails all in the greatest good humour – except the mules . . .

I have been working hard looking up the Medical Authorities and taking stock of wants etc. I think we shall be useful, but the great thing which takes everyones fancy is Allen Young's yacht. They say it will be a godsend. I hope that I can be on it from time to time. We had the first hot day today. A warm wind which sent up clouds of dust. I enjoyed the heat immensely, but not the dust and now goodnight dearest and God bless mother and child.

Shepherds Hotel   17th March
Cairo

For you only
My own dearest wife,
I slip in a line to say how often I am thinking of you and dear little Guy
even during my most busy moments. Poor little fellow, he seemed so
affectionate before I left as if he knew there was something up. I went to
Church yesterday and thought more of you, I fear, than the service, but I
prayed for you and Guy and felt that I too was in your thoughts at the
moment. I do look forward to a happy return in May and think that all
points that way. We expect an advance to be made about the 1st April and
then when Osman Digna[32] is pushed back the troops will be encamped on
the Sinkat Hills, where there is heat but not the moist heat of Suakin. I
have no personal apprehension as to my health, you know I am a
salamander!! Yesterday many people here were overcome with the hot
wind; the only effect on me was to make my eyes smart with the dust. I
shall begin today to wear the blue spectacles. Goodbye my own dear girl
and ever believe me your loving husband.
 Vincent.

Suez Hotel   19th March 1885
Suez

My own dear Wife,
I arrived here at 6 p.m. after a very dusty journey down from Cairo. I
almost forgot whether I told you in my last letter of my visit to the Princess
Nazri. She is a sort of cousin or sister or some relation to the Khedive; as
you know relationship is very mixed here, there are so many step brothers
and sisters. This worthy princess sent me a message that she would be
happy to receive me yesterday at 6 p.m. I accordingly called at the harem,
and was led through various passages by a black servant and finally reached
a beautifully decorated boudoir. A discreetly aged dame de compagnie
received me, and afterwards in came Madame. She was about 30, very
pretty but, of course, rather got up, dressed in half Turkish half European
dress. She talked English pretty well and we had a long chat, interrupted
for a while by the visit of some European ladies. Afterwards her husband
arrived, a very old looking man, too old to be her husband, but very polite

and agreeable. Of course this is not strictly harem life, the Princess goes in for living what Turks would call 'a la Franque'.

Yesterday I wished goodbye to Gen. Stephenson and Sir E. Baring, and at 6.30, just after posting my first letter to you, I went to the station to see my 'cavalry' start. The two horses plunged and kicked violently at the station and the dear donkey (which I think I shall Christen the Mahdi) became very lively too. As I sent them free by the military train I had only a military horse box, quite open; we put one horse at each end and made a sort of barrier with my tent and the poles etc. The 'Mahdi' stood meekly in the middle, quite happy eating straw! The poor animals got very much knocked about while the truck was being shunted about the station; it was a relief to me to see them well on their way.

This morning I followed them and find that they have arrived safe and sound at their destination. The donkey however is very talkative and makes an awful row at night braying.

I find that my transport the *Geelong* is detained here for two days owing to the *Navarino* not having arrived yet at Suez. We take on a draft of marines and some animals from the *Navarino*. I shall therefore remain quietly here, which will do me good after the fun of Cairo.

Fancy clever me leaving London without a pocket filter!! I could not find one today in Cairo and must trust to Major Young sending one after me! Note 1, when you go out to war, firstly buy a pocket filter in London.

They have 7 sick here and are in want of ice, so I hear; though today the weather was quite cold. Fancy I had a flannel shirt, my thick dark winter shooting coat, and flannel lined waistcoat, and thick flannel cholera belt and I was not too hot! I believe that people exaggerate the horrors of a hot country 'Mais nous verrons' (?properly spelt?).

Goodnight dearest, and do not be in the least anxious about me. I am perfectly well; fancy your letter which I feel is coming, is not 100 yards from this hotel on its way to Suakin and I cannot get at it. The Indian mail is just coming in and your letter, posted I suppose on March 13 must be in it.

SS *Missir*   20th March
Red Sea

My own dear Alice,
I have at last entered on the first 'roughing it' of the war, and a rather bad time we are having of it. I had arranged all my plans so beautifully at Cairo,

horses and donkey going by military train gratis. I follow by ordinary train half price; we were to be forwarded from Suez by the SS *Geelong*, gratis, the four nurses were coming by *Navarino* which would meet the *Geelong* at Suez so I would have had the opportunity of seeing and posting them. Alas for the irony of fate! I arrived in Suez on Thursday evening and all plans being made on Friday morning I inspected the Suez hospital with the Prin. Med. Officer, took down the things they required with letter of requisition and after lunch was out for a ride with Capt. Robbins, an old friend of the Kingslakes and myself, when a telegram was put in his hands to say that Suakin harbour being blocked no transports were to leave until further notice. I was then blocked myself at Suez with doctors and stores gone on to Suakin!

I had heard that a small Egyptian steamer was going to start in a couple of hours and so in the twinkling of an eye I galloped off, routed out my two men from the bazaar and in an hour we were all on our way to this dirty disgusting ship. There is no proper accommodation, the horses and donkey had to be slung on board and are standing on the open deck, the donkey of course quite at home and already a favourite with the whole crew, including three robbers and a murderer all in chains but without any visible guard! It seems quite ludicrous to think of our position at the moment. The little steamer's decks are piled up with huge bags of cut chaff, a long way above the bulwarks, rascals of various nationalities are lounging about and smoking among all this stuff, so much so that it will be a Godsend if it does not catch fire unless some severe precautions are taken. The Capt. of the ship is an insouciant Egyptian, always smoking himself, and at my strong representations he has had sails stretched across the more dangerous part of the bags. He said himself that it was very dangerous. One single awning covers a part of the ship and under this crowd all manner of strange people. Two Greeks on way to get bakers situations at Suakin. Three rascally looking Italians on their way to rob, steal, murder or make a fortune, perhaps all. My immediate neighbour consists of a Major C— who has suddenly been sent for to join the staff and therefore risked the passage in this boat, one man whose business I do not know, one adventuring engineer from the Caracas & La Geniana country out on 'spec' and one a traveller of Ellington the tent people.

Let me look round at some other passengers. Lying all in a heap on some bales of chaff are three dirty looking Egyptians going to serve the remaining term of their imprisonment at Suakin. They had made a raid on a neighbouring village and carried off some cattle. I had a long chat with them thro' my dragoman [interpreter] and they told me their history – A yard off lay a handsome Arab, scowling at me; perhaps he had heard me call my donkey the Mahdi! He also was in chains suffering a term of 10 years for having killed another man. Close by on the deck my donkey is braying and the people are playing tricks with him. They will get bitten soon. Alongside stand my two steeds with piles of bags between them to make improvised stalls.

Let me describe my 'staff'.

No. 1 Abdu (Marionite) [i.e. a Maronite Christian from the modern Lebanon] rather proud and sulky. When he does not like to do menial work I do it myself and he rushes to it at once.

No. 2 Hills – Cross between English and Gibraltar – Hispano-Italian has resided much in tropical parts: 2 years with 42nd Regt. position Groom, looks half a light-weight prize fighter and the rest a jockey – lent to my by an attaché of Sir E. Baring.

No. 3 Don Pasquale! – Race half an Italian and the rest query, but a touch of Arab or Egyptian, I should think. Speaks lingos accordingly. Was for 6 months with my friend Lord Melgund during the last war and has good character.

Last night while making my inspection I found to my utter astonishment another Italiano-Egyptian cuddled up under the horses. I thought at first Don Pasquale had played some Zotifwer trick and made himself into two. Quite puzzled I went to bye-bye and this morning solved the mystery. My occult friend was a stow-away who had run away from Cairo mixed up in a luggage train and had somehow personated Don Pasquale so as to get on board this ship unobserved. He has not yet been found out and, poor devil, I do not intend to denounce him. I believe my men feed him on the sly. He has no papers and no money and would starve if it were not for the crumbs which fall intentionally from their rough hands.

Looking round close to where I sit, I see a rather handsome Greek woman with a little boy, a month or two older than our boy. She had crept up to our deck to get shelter from the hot sun, and my fellow 'firsts' wanted to clear her and the rest of the poor devils out. I protested and the poor woman is now in a sort of a blanket rolled up with her bairnie, so happy, she is evidently very fond of it and smiles approvingly at me as if she knew I had pleaded her cause. She is some near relation of one of the Italian scoundrels but of which I know not as no one takes any notice of her – stop – one of them swore at her when the baby cried, so I suppose he was using the jus parentis!

I could write to you by the yard of the amusing scenes around me, of the horrible smells, of the still more horrible insects; two of the 'horriblest' I killed myself (one, I fancy, carbolized thanks to a bottle of pure carbolic acid with which I freely bespattered my berth), but you can imagine what are the constant inhabitants of the dirtiest boat I can conceive. My sleeping sack is invaluable. Rolled up in it I enjoyed a night of pure repose defying my enemies with better luck than poor Gordon.

I need not describe the food, a kid was being slain on deck before us all which I suppose we shall get through somehow, and I see one poor solitary hen in a coop looking very hungry itself. Last night something went wrong with the furnace of the ship and the engines had to stop. Something got red hot and was melting so the English engineer tells me.

I would not have come on the ship had I not thought it very necessary to push on at all costs to Suakin. Reports say that fighting may begin on 25th, and if I waited for the proper transport I might not be able to reach there in time to make the necessary disposition of our medical staff. I had provided for the contingency by giving orders to Dr Squire whom I sent on attached to the mule artillery battery, when I remained behind to buy horses and a donkey and various essentials for the ambulance, also to get certain official papers from the Khedive and our English Authorities.

The horses and donkey are my chief care on board ship. They will be all right unless there is a 'sea' in which case we shall have some hard work holding them up. Have arranged that we shall take our 'watches' day and night at their heads to prevent them from coming to any ill – and now goodnight.

22nd March 1885

It is Sunday. . . . I was reminded of the day as I saw Major Collins with a little prayer book on deck. Sunday reminds one of home sweet home and that little boy on deck reminds me of the bright jewel which adds one more happiness to ours. I find he is just the age of Guy, and so I am the more interested. My instinct patenal made me observe that little 'Homer' as I call him had not food enough, the poor mother having done her best with natural food and having no money to buy other. I luckily had with me a tin of cocoa and milk which I have been administering with great success. I was wrong qua father, he is at Suakin.

The Mahdi [his donkey] is such fun, I have taught him to bray by holding a carrot up in front of his nose, and he is just like a dog in affection following one about. He lies down on deck when tired and is in every way far more sensible than the horses. Last night, after finishing my letter, the wind got up and by the time of bye-bye it was blowing hard. As we reached the opening into the Red Sea proper we began to roll. The wind then veered round to the east and we rolled badly. The poor horses had no horse box and I piled up some sacks of chaff, part of the cargo, alongside of them and took the responsibility of breaking open one of them and strewing the contents below them to make a bed. This little steamer is only about 500 tons and should it blow really hard it would fare ill with the horses. Happily about 2 a.m. the wind changed to the north and the waves were calmed, it was Sunday morning and 'Allah is good' as our Capt. is wont to remark. I do not know why, but I feel quite confident that we shall reach our destination safely tho' of course there is a little risk for the horses should the weather become bad again. It was a lucky purchase of mine, that Cawnpore tent (officers double tent) it is the very best that I could possibly have. So please do not be anxious as to my comfort. We do not know what is going to happen at Suakin, but it will not be long before decided action is taken and after that the troops will probably encamp at Sinkat, a fine breezy height, hot but not unhealthy. I cannot imagine why the soldiers helmet is made so close to the head, they lose the important protection of the well made helmet and of course suffer from sunstroke and other abominations. That love of 'smartness' will cost many a life. There may be some reason for the absurd shape but the only one I have heard, namely that the broad helmet interferes with shooting and sloping arms, has been flatly contradicted by a staff officer.

Vincent's drawings of army helmets

23rd March

I had such a good night's rest, I acted cuckoo and slept in a spare berth of the state (!) cabin occupied by the commercial gentleman, yclept Sharpe. He did not object, as I told him it was simply necessary for me to sleep. The weather remains beautiful and today a.m. we have just caught sight of Mt.Elba [in Egypt]. We are cautiously keeping out in the middle of the sea, as if by chance we ran ashore the Arabs would cut our throats to a certainty. I have been giving the prisoners some oranges and the murderer smiled so sweetly at me and thanked me. This afternoon I shall distribute more. 'Homer' is better today and has just taken his cup of 'cocoa and milk'. He has a very bad cough and his tongue is ulcerated. I pronounce this malady teething cough with thrush! Ask our medico if I am right.

I have been learning Arabic hard this morning with Abdu, the dragoman, and Major C. We have really made progress and can ask the way, the name of the towns and streams, etc. and food, some words I remember by Memoria Technica system.[33]

How odd that such an old campaigner as myself should forget in the scurry of departure to take with him certain important things:

1 Thermometer
2 Pocket filter
3 India rubber bath
4 Extra pair of braces
5 Leather writing case
6 Flea powder
7 Strong field watch, instead of gold one
8 Bag to hold brushes etc. in ship
9 Pocket case of personal medicines
10 Carbolic soap
11 *Canvas shoes for ship*
12 Pocket aneroid or barometer
13 Can containing knife, fork and spoon, pepper and salt

and all these can be obtained at the stores. I write as I think of them and please *file* the list for reference should fate take me out to another campaign . . .

By the way our boiler pipes came to grief again last night, two of them gave way and they could not use the boiler for two and a half hours. The current sets in at the rate of four miles an hour towards the land which is infested with hostile Arabs, so it is not pleasant to have these little accidents happening so often.

Suakin   25th March 1885

Just a line to say that we reached Suakin last night at 6 p.m. – We steamed most cautiously the last 10 miles between horrid reefs where

Map to illustrate activities during the Suakin Campaign between March and June 1885

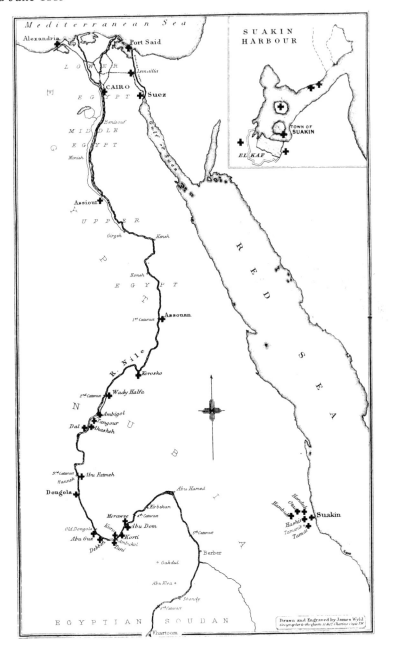

several ships have had narrow shaves and more than one have run aground on them.

They have begun the fighting and some 60 of our men are wounded. We lost 300 camels in some affair on Saturday or Sunday. Our doctors are at work so I hear, 1 is at Headquarters and 3 at base hospital.

26th March 1885

My own dear wife,

I'm writing this after a hard afternoon's work. I was tired last night not having had a good nights rest for sometime, that awful *Missir* SS still haunts me. I accepted Dr Gibbon's invitation to take a berth on the *Ganges* last night and I did rest most sweetly. So calm so quiet, lulled to sleep by the monotonous refreshing thud of the refrigerating machine.

I spent most of yesterday at the front at Headquarters. During the previous night there had been an uncomfortable feeling in the camp. The recent operations have not been very succesful, in the sense of our losing a good many men – Our force evacuated the hill of Hasheen and returned to camp while I was there but we hold Bahu Pacha's Zeriba [animal corral or fortified stockade] now called Mer Mieh Zeriba. Sundays affair was most unfortunate as we lost so many camels and mules. This makes my two horses and donkey of inestimable value . . .

This morning I was up at 5.45 a.m. and rowed to the *Australia* which sailed with Lucas on board a little after 6 a.m. Then back to the *Ganges* for breakfast and delivered over some stores to Piggott. Interviewed various people and after lunch went off to report myself to Gen. Ewart who commands the Suakin district now that the main force will advance. As I have to ply between the harbour and Headquarters and the stores etc. the horses will be attached to the base hospital for rations etc. and I shall nominally be attached there too; the base means Suakin and lines of communication to the front that is our sphere of work. Our surgeons are well placed and as far as our Soc. work is concerned I can say confidently it is a great success. You see we arrived in the nick of time and I have worked in completely with Govt. Authorities. They, on their part, have acted most *cordially* with us, giving us every welcome and encouragment. Our ten nurses arrived tonight and will be at work in two days – all well.

The weather is charming, I do not find it too hot; nights lovely, goodnight my own dear wife and may God bless you –

28th March

Lots of work, nurses arrived from England yesterday, posted them at their places. Some at base hospital and our Princess of Wales nurses at the auxiliary hospital. Breakfasted with Sir G. Graham yesterday at the Headquarters. There was another little fight on March 26th. Very few losses on our side. Have no time for more as I am immediately connected with Gen. Ewart RE. His tent is only *10 yards* from my Headquarters where I keep my horses etc. Dr Hind, the P.M.O. at base, and myself have made great friends, all going capitally. The General, Sir Graham, has written me already an official letter thanking the Society for what it is doing. I am working in rapidly wherever there is a strain or want to help in the Govt. organisation. Thus, two days ago auxiliary hospital was found – yesterday I popped in our two nurses to look after the sick, superintend the cooking etc.

Suakin   3rd April 1885

My own dear Alice,
I was most distressed today at missing the mail as far as your letter was concerned. The ship carrying the mail started before her time, as the director of Naval Transport was so anxious to get her clear of the reefs before night came on.

I am quite well and really do think that the dreaded Suakin climate has been much exaggerated. Men do suffer from sunstroke etc. but then they have constitution[s] different from mine. I believe that I am a sort of 'Salamander' or perhaps being born under a Southern sky may make a difference.

I never worked harder in my life than I have been doing since I landed at Alexandria. It is rather tiresome work in some ways as I have to be so careful not to tread upon other peoples toes. I will tell you one instance. I found that with all our splendid hospital arrangements no provision was made to give *fresh milk* to the sick and wounded. I accordingly bought two cows and this was hailed with welcome by the surgeons. The heads of the Med-Service at once saw that some comment might be made and have now, one week after the event requisitioned to have fresh milk supplied at Govt. expense! Of course I am well pleased as my object was to get fresh milk supplied. Many other little things like this occur but we all get on very well and the steam launch which I bought is used all day long by the Medical Authorities. It takes large numbers of sick and wounded to the hospital ships every day almost.

I will not talk of the fighting, we are all rather distressed about it here, so many unfortunate things have happened and I do not think that they will find their way to the papers. . . . Better not. . . . I asked L.-Lindsay to send to you my long reports to him which will tell you all news. I do hail your letters with the greediest satisfaction dearest and every night I offer to the Almighty a prayer with your likeness before me, the symbol of all that I think best and highest in the world. I was so pleased that you anticipated my request about dear little Guy's photo. Any little details about him interest me immensely.

7th April 1885

SS *Ganges* – Suakin – You may depend upon my keeping my promise to look after myself for your sake.
My own dear Alice,
It is *so* refreshing to sit down and write a letter to you, and you only with our darling boy. The little details which you so thoughtfully relate in your letters bring tears of some sort of feeling which it is hard to define into my eyes. What a dear child he is and how fully he is realising our most cherished hopes.

You say, dear Alice, that I am work [*sic*] relieving the suffering of others, well I am trying and have to work as sharply as ever fell to my lot to push forward the schemes which we conceive. There is, of course, a great mass of inertia and insouciance inseparable from the climate, and hammer hammer, screw screw is everlastingly necessary to put life into the work. My letters to the Society, copies of which will be forwarded to you, will tell you of the details of our operations. We have done, I think, fairly well, and fell into our places quite naturally. One war is just like another and so I felt quite at home.

It is so satisfactory to see the wounded doing so well; they are *all* recovering and in such good spirits. The sick look far more miserable as they come down dusty and haggard from the front. One poor fellow was brought down in the scorching sun very ill with sunstroke just as I was landing in my small boat, so I took him off to the *Ganges*; he fell down as he entered the boat. Our steam launch which I bought for £220 has done excellent service but the engines have been going wrong and she is now undergoing some overhauling.

We have plenty of ups and downs. The cows are rather a failure!! Serve me right for thinking I was so clever! They kick and lie down when the men try to milk them and are as wild as tigers. One gave my groom a good butt.

I have not been quite the thing the last day or two but am practically right again – I only tell you this in case anyone should tell you that I have been seedy. It was nothing at all and I am at my work, but shall in future work thro' the Doctors more. You see for the first ten days I was in the saddle all day long, finding out what were the wants, how I could relieve them, what I could get in the town, interviewing the various authorities, presenting letters of introduction and what you may call establishing the foundation of the work . . .

The hospitals being well supplied we are distributing large numbers of medical comforts, oranges, tobacco etc. to the soldiers through their officers. During the last four days we have given out 3,000 oranges and 4 cwt of tobacco! The tired and worn out men are so grateful for their presents. Perhaps I may be criticised for this in the press but I consider that what I am doing carries out the spirit of adding to the comfort of our forces in the field. The poor fellows come in *loaded* with dust and so thirsty, so parched. An orange is indeed a blessing to them. The limes which I sent out on the Tamai march were greedily sought after, and now goodnight – God bless the apple of my eye and her darling boy . . .

I was, as I have said, a bit seedy a few days ago, but I did not think much of it. I had been working hard and sat up late to write a long report to the Society. They gave me some medicine on board the *Ganges* and I got well rapidly, in fact it was only one day off work, as my 'heads of departments' [others N.A.S. representatives working under Kennett] came to see me instead of my seeing them; a plan which I shall follow in future, now that their respective spheres of action are defined. Now today I hear that I had been reported by some sympathetic correspondent as sick, so I took care to have telegraphed home that I was well again so as to avoid any anxiety. You may *trust* me to let you know dearest if I am really ill as I promised I would. It makes me feel uncomfortable to think that you may think that I have not kept my promise. Out here a little coup d'estomac which we think nothing of in England is at once treated in hospital to prevent it going further and so many are reported on the sick list on account of such a matter combined with exhaustion from overwork and get perfectly right after two days.

15th April 1885

My own dear Alice,

Your numbers 7 & 8 received in due course. How can I thank you sufficiently for your most welcome pages. The only fault I find is that they are not half long enough and so I read them over several times. I am so thankful that the news of poor Fleetwood's convalescence arrived contemporaneously with that of his illness, as I should have felt very anxious for him. I am not in the least nervous about dear little Guy as there is no appreciable link in such cases. It is generally the case when two or three cases of Typhoid occur in the same house that the victims have got ill from the same cause, impure water etc. – and not from one another. I wonder where F. contracted the complaint. I suppose from some hotel during his return home . . .

To revert once more to old F. How I wish that I could have been at H.P.G. [Hyde Park Gardens] to relieve you and sit with him during his convalescence. It is so tedious for a patient when he is wanting to get up and is not allowed to; I can imagine him in the nursery surrounded with papers and you sitting by his side; a nurse whom I think he appreciates. I feel anxious for him and I do hope that he will not take exercise too quickly as sometimes people have relapses. Tell him this with my best love and earnest wishes for his early and complete recovery.

You pitch into me re Princess Nazri! Well, sometimes a Princess is an agreeable companion and this lady was one but then you know that for the moment I was just in favour going to the dreaded Suakin etc. Tomorrow another war etc. . . .

I have been simply frightfully busy and have got thro' the greater part of my work. We are tumbling into a sort of system, but every day brings something new and so as we have so small a staff it is difficult to meet wants without hurry.

The enemy has disappeared and there is a sort of feeling that the end is coming. Friendly natives come in by twos and threes and are set to work on the [railway] line, so I hear. All goes on smoothly and the railway like a magic snake is creeping over the plains and turning its head towards the mountain pass which leads up to Hambuk and Tambuk. I suppose that we shall soon be able to take our tickets to Handoub.

The yacht *Stella* arrived on Sunday and the same day Young and I distributed a number of oranges with which her decks were heavily laden, among the patients of hospital ship, *Ganges, Bulimba* and *Czarewitch*. The next day we distributed some thousands of oranges among various corps and field hospitals, also medical comforts etc. to other battalions and ambulances etc.

I am sure that the great mass of the men out here are very much pleased but there are others who *I hear* think that the Govt. ought to supply the surgeons etc., perhaps jealousy must work its wicked way a bit. We have done a good deal quickly and perhaps it would be as well to steady down a little.

The day after Young's yacht came he rode to inspect Handoub and came back not well, as he had been all day in the sun and drank too much Handoub water. He is practically well and will be able to help me in the work. He has a good head.

Handoub   17th April 1885

My dearest Alice,

I hope you will not mind catching me out here what you call near the front but I was obliged to come as the doctors have made rather a muddle of the front distribution and so this morning I jumped on my white arab and meant to join an armed convoy which I was told was coming here from Suakin. The convoy started at 5.30 a.m., I at 7 a.m., but so slowly did the former go that I caught it up in half an hour and getting bored and dusty passed it and rode here alone; there is no danger as the bushes have been cut down so as to make a broad track and no one would dare to attack one in the open as one could kill him before he got near. They have very few rifles and I am sure they have retired into the mountains.

When the Tamai column advanced there was some apprehension at Suakin as all the good troops were taken (and we had only some Indian and the Australian artillery as far as I could hear) the column was the safest place!

I have been having a long chat with Generals NcNeil and Freemantle and we have been arranging details of a large refreshment hut to be erected and moveable at the extreme front of the line. The sutlers here sell most awful stuff called lemonade at –/4 [four old pence] a glass. It is composed of nasty tasting water, sugar, some cayenne pepper and a wee little lemon or lime juice. I shall either make them improve or simply establish our refreshment booth over their mercenary heads.

A dust storm has this instant passed over us and I am smothered in one moment, all down my back etc.

This place is very pretty. The mountains are close by and there is a steep hill at the edge of the camp whence they say the view is perfect. Suakin and the neighbourhood being like a map before you.

Suakin   22nd April

My own dearest wife,
I cannot describe to you the intense pleasure which your letters give me. I
am looking forward every mail to those details of our happy house and tho'
Fleetwood's illness made the letters a source of some anxiety on his
account yet the fact of your being useful and a comfort to him and his rapid
convalescence gave additional pleasure. I do hope that you are getting on
all right.

I returned from Handoub ride all right but was let in for a darkish ride
home across the plans which I did not appreciate tho' it was a delightful
change after the base. I took back a bottle of water to analyse and the cork
coming out soused my pistol and cartridges. The good people in the Zeriba
halfway would not allow me to leave until they got me fresh cartridges and
so I was delayed until dark. I confess to riding through the deserted plains
with my pistol in my hand!! I saw Gen. Graham yesterday and he said he
did not like to let convoys pass the plain unless guarded by an armed party.
I shall not do the same again as in fact my horse got tired after 15 miles and
the dry watercourses were troublesome when dusk came on.

Please ask for my report from Mr Vokes which will tell you all my work.

I am perfectly well but Sir Allen Young and Dr Piggott are both down,
the former with dysentry, a common complaint here to which I am not
subject.

I had a little sun touch but three days rest set me straight; lying on my
back with some iced bandages was a speedy cure. Have been out all day in
sun since but with the precaution – eat well before exposing yourself to sol
effulgens.

Rumours of peace – or rather abandonment of campaign. Everyone so
pleased. There is no go in the affair and sickness is increasing. How I look
forward to seeing you again.

Tambook   26th April

Here I am at a lovely spot yclept Tambook, our extreme outpost. Our
stores were so detained and sometimes robbed coming up to the front and
doctors are so unused to looking after their transport that I was determined
to take a convoy up myself, especially as Gen. Freemantle had sent me
some urgent telegrams on the subject.

Well on Thursday night I got 7 camels together at our Nat. Aid Zeriba at Suakin and sent about 20 cases of cocoa, milk etc. on shore to meet them. Early the following morning I started off but too late for the armed convoys so the groom, Hills and I acted as the 'guard' with our revolvers. It is really quite safe and no armed escort is really required but still the General has not relaxed the order. That day we arrived at Handoub and we slept in the Zeriba there. The next morning I had rather a scuffle as the Aden drivers and Hills got ready too late again for the convoy. Our previous days tactics were repeated and Hills and I brought our seven camels safely to Otao where we saw our armed convoy just starting for the outpost Regt. at Tambook. I tacked on our seven camels with Hills to this convoy which had a guard of mounted infantry. Unfortunately my horse had lost a shoe and two other shoes were coming off so I remained behind and had breakfast with the Coldstream Guards, intending to catch up the convoy afterwards and have my horse shod. However when all was ready the convoy was way out of sight and an Australian, Capt. Laing, joined me and we agreed to ride together, alone (rather an Irishism). A stupid soldier put us on a wrong track and we had a long two hours ride into the mountains. At last the Australian found that we were on a OLD Arab track so we did not like the look of affairs and turning round we retraced our steps to Otao. After resting a bit we started again, this time on the right track and being joined by two other Australians all armed we rode safely to Tambook. I found my 7 camels returning with Hills and the convoy after having deposited the stores with General Freemantle. The Gen. had kept my saddle bags and wished me to stay with him and see the things distributed. It was very interesting and the soldiers were so pleased at the tobacco, cocoa and oranges.

The Zeriba is such a contrast to the others, there is only one regt., the Scots Guards and everything is so neat and tidy. We cannot see anything of the mass of the Arabs but today Inigo Jones caught one near the camp and took his spear and knife. He says he is a friendly man. They come in now and then – but what prevents them is the uncertainty as to how long we are going to stay here. If only we hoisted the *British* flag they say that masses would come in. The feeling that we are only acting as it were under the Khedive prevents the blacks from trusting us. They sometimes fire into the camp at night; last night they fired into Otao Zeriba and the night before into this. Tonight we expect a visit and if they come they will be nicely caught by some guardsmen who go out in black greatcoats and nightcaps so as not to be distinguished!

Today is Sunday and I attended with great interest and I hope profit, the Church Parade. Service was read by Col. Trefusis to the troops consisting of Scots Guards, a Co. of Engineers, the Bearer Comp. and Balloon Corps; quite a little band but a brave set of fellows. The health of all is *excellent*, only 7 ill out of over 1,000 men. I feel *so well* here. Yesterday I rode in the sun from 7 a.m. to 1 p.m. and felt none the worse simply because I always eat breakfast, lunch and dinner, and allow nothing to stop my food. This and moderation in drink with preventing chill are the great secrets of keeping ones health.

Let me try to bring you to this place. We are in a valley or plateau some 1,300 feet above Suakin which is 23 miles off. Beautifully shaped mountains surround us on all sides and the colours of their sloping sides in the early morning are exquisite. The plain is formed of the debris of mountain streams and is scattered over with mimosa shrubs and boulders while some two miles off is the bed of a large river, now quite dry. I am sitting in the Generals tent with its sides all pulled up, he is dozing and reading in an arm chair, close to which sits Stopford, his Aide de Camp. The scene is now quiet only interrupted by the bleating of goats seized from Arabs and the buzz of conversation in the tents.

We have just received a telegram from England which leads to the impression that the expedition will not be proceeded with. Everyone is so glad at the prospect of returning. You see that there is no 'go' in the business. No one dislikes the Arabs, they think them splendid fellows and there is a feeling that we are doing no good staying here. Then there are various differences of opinion as to the possibility of making the line (the Rly) and we all know that in another months time the heat which was tolerable will be intolerable. After all it is only 95 or so in the shade today and there is a fair breeze blowing. At 10 a.m. it was far hotter than now at 1 p.m.

I need hardly tell you that I am tired of the dust etc. and the necessity for our presence here is diminishing, if the troops do not advance further. There appears no indication of any advance except as to the line, one mile off, which was made yesterday. It is amusing to see how at the prospect of abandoning the railway the faces of Lucas and Aird men lengthen, while the whole army without exception hail the news with joy.

I have not your letters with me up here or I would read them over and over again. My traps were put together quite rapidly as usual and are limited to a very small compass indeed. In fact I left behind my camp bed etc. and sleep on a stretcher which I borrow from the hospital.

This morning I breakfasted with the Scots Guards after passing a most pleasant night on a stretcher. It became so cold in the morning early the thermometer going down to 45 degrees. I was rather disturbed by a stray goat which came bleating close to my head as all the sides our tent were open and we are really more under an awning than in a tent. I was from time to time bombarding the goat with stones and this morning we caught it and tied it up for the benefit of its milk and its silence.

Just had lunch. I am going to stay quietly to rest instead of going out with the Gen. and the Australians to 'prospect' some auriferous deposits and quartz which has been found here.

PRIVATE   26th April
Tambook

One line my own dear Alice to say how I am longing to be with you again. I am so often thinking of you and wondering if you are well and happy. Dear little Guy too is constantly before me. When you receive this I shall be back again at Suakin or possibly on my way to arrange for my departure.

It is so unfortunate that I could not arrange to leave as Sir A. Young was ill and the confounded doctors are so jealous of each other. Next time I go out I shall select *all* my staff and let Sir W. MacCormac go to [*illegible*] with his patronage and appointing men like Newby. He is rather a thorn in my side though a most hardworking man. He is not a gentleman and does all manner of stupid things, chaffing soldiers etc. and arguing with sailors, in fact he does not keep up his position.

Well to turn to agreeables. I am living in the prospect of devouring your letters. Every line and blot is of intense interest to me.

I told you all about my doings and conceal nothing from you. I am in no danger here and remember that I am doing a [*illegible*] and proper work and the God to whom we both pray who forms the union of our hearts and souls will protect me or not as may be his will, whether I am crossing a crowded street or carrying out the work of my heart out here.

I attended Church Parade and as usual when I heard the service I thought of you and prayed for you dearest and for our dear boy. God bless you and keep me worthy of your pure and holy love.

PRIVATE

My own dear Alice,
I am so sorry that I have missed your letters or rather some of them. I received one date Ap. 11 and another of Ap. 14 but I expect that *Brindisi*

letter is one of a packet which passed me at Handoub. I am so annoyed. I have been reading those precious lines over and over again and feel so relieved that you had no anxiety on account of my being ill . . .

I am sorry to say that Mr Burrell [the clerk who had solicited his help while working for Cocks Biddulph and Co.] has turned out a complete failure. He is either half-witted or is the laziest stupidest fellow I ever met. He evidently thought he was coming out to amuse himself. I could not get him even to get up in the morning and he is utterly incapable of helping me in any way except that of taking down my letters at my dictation . . .

It interests me immensely all that you tell me about dear little Guy and what a good little fellow he is. How blessed we are to have such a child. It is the same as with you, dearest, absence makes me realise in a peculiar way how fond I am of him and of you also who have given him to me . . .

How refreshing to come to the next paragraph of your letter, the darkened room and the little child sleeping peacefully. I am there, dearest, in the spirit and that is the best part of me. It is such a comfort to me to know that you are not much inconvenienced; I am sharing your burdens in my sympathy and anxiety for you. Would that I could take a greater share. How willingly would I do so.

And now, what can I say about my return? The war is practically over and I am thinking of winding up our business. If there is a war in the North of India[34] I shall send off two of our surgeons, Piggott and Lake there. I shall not suggest the employment of Squire and Newby, they are neither of them satisfactory. The former has, I think, a very disagreeable manner, rather satirical, and half suggesting he could do things better but when asked for suggestions making utterly impossible ones. The latter, Dr Newby, is a very common individual, hard working but utterly ignorant of all 'gentlemanlike' manners. His sayings are made a joke of as far as Handoub!! In our mess an officer said he could not imagine how I could have selected such a man. What a shame it was of McCormac to fix me with him. However he works hard and well and I keep him at it constantly.

Piggott and Professor Ogston are the only two thoroughly satisfactory men. Lake is very fair. On the whole I shall be glad to get out of it all.

And now you good unselfish girl you have indeed helped me about the ambulance classes. It appears to me that they go on better in my absence than when I am there. You are sure to manage the affair all right and if I reach England in time to wind up when you are laid up it will be a most successful season.

And now to come back to that odious chance, now almost certain, that I shall not be in time for May 11th [when their second child was due]. I cannot leave affairs here to be wound up by Sir A. Young, unless I can give over that Docker hut to some regiment. This hut was sent to me by the Princess of Wales and the wretched thing has only just arrived! I am hurrying it on and want to get it stuck up and give it over for management to some regiment. The Regt. which may be ordered to stay here. Then I have to get the house sold and settle accounts. Our stores are nearly all disposed of except some clothing and medicines. These will keep. If only the authorities would say what is to be done with the force I could make our plans at once, *but we do not know* what is going to happen. Immediately we do I can wind up. I have received from Loyd-Lindsay leave to send staff to India but of course I shall not go there without returning to you. In fact I am not anticipating that contingency but telegraphed to know what was the wish of the Council.

30th April

My dearest Alice,

It is 4.50 a.m. and I have got up to add a line or two to my letter and wish you good morning at the last moment. The mail boat leaves very soon and I only wish I were going in her. I hope to be able to telegraph to you as to the date of my return before you receive this. I am utterly disappointed that I shall not get back by the middle of May, my presence is required to decide what course of action shall be taken by us in the event of hostilities with Russia. I cannot well delegate this work to anyone else. Immediately the decision is taken I can in a few days settle our plans and probably leave myself.

Lord Wolseley is coming here in a few days, in fact he is due on Friday. He will perhaps tell us what is decided. How clever he is, he has not allowed anything to be said officially as to the abandonment of the Rly and so all eyes are fixed on him as the herald who is to bring news of home sweet home, or at any rate release from this weary campaign.

Splash, splash, thud thud, I hear from my cabin window. The mail steamer, which never leaves before 9 or sometimes 11 a.m., has gone this morning at 5 a.m. What a shame and all this letter and contents must wait for a week in Suakin. My labour has been in vain. The wish to add the little note this morning has spoilt the whole and you will not get the letter until another mail. I am a bit tired so shall recline and take another snooze.

Suakin

My own dearest Alice,

I am writing from the *Ganges* where I am sitting in rather a hot bath. The weather has taken a turn for the hotter but I am all right and feel perfectly well. However I hear of nothing but murmurs and groans from my surroundings as to the heat and also on shore the masses of flies.

As you will have known from the papers Lord Wolseley arrived here and yesterday I had a long talk with him. He is not well and looks so much older than when I last saw him. Of course we are all anxiously awaiting his decision as to the 'Military Situation' which is supposed to be final.

I was at Handoub yesterday on business and was breakfasting with Col. Huysh who commands the Berkshire Reg. Everyone is so hospitable and kind and it is quite a pleasure to find oneself a welcome guest wherever one goes.

Since writing my last letter to you I have been at my old work keeping things together at Suakin. We have had strikes among the sailors on the launch and worries in the stable. My dragoman and Hills, the good groom, and Pasquale assistant have all given notice, they cannot stand the weather and money will not tempt them . . . all eyes and wishes are turned homeward. I am making all arrangements for disbanding our ambulance but I hear that a little reconnaissance is to start today on a 3 day march to try and catch Osman Digna. They won't do it I fear, and the result may be the sickness of many men.

I am longing to return home, the excitement etc. is over. Of course if they begin to march about we shall be crowded with sick again. They are beginning to come in. The *Ganges* is full and the doctors of the Indian troops are sending to me for milk etc. which means sickness. Whenever we have pressure of work I find that the heat etc. make no impression but three days rest makes one think of oneself.

Now I want to explain why I could not get away. Lord Wolseley was expected every week for a long time and all depended on his dictum and Russia's movements as to what we were to do. Loyd-Lindsay left decisions in my hands. Now I could not leave my post at such a moment. It would have looked so bad, so I *most reluctantly* decided that it was my duty to stay, and I think you will approve my decision.

Today we take stock of our stores and I am settling as to destination of horses etc. in case the expedition collapses which we all think will be the case. Burton has been working very hard and very well and I am quite satisfied with him but I cannot say the same of all my staff. I have had more trouble with them this time than I ever had before. The British sailor has not gone up in my estimation from what I have seen of them on the transports. I would far rather have natives to man the steam launch if they understood the machinery. The sailors have no idea of the higher objects of ones work and only think of how much money they can make, striking for another £1 a month because Lucas and Aird (at Govt. expense) overpay their launch men. I was very much disappointed with my crew. . . . I am sorry to say that the 'clerk' [Burrell] is not satisfactory either. I do not suffer from the heat in health but it enervates one unless one is doing some active work. The sick on board are suffering from the moist heat very much, not that the thermometer is so high but the moisture in the air keeps a peculiar gummy feeling on the skin.

I was about today on shore twice and walked about with Lord Wolseleys private 'medico'. The former told me he was not well and the medico was evidently in a most uncomfortable state saying that he (medico) felt the peculiar heat so much, that it was different in Egypt and that he felt the warm nights so much.

The mail is just in and I am anxiously, so anxiously, expecting my letter from you dearest. It seems to be the one event of the day to me, the one thing worth living for.

Our real work is just now slack, and the sick, when once in hospital, are well cared for, except the Indians to whom we supply a great many things. We have a good system of doing our business now which is easier work as we have more time. Of course if any action takes place we shall be all hard work and hurrying up again. The chance of further action is however in my mind very remote.

I dined on Saturday night with Col. Chermiside[35] who gave me a long account of his life here. He is going to leave I hear, having had enough of it, but he has succeeded in relieving some of the besieged garrisons in the interior and I see some of the poor refugees here huddled up in hot steamers. The women and children are in a very deplorable condition and have scarcely any clothes, but Chermiside is doing his best for them. I offered to give some tinned milk from our store for the babies and children who have my first care and Chermiside is going to see if this is practicable. Of course they do not understand anything about tinned food. As regards dress they are perhaps not so badly off; I sometimes wish that I could go about like them! However I am thinking of giving them some cotton for making a few garments. People are not over-particular over here.

I am so disappointed Lord Wolseley did not come here a few weeks before as I could then probably have been with you now.

Chermiside's palace I have described to you before. It is built of blocks of coral, I think, and mud. He lives quite au Pacha, surrounded with obsequious blacks who do his bidding with alacrity. He has the whole government of the town from registration of births and deaths to compulsory vaccination and arranging the domestic rows of mistresses and their slaves; a curious position.

8th May 1885

My dearest Alice,

I am writing with a heavy heart and my thoughts are, as usual, with you. There has been great jealousy here about those reports in *The Times* of our work and I am much annoyed that they were published; particularly the one on the 21st which said more than I ever stated, meaning that much inconvenience existed *until* I came with the Launch. I have contradicted it in a telegram sent through Huyshe [*sic* Huish, *The Times* correspondent at Suakin]. The fact is that very little ought to be said about our work in the papers as after all it is only a flea-bite in comparison to what the Army medical has done, moreover the Army medical has been so kind to us that I am sorry to see them offended. But dearest what is all this to *the* event uppermost in my mind, your own dear self. I feel such a longing to be with you that I am almost inclined to throw up everything and rush off.

The reason which prevented me I have told you. Everything combined to prevent me. Burrell turning out a complete failure, jealousy between Squire and Newby etc. Sir A. Young was also inclined to advise me to stay on. And now this bad feeling got up against us by the Army Medical owing to the printed reports in *The Times* make it imperative for me to see the affair through.

I am sorry, very sorry, that I ever left as I cannot keep my promise to you. As usual I have tried to do too much, trop de Zèle, my nature at 40 and I fear my nature for life.

My own dearest wife, may God protect you and give you a happy deliverance from your troubles. I would give my right hand to be with you. Good God how fervently I pray for your safety – never again dearest shall I leave you, of that I am determined.

I am well and though full of anxiety am kept up. I try to console myself by thinking that you approve of what I am doing. All danger, if ever there was any, is over and I am winding up to prepare for leaving perhaps two doctors here and the boat and launch and Docker hut. I shall certainly return myself as there will be nothing for me to do . . .

It has been raining during the night and I am sitting quietly on the *Stella* at the mouth of the harbour. The little nigger boys are gaily prattling as they fish from the pier close by and a cool wind is blowing through the open hatches of the deck cabins where I am. My thoughts wander far over the Red Sea, through Egypt away across the sea again and fly over Italy thro to belle France to the fairest thing in my eyes, my own dear Alice. How sweet will be our meeting. How I long for it my own dear girl. How far deeper and holier is the love I have for you now than ever I had before, though every year I think that I love you as much as man could love, as man ever had love . . .

No one knows about the prospects of an autumn campaign, but I do not think I shall go with this work again. I have had my fair share of it and shall devote the rest of my days to you. I think that I am rather played out at it and am not diplomatic enough. I am too much prone to speak out what I think and to write rapidly first impressions. All very well when there is great pressure but not when there is not. The Med. Authorities are rather annoyed and Dr Barnett, who is ill, is much annoyed at the report in *The Times* of Apr. 21.

Suakin   9th May 1885

My own dearest Alice,

I was ill at ease and uncomfortable about you yesterday – very much so. I was thinking about you the night before last and woke so early at very little figures indeed. I had a presentiment that you would like to hear from me and dearest I could not resist the temptation of telegraphing to ask how you were . . . Thank God my darling is still well.

We had a fearful night last night. Thunder, lightening, rain in just torrents. I was half awake as usual at 3.30 and walked out. The rain was quite hot and the wind from the south seemed like the breath of some huge monster which was spitting fire at us. All this is most unusual at this time of year. I fear that thousands of pounds of stores will be spoilt.

We are quite slack here now and everyone is longing to get away. Home sweet home is the one thought and we have all quite forgotten the native and Osman Digna & Co. They [the British forces] had a raid about a fortnight ago and burnt a village carrying off all the goats and camels and driving off the inhabitants to the mountains, even women and children. They will find their homes burnt and their source of water (and water is life here) blown up. I hear that the well was made use of to pitch the bodies of the dead into and then it was blown up. The village was attacked because some of the men had been firing into our camp at Otao and Tambook. However there was no excitement, no one was pleased to hear of it, the spirit of the war is *dead*, even Lord Wolseley cannot put life into it.

He goes about quite 'en grand' on a large white Arab which has been lent to him. He inspects everything and flatters everybody, quite like a Royal personage . . .

Now I wrote in rather low spirits last mail as I was awfully annoyed about the summary of my report. I have worked *so hard* to make this thing a success and it was horrid to see that Army Med. Dept. do not quite trust us. They dislike Loyd-Lindsay immensely, and in one sense they associate us with him, although they are afraid to do anything. However they have been personally very friendly and I am the more sorry that they exaggerate what I put in my report.

I suppose you saw my telegram in *The Times*, or rather the one I requested the correspondent to write, I thought it only right to tell the facts. I bought the steam launch in order to do the carrying work of the sick and wounded, but before it was really ready, as it required some repairs, the P.M.O. of Base had made his own arrangements with the *Ganges* launch which he had finally placed at his entire disposal. Now there was loads of work for our launch to do in carrying about stores etc. and taking occasional sick and friends of patients etc., so it has been *extremely useful*. However it has *not* been used for the purpose which it was represented in *The Times* as doing.

Well enough of a disagreeable subject. I hope that we shall all make friends again and that the sick and wounded will not be sufferers. You know that I have no jealousy etc. in my nature and hate being on bad terms, so I am determined to let the Army Med. know that far from wishing to crab them I would like to do them a good turn.

PRIVATE   13th May 1885
Suakin

My own dearest Alice,
It is just day break and the sea is like a smooth glass on which someone has breathed here and there. The thermometer is at 82 degrees and I rise not quite refreshed from the impromptu bed which was rigged up for me on deck.
    We can none of us sleep in our berths now and turn out on deck to get a

little chance of sea breeze; there is little enough of that during the night, but it gets up about 9 a.m. and there is always a breeze in the afternoon . . .

Dearest I am thinking much of you and pray God to keep and preserve you through the trial you are about to go through. May He give you all that sympathy, consolation and support which the husband who loves you so deeply would have offered and may He bring us together once more before long, and this time to part no more. I am not happy away from you dearest and long to get back.

You ask me what keeps me in this place. The answer is this. In spite of telling the good ladies at home not to send out any stores without my ordering them, they are inundating me with stores. Five ships are bringing out great lots. What am I to do? I have a perfect *fool* and what is more an *indolent fool* in the person of Burrell. He has made me swear like a trooper and lose my temper several times. In the whole course of my existence I never came across such a provokingly stolid, stupid fellow who does not try to work. Then Newby has such fearful manners that I have constantly to apologise for his behaviour. I never saw a man with such bad manners. It is quite impossible to leave him in charge. Squire, Piggott and Lake are at the W. Redoubt and I cannot utilize them. What is more I hear that Piggott and Lake are to be asked to accompany the sick back to England tomorrow so I shall lose the chance of having him [*sic* them].

Then there is that disagreeable affair about the paragraph in *The Times* as to our work, which created such bad feeling and jealousy. The very thing which I wanted to avoid. It is so heartbreaking at the end of ones ambulance career to fall into the fated trap of making the Med. Dept. jealous. If only the Soc. had published nice things about the Army Med. Dept. instead of too much about us, it would have been quite different. Too much has been written about us, too much telegraphed. I must square this matter before leaving.

Sir A. Young is a good fellow but he, of course, has his own great friends here. He knows intimately one of the Aides de Camps of Lord Wolseley, Lord C. Beresford and he dines etc. with Lord W. and yesterday accompanied him to Tambook. However Young's yacht has not been used, I am sorry to say, and what is more I do not think the Medical Authorities will use it! It makes a rather ridiculous position! I cannot well leave Young to do the drudgery work which I am doing.

Half Commissariat Sergeant
Half light porter } That is what I am

The *Standard* newspaper says that we have exaggerated notions of our functions! I wonder what lower functions they would impose!

20th May 1885

My own dearest Alice,

I am lying on the deck of the *Ganges*, once more on the sick list, but this time from an accident. I had a lucky escape and this is the best way of looking at it! We had just finished our *final* distribution of stores in hand and I went down into the lower deck of the *Calabria* to see after some cases. The brutes of sailors left a hatch open in the dark passage. Dr Newby who was walking before me said 'mind the hold' but before the words were out of his mouth I was in it! My leg caught on the edge of the hatchway which stopped my tumbling right down as did the vigorous grasp of little Newby. However I have wrenched my leg a bit and am now in the unhappy position of being 'splinted' quite a la St J.A.A. and bandaged. I can hobble about but am advised to keep quite quiet for a day or two which I shall do. Nothing is broken but my leg is strained. Newby is a first class surgeon and must from the nature of the case be in constant attendance!

I have made all arrangements to leave this at the end of next week. My unfortunate accident will, of course, delay me for a few days longer than I intended as I cannot get about. I am leaving Piggott behind and I have regularly wound up all our affairs. Two horses, one donkey and a groom have returned with Sir A. Young and Lord Wolseley etc. on the *Queen*. I was invited to return at the same time but hardly liked leaving matters here unsettled. I am sorry that I did not do so now, but I am always so slow winding up. I am *determined* to go next week. I do not think that the weather is good for the strain I have.

By the way we had a boat accident here, just opposite the *Stella* in the mouth of the harbour. I was quietly sitting on the *Stella* when I heard Sir Allen say 'shove off quick that launch' and then 'by jove they're over'. I ran out and jumped into the launch which was our *Princess* and seeing three men, two clasped together in the deep water struggling and one sinking close to the screw of a powerful tug which had nearly run them down. I went in after them with the skipper of the *Stella*. The one man got hold of a life buoy thrown from the tug, the other two were left behind struggling; one could not swim and he clasped the one who could. They were the Capt. of the *Vito* and his chief engineer. Well we got hold of them and the launch came up and ran into and nearly over the lot of us! We got the men into the launch all right, one was very much exhausted and both done. The water is so warm and buoyant that there was no difficulty in swimming especially as I took the precaution to slip off my shoes and trousers. There was really not much in it but they made rather a fuss about it on the *Ganges* as all the people rushed to the side to see what was happening.

We have got over that little row about the exaggerated summary of my report in *The Times* of Ap. 21. I was so much annoyed – one creates so much jealousy by being brought too prominently forward. In fact if you do nothing then that would make you most popular with certain people, especially if you at the same time flattered. Ah flattery can open the door of many hearts that one would think impervious to it!

Queen's Birthday – God save the Queen!   24th May
and by chance the General Sir R. Greaves is dining with me tonight.

My own dear Alice,

It is with a mass of confused feelings that I write to you my morning letter, lying in an Indian cane chair on the deck of the *Ganges*. The sun is hidden behind some friendly clouds and on the coral reef just opposite our ship the white tents of the troops destined to form our summer garrison are fluttering in the breeze. All round is full of life, the sea swarms with myriads of fish of all sizes, shapes and colour, the air with gulls and other birds to say nothing of the domesticated flies and knats [*sic*] with an occasional visitor in the person of a large moth, while the very shores on which we tread is the work of those mysterious coral insects which besides creating land afford the materials out of which the white palaces of Suakin are constructed. In truth they look like palaces, those few fine houses which belong to some of the richer merchants and Govt. officials, especially in the early morning behind the forest of masts as you look westwards up the harbour.

I am getting quite happily practical, tho' my feelings are not all happy ones. I have had my disappointments here as well as satisfaction. My chief one is that I have not succeeded in what was one of my objects – to allay completely the feelings of quasi-jealousy which exist against us on the part of the Medical Dept. Too much publicity has done harm to the work and perhaps one ought to have seen that this was natural and ought to have provided against it. It is difficult however to ask the press not to mention names or report our doings, as I have done on certain occasions since the 'incident' of Ap. 21st. Again there is a certain amount of feeling about my having secured Prof. Ogston's services after he had obtained a letter accrediting him to the Govt officials here. You remember that his services had been once declined by the Society and afterwards I secured them. This I *could not possibly* forsee. The ways of the department are mysterious indeed!

But what is all this to the one great wave of joy and thanksgiving which sweeps all else before it; that dear hope of my happy life with you, to see a little daughter born to us [on 15 May 1885]. Quite spontaneously I hailed her as my Desiree – my longed for one, though such a name is not quite in harmony with the terrible state of sin and wickedness in which the dear spotless babe is, according to some people's religious convictions, steeped. I feel so poetical this morning that my thoughts run to rhyme; the good old communion service is being celebrated below, I would attend but I cannot bend my knee which is all bandaged:

Here are my thoughts written off hand:

> Can he who's seen a spotless babe and heard its first faint cry
> Believe it born in taint of sin and vile impurity?
> Remember how in days of old, Jesus the just though mild
> Abhorred the evil deeds of man, but loved the little child.
> Sweet babe I recognise in these the good, the true, the pure,
> The way to holier things, the mean worlds trials to endure;
> Reflected in thy little face I see, instead of woe,
> His love too great for Heav'n above and hers for earth below.

I fear this is unorthodox but at some times and seasons ones soul escapes from the trammels of education and tradition, and tries to soar above to the God of ones own longing, to the spirit which responds to ones own hearts desire.

The sweet little reverie is over. Here comes that stupid Burrell. I know, I feel, that I must scold him, he is sure to have done something awfully stupid . . .

He has gone, my prognostications were perfectly correct. He brought me a completely incomplete (!) list and I have sent him back to his ship with a large, what I was taught to call 'Musquito' in his clumsy ear. What a descent from the ideal to the practical.

And now dearest how do I long to know what our little Desiree is like! Is she like Diana or the Careys or Alfred Marten or Lady Brassey? Has she all her dear little toes on? Bother, here comes Burrell again! He can't find a pen in the whole ship! He does annoy me immensely.

Well tell me dearest in your next letter the minutest details of that little stranger and if it has the cross of the St J.A.A. marked on it by any chance.

> Is she fair or is she dark
> Is she like my darling Alice
> Good and true and free from malice

If she's not, I don't care at all
Whether she's short or whether she's tall
Whether she's child of the snow or the sun
For babies are many but Alice is one!

There, I am running off into rhyme again! There must be something in the air, or perhaps Burrell is a muse in disguise!

You will wonder what I am staying here for. The fact is I *cannot* leave my work unfinished. I had telegraphed to stop further stores coming but to my surprise the day before yesterday I received 220 cases! I have to distribute these judiciously and to see the launch and other things taken over, to *see* our doctors off etc. Entre nous the troops are delighted with the Nat. Aid but I don't think that some members of the Med. Dept. few I am glad to say, are. They cannot or will not realise the broadness of our mission; they perhaps cannot, owing to ingrained routine, take the higher view of our motives.

1st the good of the patients, 2nd the good of our Society, 3rd the good of ourselves. Conscientiously and entirely have I endeavoured to carry out the principles of that non-equal Trinity, tho' I am too well aware that I have fallen far short of what my ideal is.

I shall try to make a sketch or two of scenes around this ship. She sails on Tuesday. I leave her Monday to take up my quarters on the *Edinborough*. Funny as I have never been to Scotland.

I have enlisted for the Society the services of Mr Brewster, the deputy Govr. here. He will see our stores safely looked after and distributed in my absence. It is a great find and will enable me to leave in a week or 10 days.

Suakin   30th May 1885

My own dearest Alice,
Today I told General Greaves that I had made arrangements to leave by Wednesday, and he at once arranged that I should go by the *Queen* starting that day or Thursday morning. I shall go by Cairo to settle accounts and see Young.

I have formed a committee consisting of:
Gen. Hudson – Commodore of the Forces
Capt. Molyneaux – RM Commander
Capt. Duferin RM who will succeed Molyneaux
Surg. Maj. Reordon – Chief Med. Officer English Forces

Brig. Surg. Thornton – ditto of Indian Forces
Colonel Woodcote – Chief Commt. Officer Indian Contingent
These have accepted the responsibility of receiving and distributing the stores, erecting huts etc. This acceptance by so powerful a committee is some recognition that the work is no piece of sentimental folly, but a good honest work of which the General and Commodore commanding the forces are willing to take a share!

31st May

I have been settling business on shore and now the sun is coming out with a vengeance. The air is like an agreeable tepid, or rather hot, bath. Ones skin gets into a sort of slimy state as if covered with railway grease and remains so whether one sits in a draught of air or washes or anything. I have an idea that violet-powder would be good out here or some open grate or stove to dry the air.

The Indians of the contingent are suffering a good deal but really I do not mind the heat in the least. The only drawback is that the muscles of my leg and knee will not get strong again and I feel my leg very weak unless I bandage the knee up tightly.

The water etc. round the cap has almost disappeared and there is no apprehension about my getting quite over it – which is a blessing. I walk with one or two sticks not crutches.

My mind is so full of home sweet home that I have not the heart to tell you of all the plans I have arranged for the comfort of the troops during the summer – Briefly they consist of:

1   The launch *Princess* for the use of convalescents of the British Forces and general convenience of hospitals.
2   Two rowing boats for Shropshire regiment.
3   One large rowing boat (to be towed from time to time) for convalescents of Indian forces.
4   Docker hut for invalids etc. recreation room, fitted up, on quarantine island.
5   Pratt club hut (present) as recreation room for garrison.
6   Sodawater machine from Cairo.
7   Stores handed over to powerful committee and lodged in the large caravanserai.
8   Provision of newspapers etc.
9   Books etc. given to Chaplain as Librarian.

SS *Erin*   9th June 1885
arriving at Suez

My own darling Alice,
My first letter, like my first thoughts, on arriving at Suez shall be to you. Somehow I do not feel that 'jump' which joy ought to bring me, though I long to be with you, my dearest. I have not been well since about 2 June. I expect the reaction etc. and perhaps the sudden changes in the Suakin weather told against me. It is also depressing to see poor Burton in hospital on the ship with fever which he caught the last two days at Suakin, funnily enough the very day I began to run down. Then those *Standard* letters, a collection of most deliberate (I think) falsehoods were not enlivening. Loyd-Lindsay wrote me such a kind letter about them saying they were not worth while answering, no more they are. No gentleman with the service could ever think of writing against anyone serving with him; *anonymously* above all. I suspect the man, a man who I know hates our Society and hated me as soon as we were doing good work, and the papers took notice. I may *be wrong*. I said openly before a friend of that man that I thought the writers were devoid of every feeling of officers and gentlemen. I assure you that my blood was up at last and if I could have found out the men who wrote the letters I would have struck them. I *could* not have prevented it I fear. However I have reason to believe that these 'strike in the dark' worthies were all out of Suakin.

General Greaves who was commanding and all the staff etc., in fact all the authorities including the medical ones were extra kind and civil to show they did not approve of the cowardly attack; they said some of them that a man who could be such an 'outsider' as to write anonymous letters such as these would do or write anything, and it was far better to leave the dirty letter unanswered – this I also think, but it is a bit depressing all the same!

My knee is better, dearest, but not well; it must have more rest than what I have given it.

That General Ewart RE is, I think, a regular timeserver. He never assisted me in the least, tho' he was one of my oldest friends – He seemed only to think about himself and how he could save himself trouble or responsibility. This was my impression.

I liked most of the officers I came across very much, except the Engineers, these are cold calculating men compared to the others, and seem wanting in bonhomie altogether.

Fancy the letter signed 'officer' contained 6 distinct untruths in 5 lines. Some men are rather indignant about it but men are too anxious about their own promotions etc. to think much about other peoples affairs.

I have an easy conscience myself and *know* that our Society has done a great deal of good. The mere presence of our surgeons wakes up the army medical men, they hate it I know. I have plenty of stories to tell you about these matters when I return. All that I write now is *private*.

FIVE

Letters from Bulgaria, December 1885–
January 1886

CHRONOLOGY OF THE SERVO-BULGARIAN WAR,
SEPTEMBER 1885 TO MARCH 1886

18 September	Ottoman Governor and officials at Philippopolis, capital of Eastern Roumelia, arrested and expelled and Prince Alexander proclaimed sovereign and Prince of United Bulgaria. On the same day the Bulgarian army is mobilized.
19 September	Prince Alexander goes to Philippopolis.
20 September	King Milan of Servia, in Vienna, is reported to be excited by the news and there are rumours that Servia will invade Macedonia, still part of the Ottoman Empire, to secure 'Old Servia', the district of Kossovo.
21 September	Bulgaria orders a levee *en masse* of all men aged between eighteen and forty.
23 September	Servian mobilization starts.
24 September	Bulgarian units start arriving in Roumelia. Increasing Servian belligerence against Bulgaria and claims that the Balkan balance of power has been upset.
27 September	Talk in Vienna of need to compensate Servia by frontier rectification at the expense of Bulgaria.
29 September	Milan increasingly out of control of events and Servian

Map to illustrate activities during the Servo-Bulgarian War in December 1885 and January 1886

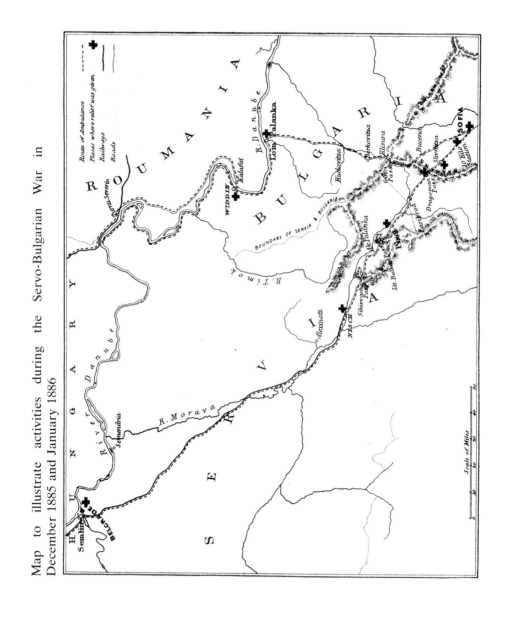

	reservists called out. Railways taken over for military purposes.
5 October	Servian military concentration confirmed at Zajcsar and Kajazevacs on Bulgarian frontier.
6 October	Reports of Servian agents active in Bulgarian frontier districts creating unrest in Widdin area.
11 October	Considerable Servian orders placed for munitions with French and German firms. First news of frontier clashes between Servian and Bulgarian outposts.
15 October	False reports of Servian invasion of Bulgaria.
21 October	Ottoman Government issues invitation to Powers to a Conference at Constantinople to resolve Roumelian question.
25 October	Further false reports of Servian invasion of Bulgaria.
November	During the first two weeks border tension between Servia and Bulgaria remains high, the border is closed and there are repeated exchanges of rifle fire. Despite this, the Bulgarian forces remain concentrated in Roumelia, on the frontier with the Ottomann Empire and none are regrouped on the Servian frontier, which remains defended by reservists and militiamen.
5 November	Conference at Constantinople opens.
14 November	Servian army invades Bulgaria at midnight forcing back opposing guards. Success continues until 17 November, with Servians securing most of strategic Dragoman Pass on main road to Sofia.
17 November	Hastily recalled Bulgarian forces under Prince Alexander halt Servian advance at Slivnitza and retain positions despite renewed attacks on 18 November.
21 November	Bulgarians regain Dragoman Pass as Servian forces retreat. Morale of latter soon collapses and retreat becomes a rout.
28 November	With Bulgarian forces firmly entrenched in Servia, Alexander accedes to Powers' call for a truce already accepted by Milan.
7 December	Vincent arrives at Sofia.
1886	
23 January	Vincent leaves Sofia.
February	Peace negotiations leading to
2 March	Peace of Bucharest.

Turn Severin on the Blue Danube   1st December 1885

My own dear Alice,

I hear such bad accounts of the state of the wounded. The sleeping car conductor who has just come from Belgrade tells me that, three days before his arrival there, the Servian Authorities had one man in every ten prisoners shot. I suppose that there were 2,500 Bulgar prisoners and that they revolted on the sore point of being mixed up in the prison at Belgrade with common felons in chains. He saw the prisoners and said that they were in a dreadful state without shoes or stockings. I am afraid that we shall have more than enough to do with the sick and wounded but why should not the Princess of Wales Branch send out to the British Minister at Belgrade 1,000 pairs of warm socks and shirts for these poor fellows? However, by the time they come perhaps the prisoners will be on their way home for the Servians will not care about feeding them a day after peace has been settled . . .

All Sunday we were travelling up the Rhine and down the Danube, unhappily through mist and rain which made the mountains look 'invisibly wild' as our Irish friend put it. No adventures but we gradually made more acquaintance with our Royal nurse and have all come to the conclusion that we like her very much! She is well-informed, most anxious to be useful, and has any amount of pluck. When I thought of pushing on through the Servian lines via Belgrade and Nisch and thence across to the Bulgarians at Pirot she was not in the least afraid. My plan was to do this to save 3 days in time but they have 'come crash' owing to the probable impossibility of procuring waggons at Nisch and the fact that I was informed only yesterday by the Servian Minister that altho' papers cried 'Peace, Peace' yet there was no peace – officially, not even an official armistice, only a cessation of hostilities.

I am accordingly taking the longer route: the worst difficulty in store being want of waggons again. However at Lom Palanka we are in Bulgaria and would then have a better chance than at Nisch.

The people of the Hungarian plains are so poor; they seem dressed in rags. The land belongs to the large proprietors of thousands of acres, a wealthy hereditary nobility who seldom look after their properties, seldom reside there except for a few weeks sporting and spend the rents in Pesth,

Vienna or Paris, result misery and nursery of evils. This is the information which I picked up on my way. As we progress in Roumania we find
affairs different. The peasants have small holdings. Their worst enemy is
the Jew who lends them money on the security of their little estates and
holds them fast to work out exorbitant interest. I shall be interested to
see how the peasant proprietors of Bulgaria have been getting on under
their improved conditions since the St Stephano and Berlin treaties.

Kutlouitza ⅓ of way down from   4 a.m., 6th December 1885
Lom Palenka to Sofia

We started from Lom Palenka at 12 noon yesterday and had a most
interesting drive over wild open country to this place. The roads near the
villages are absurdly muddy and we can only go at a foots pace. We arrived
here at 8 p.m. and partook of good Bulgarian fare. As we timed our
departure at 3 a.m. we lay down in our clothes and were up in time.
However the horses are not ready yet.

Everything has gone off well. I was just in time to relieve wants at
Widdin and gave what was most wanted at Lom. Also visited hospitals and
made arrangements for future wants at both places.

Our stores have gone ahead in ox-waggons and cross the Balkans this
morning. We shall be at foot of Balkans at 10 a.m. and cross by 5 p.m. I
like Miss Stewart very much, a first rate traveller. She got into hot water by
exposing some of the abuses in our hospitals!! I shall write often.

Vincent.

The people receive us with open arms. One old man said – so you are
coming to heal our poor wounded then God be with you. My amen was
perhaps more sincere than that which I have so often repeated in
Church. There is something elevating in this work when one sees a whole
nation facing danger and death for their liberties and a righteous cause.

Sofia   11th December 1885
c/o British Consul General

My own good Alice,

As I feel you must know want of time, not inclination, was the only reason for my not writing to you at the same time as to the Society. You once said you wished you were a Voluntary Aid Society! Well, in order to carry out your desires I have asked the Sec. to send you copies of all my letters rec'd by him.

I have been *so* busy, we arrived here on Monday December 7th. Dr Fetherstonhaugh began hard work on the Tuesday and Miss Stewart on the Thursday, December 10th. While yesterday also our depot was opened and hospitals were supplied with relief in various kinds. No time has been lost but the pressure has been great, very great. This morning hearing that the great frost had set in with a vengeance, I suddenly remembered my 1870 experience, and ran down to our depot to see if the carbolic acid had frozen. I was only just in time. The acid had begun to freeze and in another day the bottles would have burst and then woe betide us! Now it is impossible to warm our depot so today I have had to move our stores up one storey to a room in which there was means of warming.

I have so much to write that I do not know where to begin. Such a complication of relief societies; let me write down a few:

Railway administered Hospital	Founded and supported almost entirely with the money supplied by the Nat. Aid Soc. to Mr Lascelles thro' Coutts. Nominally under an International Committee of French, Italian, English and Belgian Consuls
Sisters administered Hospital	
Monks administered Hospital	
Italian administered Hospital	
Italian Transport Corps	(which picked up 800 men)
Greek Hospital	supported by Greek residents
Jews Hospital	supported by Jewish residents
Austrian Hospital	supported by Austrian Government
German Hospital	supported by German Government
3 Red Cross Hospitals	Bulgarian Red Cross Society
Bulgarian Mission Hospital	worked by Austrian Teutonic Order
Bulgarian Mission Hospital	worked by German surgeons
Bulgarian Military Hospital	taken over by Austrian Red Cross Society
Bulgarian Military Hospital	taken over by Darmstadt Red Cross Society

and about 10 more military hospitals established in the:
Gymnasium
Ecole Militaire
Artillery Barracks
Ecole des Garcons
Banque de Bulgaria
Ministry of Justice
Ministry of Finance
Ministry of Interior
Assemble Nationale
etc. etc.
also at The Alexander Hospital
(I have enumerated 23 in all and there are, I know, several others. Don't
be nervous if it is reported that typhoid or enteric fever has broken out.
There are a *very few* cases at Pirot, I believe. None here. The reports were
quite unfounded.)

In fact the whole town is one mass of hospitals as may be imagined when
the total losses of the Bulgars were nearly 5,000 killed and 2,700 wounded
thrown suddenly on Sofia! Some of the hospitals are small with only 35 to
70 beds, others have 100 to 250 beds.

And now to my sphere of work:

I had one *most awful bother* at first. There were many difficulties and
rocks ahead. Many jealousies etc. to avoid but I shall tell you when we
meet what my worst bother (now completely over) was and you will laugh
with me over it! It had nothing to do with clothes! Well, the result is as
follows:

1. *Dr Fetherstonhaugh* is attached to Professor Gluck,[36] a great operator
from Berlin. He begged me to attach him to the hospital as he had so many
fearfully wounded and neglected cases and had 16 most important amputations etc. to undertake. Dr F. is at work from morn to night fighting to
save the lives of these poor fellows, so many of whom might easily have
been saved had we been here a fortnight ago.

2. *Miss Stewart* – I could not give *orders* to HRH's nurse, but she was, of
course, thrown entirely on my advice and not being able to speak a word of
anything but English would have been much isolated. She did not fall in
with my wishes of attaching 6 Bulgarian English speaking girls to her and
for her to take over the nursing of the huge Assemble Nationale Hospital.
All was arranged and I fondly hoped to establish a school of nursing which
would do permanent good. However Miss S., when I called to þring her

and 'install' her, objected. She said she would obey if I insisted but that she was not sent out by The Queen for that sort of work. Of course I did *not* insist. I reminded her of her position as The Queen's nurse, that I would be only too glad to make some other arrangement. Perhaps I was too hurried and ambitious in my scheme and after all Miss S. was right – she could not have carried out such a large work satisfactorily. So I arranged in 4 hours that she should be placed under the celebrated Professor Langenbuch[37] at the Bank Hospital. He speaks English and also his assistant, and I have engaged a (National Aid Soc.) interpreting nurse, a Bulgar who speaks English, nice widow, to be always at her side. She is promised by me every assistance and protection by our Society and has the run of our stores. She is quite happy and expressed warm thanks for my arranging the affair so comfortably. She will do good work at the Bank for there are many cases of the worst sort of wounded. It is terrible, legs and arms are cut off every day – the want of a sufficient number of skilled surgeons has cost many a life, and now that there are four or five first class Germans etc. operators they find, alas, only too much work to do among the neglected cases. *Most careful* nursing is required. A man whose leg is cut off while he is in the prime of health is very likely to recover even with rough nursing, but when he is half dead with pain and exhaustion before the skilled surgeon has a chance of seeing him, then indeed he has to be most skillfully and tenderly nursed to give him a chance.

Dear Alice, if only you could walk through one or two of the twenty-four hospitals and see those who only a little over a fortnight ago were fine stalwart lads, glorying in their strength, now lying side by side, racked by fever and wounds – you, I know, would not think it waste of time and money to soothe the sufferings of those who must die; to add something to 'wee' chance of life which is all that is left to many a brave fellow here.

I cannot tell you how glad I am that The Queen sent the instruments by her messenger.[38] He arrived here very quickly and they were all *immediately* distributed and put into use. Every day – every hour – makes a difference when an operation is really necessary. Death and the Doctor have had many a hard race. The Bulgars aided by the foreign residents here have really done wonders in providing for so many wounded.

I must now go on with the Nat. Soc. Work.

3. *Four hospitals of the Soc. Internat.* These are being entirely sustained by grants from the National Aid which I am continuing. I am informed of expenditure but keep on same administration.

Dr Fetherstonhaugh is *consulting surgeon* to the four.

Vincent's drawing of his hotel

4. *Depot N.A.S.* I have taken five rooms in fact a wing of a little sort of hotel, stores are being already distributed from the depot.

There was no room in the first class hotels except for Miss Stewart, so I put her at the Hotel de Bulgaire and Dr F., Herk, self and stores were duly established at the *Vitosh*. One cannot even get a cup of coffee, dirt was supreme. But we have cleaned it out and now all are comfortable and *on the spot* . . .

PPS Dec 12
Lumley The Queen's messenger has just come in from Pirot the Bulgarian Headquarters. He tells me that typhoid and dysentry has broken out at Pirot. I have been begged to go there by Madame von Rosen whom you remember at St Mary's Hospital. I start tomorrow by sledge with medicines and disinfectants – leaving Fetherstonhaugh and Miss Stewart here. The Prince[39] says he would like to see me. Dined at Consul-General, who gave dinner for me. Miss Stewart and I the honoured guests!! How the world repeats itself!!

Sofia   12th December

Dr Mirkoff, the head surgeon of Bulgaria, has just been to see me. He says that there is no dysentry or typhoid at Pirot. Hope he is right.

209

I leave for Pirot with medicines etc. tomorrow at daybreak or rather an hour before unless something prevents me!

Dr Mirkoff gravely assured me that all the Bulgarian wounded were most carefully attended to!!! And this in the face of the regrets of the eminent German surgeon here, that so many poor fellows must die owing to their not having been operated on at earlier stage.

However we must make allowances for a young people and for 30 generations of semi slavery under the yoke of Turkey. Should we be any better under similar conditions?

The sun is coming out. Hail my best friend after my cara sposa. I put him next to you. Am in good health and spirits, only a little cold which everyone has. It is normal here.

Yours ever dearest

Vincent

PS

Lumley is kindly taking this letter. Please ask him to dinner as he said he would be glad to see you and give you my news. He has an awful cold, poor fellow, and has to cross the Balkans by the Ginci pass tomorrow. The snow is coming down heavily and it was up to my knees in places today! I fell down trying to wade up to the Lascelles tonight . . .

Herck is simply *perfect*. He looks after me in every way and is by far the best assistant I ever had. What would I have done for such a man in Suakin!

Headquarters   14th December 1885
Pirot

My own dearest Alice,

Hearing that an epidemic of dysentry and typhus had broken out at Pirot I made arrangements on Saturday last to start at once with some special medicines.

After many delays on Sunday morning owing to the Minister of War not fulfilling his promise of sending me conveyance for the medicines, I made a start at 9 a.m. The snow lay thick on the ground as our two 'phaetons' drove up. Both were of the ordinary country type and were drawn each by four sturdy Bulgarian ponies. In one we placed our stores in the other ourselves and soon left Sofia behind us. The carriage being light our little horses pulled us easily through the snow which in places was nearly up to the axles. All went well until we arrived at Alimnica, the nearest battlefield to Sofia. It was here that Prince Alexander made his gallant stand against overwhelming odds, the first day with but four battalions he checked the Servians; in the night four more battalions came up to his assistance by forced marches from Philippopolis, another battle followed in which he held his ground. The next day more battalions came up until at last Prince Alexander took the offensive and drove back the Servians to the Dragoman Pass. He pressed them again here and forced them back on Pirot and there took place his last and successful battle in which he drove the whole Servian army helter skelter from Pirot across the hills to Ak Palanca.

Slivnitza was full of ox waggons; long strings of them were continuously blocking the road and truly did I pity many a patient beast, toiling until he fell, along the heavy and in places slippery road.

We had some food from our luncheon basket in a little room at the Commandants who was lying ill. After this we proceeded along the ascent towards the Dragoman pass. I was just thinking how smooth the road looked when down went two of the horses of the second carriage. Imagine my disappointment when I found that those horses had not been rough-shod and saw four miles of road like a sheet of ice before me. There was no help for it but to take to the fields where the snow lay thick, sometimes *over* the axles, when the carriages came to a dead stop, and we had to tug on at the horses heads to get them to move. At times the snow was so deep that we were obliged to go back on the slippery road among the ox waggons whose wheels were frozen to the axles so that they could not turn round and poor oxen tumbling about all over the place. However we at length arrived at the top of the pass and here found a few wretched soldiers sick on their journey to Sophia. Two were lying half senseless in a little hut. We went on and turning the sharp corner of a zigzag road one of the 2nd team of horses fell for the twentieth time. The other could not stop and I really believe it was dragged quite twenty yards.

I was tired and very cold when we arrived at Saribrod where the only place to find a bed or shelter was a crowded little 'Khan' – a sort of room opening into the farmyard, full of awful refuse, was offered and greedily accepted. Here I and Herck slept clothes and all and soundly indeed. Herck has been nervous about sleeping at these places as the other night he woke owing to a rat running across his face! He felt its claws and hit it off, dead silence as the rat was falling through the air; then flop and scuttle as it hit the ground and scrambled away! Cannot you imagine and nearly hear it!

This morning I woke up fresh as a lark and had a good cup of hot cocoa made from a tin. By the way your, or Aunt Cecilia's, spirit master is *so useful.* I made such good Liebig with it and it is such a blessing being able to carry the spirit all so neatly done up.

We arrived at Pirot about 12, one of the horses fell at the entrance to the town and we were quarter of an hour before we could get it up again. A calf dropped down almost at the same time and being too weak to move was going to be sent to its rest and eaten up by the hungry soldiers, and hungry they were with a vengeance poor fellows!

The Prince received me most kindly, he asked me to lunch and dine there every day and we have planned together several schemes for the sick and wounded transport. There are many sick and wounded here and they estimate that there must be about 60 a day sent to the rear as patients.

The Prince is a handsome rather sad looking man, with a very tender expression and delicate features, but with the frame of a Hercules I was going to say.

The place is almost entirely deserted by the inhabitants, shops shut up etc. and nothing but soldiers about.

Tomorrow I go to see the state of soldiers at the advanced posts and do some hospital inspections. The day after I return to Sofia and begin a new and arduous task in organizing a series of soup kitchens along the route from Zaribrod to Sofia.

The poor sick suffer dreadfully in being transported in open waggons across the high pass and I do hope that I shall succeed in establishing the same sort of soup kitchens as did such good service in the Russo-Turkish War. I have however only myself and Herck to do it at present but I hope to get volunteers to help.

So Evatt has been writing again! He is an awful bore, always pushing himself forward and meddling in other peoples business. Why should N.A.S. spend its funds in supplying ambulance materiel to Volunteers? Was its money subscribed for that purpose. Are the volunteers likely to be sick or wounded in war for 1,000 years to come? Is it not well known that the volunteers would only be called out at the last moment of a dire national calamity? They would never be in the field except in case of an invasion. Would it be proper to lock up the generous offerings of people who were touched by the sufferings of aliens in war and invest them in ambulance waggons and red cross flags to be received and admired and reported upon by some cocked hat general on Brighton Racecourse or Epsom Down. No, let the gifts go to their proper destinations, the relief of the horrible sufferings of war wherever and whenever it may happen, and let them be as a sign of the brotherhood of humanity which knows no nations, creed or limits . . .

Had we started a week later our materiel could never have passed the Ginci pass. It would have been delayed a fortnight! Had the instruments *not* gone out by the Queen's Messenger many men *alive now* would have been *dead*. There is no mistake about this. A kind Providence has indeed prospered our work this time. Within three days of our arrival surgeon and nurse and depot hard at work, and within a week arrangements being made for the crying wants of the poor invalids who are being transported in open ox waggons 40 miles with the thermometer at 12 degrees to 20 degrees below freezing point. The night before last we had 20 degrees of frost! Rivers etc. seem all frozen almost through and my washing gloves froze inside my portmanteau in my bedroom!

Pirot   15th December 1885
Headquarters

My own dear Girl,
One line to say that instead of going back to Sophia I go through the lines tomorrow to Belgrade on an important mission. We want dreadfully blankets and warm clothing for the invalids who have to be sent for miles and miles in this bitter weather, often in open carts. We cannot buy them in Sophia or Bulgaria anywhere and it costs time and money to bring them all round by Lom Palenka and Rustchuk. So I am trying to get them through by the Servian lines. An Austrian has passed the lines with permission from King Milan to allow Red Cross stores through and I am the first to take advantage of it. King Milan has sent to allow me to pass and Prince Alexander is, of course, very pleased at the chance of my getting things thro'. Goodbye dearest – no time for more – I start early tomorrow morning and a carriage awaits me at the Servian outposts to drive me to Ak Palanka. Thence I go to Nisch and Belgrade. Then buy things and go off back.

Samokov – Bulgaria   16th December 1885

To:
Mr V. Barrington Kennett
Representative of the British National Aid Society

My Dear Sir,
Hearing from my friend Mr Sichanoff that you were to be in Sophia on
your return from Pirdoss, I have thought it good to send you this written
welcome on behalf of our American Community and to add that, if it is
convenient for you, we would be happy to see you in our home before you
return to England.

When the war was declared, I at once offered my services to the
Government (Dr Bradel is the representative). I informed him that I was
ready to go to the front, to go to Sophia to serve in a hospital, to remain in
the second class Hospital in this city or to prepare a small private Hospital
at our own charges which would afford place for 20 beds. I received a
telegram designating me to this Hospital together with Dr Dagoroff, who
was here temporarily. I replied that there was not work here for two
doctors. There were but about 30 patients including quite a number of civil
chronic cases which had lain in the Hospital for a long time. I repeated my
offer to prepare a Hospital with 20 beds and added that, if they would not
send wounded soldiers to us, I would like to come to Sophia to help. On
the following day I received a telegram 'Come to Sophia. There is work.' I
at once went. On my arrival I was told to return and prepare my hospital;
that the following Thursday (three weeks ago tomorrow) there would be
sent to me 20 wounded soldiers; that they would telegraph the same to the
American community here. I returned and prepared my Hospital. I had
food prepared and everything in readiness. No soldiers came. I telegraphed my readiness and the following day the City Govt. here telegraphed asking when the wounded would come to our hospital. The
following day I telegraphed personally that we were waiting for the
wounded. On the following day I received an official note from the city of
government that soldiers would be sent. I would be very glad to be helpful
in this crisis and would be very glad either to come to Sophia or to receive
patients in our Hospital. If there is anything I can do in any capacity in
co-operating with your Society I would be only too glad.

A case of Pneumonia, complicated with meningitis following measles
detains me, or I would go at once to Sophia with Mr Sichanoff. We have
received great kindness at the hands of Mr Lascelles and feel ourselves
under great obligation to him.

If you can in any way send us 20 wounded or sick soldiers we should be very much rejoiced. Still we would not dictate. If there is work we are ready to do it.

Very sincerely yours,
Fred L. Kingsbury

Nisch   18th December 1885

My own dear Girl,
Here I am at the Servian Headquarters having last written to you at the Bulgarian. We passed through the lines safely – It was a fearful morning; snow was lying thick on the road and as there was no traffic between the lines it had not been disturbed and was like a sheet of ice underneath. We found that the Bulgarian outposts had not received orders to let us pass but the officers of Prince Alexander's escort who accompanied us made that right and we then had a short drive, about a quarter of a mile, through no man's ground between the lines. There is a sort of pleasureable excitement in passing over the bridge which separates the two contending armies. The snow was so thick that we could not see the Servian outposts until we were quite near. We found an officer waiting for us with a carriage. We accordingly, after having a friendly chat and wishing goodbye to our Bulgarian escort, changed into the other carriage and drove away to Ak Palanka over a long series of wild wooded hills, deserted and half hidden in snow. We reached Nisch the same night, very cold and hungry, and were given regal quarters at the best hotel in town.

Today I was introduced to the General and presented to King Milan who received me most kindly and at once granted my request for permission to take blankets etc. through the Servian lines to Bulgaria. This is a generous act on his part as the lines are most strictly guarded. You see there is no armistice and either side can begin fighting at scarcely any notice. I am rather in a fright that it may break out again before I can get back through the lines with my convoy.

In train – Nisch to Belgrade   19th December

Yesterday we met the military commission at Nisch – consisting of officers of the great nations. They were on their way to the frontier to mark out the proposed line of outposts for the armistice that is to be! I called on Col.

215

Keith Frazer, the British Commissioner,[40] and was authorised by King Milan to send a message through him to Prince Alexander that my proposals as to the passage of ambulance stores had been accepted. Moreover King Milan has promised me personally to allow me his own carts to convey the stores. This is generous and should be known. I hear that the fighting has begun again at Widdin. This is bad news and I trust it may not be true as obstacles may thereby arise to our stores going through and we may be blocked ourselves.

We had to wait so long in the cold at Nisch railway station; this is the first ordinary train which has run since the war begun and heaven only knows when we shall reach Belgrade.

I am rather anxious about the result of my mission as I have taken a great responsibility on my shoulders passing the enemy lines in search of what we so sorely want. If I fail my mission may be called a goose chase but I know I was right in trying so the old proverb 'Be just and fear not' holds me in good stead!

Though we have been treated with scrupulous politeness and courtesy here, yet they look upon me as belonging to the other side. I was accompanied by a gendarme wherever I went at Nisch and a sentinel was placed at the door of the house where I slept! Poor fellow, he looked so cold that we gave him the remains of the turkey we had brought with us in our basket.

I wish I could relate all the interesting incidents of our journey. It was bitterly cold. Herck says that he never felt the cold so much even in Siberia! And this in spite of fur coats. The rapid transition from a winter–summer of the Riviera to 20 degress below freezing point is rather trying! I had rather a shave for my nose – we were driving along in the open carriage at night when I felt my nose quite senseless (rather an Irishism). It felt quite hard and had no sensation in it. I rubbed it mightily and it got all right but perhaps it was lucky that I did not fall asleep. I am getting acclimatised now and do not feel the cold so much. My grand appetite and digestion come to the front and being able to eat heartily of the common food of the peasants, which even Herck can't eat at times, is a security against running down. Tell Brackley that I have taken to a pipe at last and banished cigarettes; this will please his heart also the tobacco he bought for me is excellent.

I cannot answer your letters as I have not received any since the one dated Dec 1. They are all at Sofia where I shall be in another week. What a feast of reading I shall have.

Hotel de Paris
Belgrade

My dear Alice,
Am all right. Passed lines safely. Have bought about £300 worth of stores. Start back to Nisch tonight with stores. Off tomorrow with ox waggons etc. and arrive at outposts Xmas day or day after. Alexander's carts await me there. We transfer stores and off to Pirot. Vokes will copy a long letter of mine and send it to you . . .

Am taking some of the Queen's stores and gifts back through the lines with my convoy. I had a telegram from Sir H. Ponsonby about them yesterday. They arrived here with Capt. Lumley.

Nisch   23rd December 1885

Dearest Alice,
Just off to Pirot with large convoy of stores – 12 waggons – all right. Road quite safe as armistice has been declared. Seen King Milan again who is all kindness. We shall have interesting journey but very cold. Doctor Fether-stonhaugh has tumbled down and broken the little bone in his leg. He was taken back to Sofia on a sledge, not serious . . .

Don't be at all nervous. Dr Lake, one of my Suakin doctors, has been attached by me to our convoy – he was at Belgrade.

Sofia   27th December 1885
c/o British Consulate

DON'T BE ANXIOUS ABOUT MY ACCIDENT
MERRY CHRISTMAS AND HAPPY NEW YEAR

My dearest Alice,
My first feeling on writing to you again from Sofia is one of intense gratitude to the Father in whom we both trust for having preserved me from what might have been, and nearly was, a fatal accident. I had returned safe and sound with my convoy of 12 carts through the lines, and

yesterday morning was congratulating myself on what was a successful mission and one highly approved of by both the Prince and Lascelles. I was also so pleased at arriving in time to see the triumphal entry of Prince Alexander into Sofia. I was with Mr and Mrs Lascelles at the triumphal arch at the entrance to the town where some cannon were firing salutes. Mrs Lascelles had my arm and I was hurrying her to my sledge to take her away after the procession had passed. In the rush she left me and I fancied she had gone along with the crowd so I ran on a few yards and hardly remember any more. A cannon was fired off about ten yards from me and I was knocked clean over. On recovering a bit I felt something at the back of my head and found my hand all over blood. They took me to the German hospital where Miss Stewart was and where a surgeon pulled out two little bits of wadding which had gone into my neck in two little holes like small bullet holes. He probed to find out if there was anything more in, and cleaned out the two holes. I am now all right but of course very sore and stiff about my neck!! By a piece of great good luck the two pieces went in in the thick muscles of the neck, one each side. Professor Langenbuch, the great Berlin surgeon, who dressed the place today, says that if one had gone a couple of inches to the left it would have done for me. As it is I shall probably get well in a few days but have to keep quiet. DON'T BE ANXIOUS. I have a splendid doctor and Miss Stewart is *most kind* and attentive. I am in my old quarters at the hotel. This morning Lumley, the Queen's messenger, spent in my room an hour or so, picking out little bits of powder from under the skin of my head and a few bits out of my ear. I may have a few black marks and one of the little holes may mark my neck but that is all. My face was turned away so I am not in the least disfigured which will please you!! I feel so thankful at being preserved but as I told you before I firmly believe in the protecting hand of a kind Providence and feel quite confident that all will be right. I have written to you quite fully, as usual, not disguising anything, as you can then feel confident that you know the worst. There may be a little suppuration etc. but the Professor is quite confident that he can heal the places perfectly – therefore, please feel happy, as I do, that I have had an escape, and do not be anxious. I lost a little blood but nothing to speak of and feel *quite well* today. In fact I have just sent to the restaurant for some soup and chicken!! Mr Lascelles is most kind, he came and sat with me yesterday. Lumley also.

Dr Fetherstonhaugh, my favourite doctor, has had worse luck. He was on his way to Pirot to take over a hospital there and, while walking on the slippery ice road, fell and broke the small bone of his leg. His leg was set in plaster of Paris and he was sent back to Sofia in a sledge. He is now lying at the Hotel du Bulgarie and is getting on capitally. He will be able to walk about in three weeks. Miss Stewart's interpreting nurse has also been unlucky. She has poisoned her finger in some wound and had to have it lanced today; so we have not been lucky between us.

The sun is shining brightly over Mount Vitosh in front of my windows, and I am feeling quite well and only anxious to be out again. This morning I sent off Herck with a sledge full of soups, tobacco and other things for the soup stations on the Dragoman Pass and Slionitza. My accident does not prevent my attending to business . . . The journey from Nisch across the mountains to Ak Palanka during the night of December 23rd was wild and interesting. We had to catch up the 12 waggons of our stores which had started from Nisch in the morning and were delayed getting carriage for ourselves and by my interview with King Milan. A dense fog came on in the evening and the roads were simply like broken ice. The most picturesque scenes opened up to our view as we rounded the zigzags of the pass. Convoys of ox waggons resting for the night, the oxen tethered to the carts and the drivers sitting round large fires which they spend all night keeping up. Sometimes they have time to build up rough sheds of boughs and snow to form a shelter . . .

There was a splendid reception yesterday. I felt a great lump in my throat when I saw the Prince riding into the town through a rough triumphal arch and the cheers of the people, who look upon him with justice as their saviour. It was so touching to see the presents offered to him, bouquets, wreaths, ribbons, and one poor man offered him a photograph album. All he received with good humoured expression and kind words. Then there was a Te Deum in the Cathedral and then the march past at the palace, where I was to have been one of the honoured guests, but fate willed it otherwise. Tonight the civil population will give him a torchlight procession and gala. I cannot, of course, see this which is a great bore.

Miss Stewart has been here again. She is so kind and attentive. She has just come from dressing Fetherstonhaugh's leg and gives a good account of him. I think that I was right in consulting Professor Langenbuch altho' I could see that Lake did not half like it. I feel much more satisfied. Langenbuch has changed the treatment and said that he would not have probed or touched the wound at all if he had seen it first, but I am glad that the other surgeon did so as he got out the felt wadding . . .

Dearest of wives before I close my letter let me tell you the old old story of how dear you are to me. I often think of you in my waking hours and feel as if we were together again. I have as usual written you the whole truth about myself as altho' it may make you feel a wee bit anxious yet in the long run it is the best plan as you will always know the worst and not be plagued by the feeling of uncertainty.

Lumley has just been in again and we were laughing over his surgical operations on my ear and head. The doctor however objects to any more such operations until the two holes are cured when he can do as he likes!

Sofia   27th December

My own dearest girl,
I have read through all your letters with so much interest. Poor little Guy. I am so sorry for him and I know it must be a trial, a sore trial for you dear girl. However I knew for certain that one of his legs was bent and am not in the least surprised that splints have been ordered. In fact I am relieved as I was *so certain* that this ought to be done. You remember my saying that I thought we should have to do so. I am tired and cannot answer all your letters. I was intensely interested in all you write.

Sofia   30th December 1885

Dear Alice,
Am getting on all right. Don't be in the least anxious. The two little holes are in process of healing. They are barely big enough to be called wounds. One is a great deal better this morning. Please do not let Brackley or anyone fuss in the least as I shall be up and about before you can answer this letter. Have written long report today to Wantage. I feel such a fool having been hit by a *blank* cartridge like a little rascally boy at a Brighton review.

Prince Alexander has been in my room sitting with me; so kind of him considering all the huge amount of work he has to do. His brother came to see me again yesterday, a pleasant and cheery visitor.

I am to be kept more quiet for the next few days as so many people come in and Dr Langenbuch says that rest will get me well quicker than anything – as I shall not then move about my neck so much. I am in no pain. In four or five days I shall be up and about thanks to a perfectly healthy state of body and mind.

After I left Pirot the Servians fired upon some of the soldiers who were left in the place to keep order and there was a little fight. The Bulgarians

220

lost one and two wounded – hard lines. Luckily they let us go through before they fought.

Miss Stewart brought me the enclosed Bulgarian New Year cards and asked me to send one to each of my children! On the back of one is the Lord's Prayer and the other contains some verses of St Matthew.

The Bulgarian New Year is Jan 12th. so you will get the cards in time!!

Sofia   New Year's Eve 1885

HAPPY NEW YEAR TO ALL AT HOME – 1st letter

My own dear Alice,

Here I am lying down on a bye bye of rapid convalescence, and wishing you, my own good girl, all the blessings of the New Year. The old old story is told again. How well can I remember hundreds of times when I might have been better, might have done more good things and fewer bad ones during the 37 years of my life which I can look back upon! Often, dearest, I might have been more unselfish towards you, though you know as well as I do that my love for you has increased and deepened with the rolling years. I can indeed dearest say that I could not love you more.

The New Year reminds one of all these things and the comparative rest upon which the good Dr Langenbuch has positively insisted, gives time for reflection and thoughts of the past and present.

I am much better today. Some little feverish symptoms which I had the night before last and Monday night were, I am sure, caused by the intense heat of the room. We did not know how to manage the German stove in it, a huge erection which gets very hot and there is no stopping it but raking out the fire! On getting a thermometer I found it registered over 70 degrees. Last night by careful attention to the stove it registered 65 degrees – just right, and I slept perfectly well without morphine. Today I feel no pain. Lake has just changed the dressings, and says that all is going on perfectly well. Probably I shall go out in a sledge tomorrow with Dr Fetherstonhaugh . . .

Prince Alexander is such a good fellow. Fancy with all his work before him he came up to my room and sat with me for three quarters of an hour with his brother. The next day his brother came for half an hour and yesterday the Prince's private secretary came to see me but found me sound asleep.

Well, I know one thing now and that is that I shall never be smashed by gunpowder. At Cambridge Mr Butler nearly blew my head off with a rifle, then afterwards I got a shot in my forehead, then my head was nearly smashed shooting at Mr Bolkows and now I have had my fourth escape – I hope that I am not destined for the rope!

I am thinking about little Guy. Lake says that wood splints are by far the best and that he thinks from my description that Guy will get all right without loss of muscular development. I am so glad that dear little *Leonor* has nice straight legs like her Father. Is it not a pity that Guy did not take after me too!

I have a sort of presentiment that Brackley will get nervous and rush out here. He probably will find me gone somewhere on ambulance work. Please put a *stop full stop* to any such idea as it would be good natured but ridiculous to make such a fuss and it would do no good at all.

Miss Stewart is quite in her element dressing the places and does it so nicely. She is an A1 nurse and Dr Langenbuch tells me that she has been doing first rate work at his hospital.

We are having a days comparative rest. The first one since I left England. I have finished all my own accounts up to date and shall keep them continually 'fixed up' so as not to have the bother of a fortnights work on my return with the typical auditor in spectacles!

And now for the result of our operation so far:

1 Distributed stores at Widdin – much wanted
2 Medicine and money grant at Lom Palanka
3 Dr Fetherstonhaugh and two assistants undertake good work at Alexander Hospital
4 Assistance to Miss Stewart at Bank Hospital – attached an interpreting nurse to her, supplied her hospital with stores etc.
5 Convoy of medicines brought to Pirot by me on breaking out of Typhoid etc.
6 Large convoy of stores bought in Belgrade and passed back here through lines
7 Two carts of stores to 'rest' stations at Dragoman and Slivinitza
8 Second set of two carts of stores for same place
9 General distribution of stores from our Nat. Aid Soc. depot at Palais (!) Vitosh to:
Teutonic Order Hospital
Alexander
Bank Hosp.
Jews Hosp.
4 Hospitals of Societe Internationale

Dr Lake attached to Ecole Militaire Hosp., which he supplied with all that we can give from our depot.

Fancy over 350 of the 500 blankets which I brought from Belgrade have been already snapped up.

2nd letter   10 p.m., New Years Eve

My dearest Alice,
The New Year is close at hand and these will be the last few lines penned by me in 1885. I am again reading over my favourite book – your letters . . .

I am glad that the Wantages are pleased with our co-operation in the work of the N.A.S. It is fascinating work being able to relieve physical suffering and a touch of it now and then makes one know how such relief is appreciated. Of course, the war over and all is forgotten, but what matters that if the good is done . . .

So you are consoled at my not being M.P. and the unscrupulous side of politics has no attractions for me. If I could be returned in the grand position of M. Foster or Mr Goschen it would be another matter . . . I like this country where the Prince is the radical – the Church and Russian parts are the Conservatives. The Church here is like the Church elsewhere = against all real progress, against *trusting the people*, strongly in favour of making an Upper House etc., all the same as in England and elsewhere.

God Bless all at H.P. Gardens   New Year's Day 1886
[Hyde Park Gardens, the Sandeman's
London house]
Happy New Year to all

My darling Alice,
As my last lines in 1885 were written to you and have gone off by the mail cart this morning so my first letter of 1886 shall be to the being who is uppermost in my mind. Many, many happy returns of New Years Day to you and our chicks and may our mutual love ever burn as brightly and purely as it does at this moment. All the good resolutions of past New Years Days crowd upon me, too many, alas, broken but though, as the brave Marinoff here, one loses here a battery of artillery, there a company or two of men the great object of gaining the position may yet be attained.

Poor Marinoff – he was a brave young Captn in the Princes Army and died the day before yesterday of his wounds. He, for three days, with a handful of men stopped the junction of two Servian Corps and thereby saved Slivinitza from being surrounded and gave time for Prince Alexander to bring up his volunteers by forced marches.

The Prince feels Marinoff's loss very much. He was shot through his right lung whilst leading his men to storm an important point. The bullet went right through his body and he lived for over a month. He finally died of a complication of irritation etc. in his left lung! He was to all accounts a good man and a good example to the other young men by whom the Prince is surrounded. Does it not seem strange that he should have been the one taken away? He is to be buried today with all honours.

c/o British Consul
Sofia

2nd January 1886

My dearest Alice,

Am getting on capitally and shall soon be about. Have just received two letters together from you. Such a relief as I had not heard for a week and absence of news from you is like a very big blank in a pretty picture . . .

As to the £100 honorarium. I telegraphed to Wantage my appreciation of the vote but declined to receive it or any payment. I said I was only too happy if my services had promoted an object very much at heart etc. etc. This is true.

As to whether it appears in the accounts I should like *my declining* it to appear in the *same report* as the statement that the grant had been voted, and this can of course be done. Even if it is too late to add to the text a little note like an erratum might be added. This perhaps would give too much publicity! However if a vote is passed it must be recorded and there is no harm in that. However as I decline to receive the money they may add that as a note, or credit the Society with the £100 at my request *in the same account*. Of course I feel pleased at their voting the sum as a token of appreciation, at the same time I should not like the accounts to be published without the statement that I had wished it refunded, or as Wantage put it to be credited to the Society. I think Wantage means to do this. We dont want the whole transaction rescinded but only the fact of my declining recorded in the same set of accounts as the item showing the payment to me.

c/o British Consul General   5th January 1886
Sofia

My dear good Alice,
I am happy to say that my head wound has taken a wonderful turn for the
better during the last two days. It was a little obstinate for three days last
week, nothing serious, but it has suddenly taken to healing and Dr
Langenbuch says that it will be all right in a few days. It is now only the size
of a large pea.

We were getting on all right when alas Dr Lake had a misfortune. He
poisoned his hand while doing some operation on a very bad wound which
was in a dangerous state. His accident is of almost common occurance
under these circumstances and is a sort of blood poisoning. Of course he
cannot work any more and is confined to his room. I have sent him to the
Hotel Bulgarie where he will be near Dr Langenbuch and Miss Stewart.
This good lady has had the pleasure of dressing Dr Fetherstonhaugh's
broken leg, my old head and Dr Lake's hand and arm, and right well has
she done her duties in addition to her heavy work at the Nat. Bank
hospital.

No news particularly – Tomorrow is the Xmas day out here – old
style – the number of sucking pigs which have squealed their last today
is appalling! War or no war the Bulgars keep their Yuletime right
religiously . . .

Adieu, my own dear girl. This may and I hope will reach you on our
Wedding Day, Jan 12th. Eight years we shall have been married! And
during all those years, dearest, you have been the best and truest wife to
me that man could have. Every year makes you dearer and dearer. May
you have every blessing from our Father and my prayers for your happiness
be heard – Goodnight my own loved Alice.

MANY HAPPY RETURNS OF YOUR WEDDING DAY
Sofia   6th January 1886

My dear Brackley,
My head wound has made rapid progress during the last two days, it made
no progress three days before and Dr Langenbuch decided to make an
incision, nothing serious. I was actually in the operation room with my coat
off and like a sensible man was first going to have chloroform when Dr

Langenbuch on making a final examination, saw that the place was improving, and decided not to cut into it. During the last three days it has suddenly begun to heal; scarcely any discharge and today the hole is not larger than a pea. I shall have my bandages off in a couple of days or so. I go about now and do not feel the slightest pain or even discomfort, except that I have three or four rather sore places where bits of powder got under the skin. I have had all those in my ears picked out like little thorns and shall have no marks except two little dots on my ears and one on my neck. These will be quite faint. What a lucky escape!

We leave this in 10 days or a fortnight, homeward bound I expect. As for news I have none. We distribute our stores when required, and are just now increasing our distribution of warm waistcoats etc. to the most feeble among the convalescents who have to trudge long distances to their homes in a hard frost – a trying change after the warm hospital.

The soldiers are so grateful . . .

Prince Alexander is such a kind-hearted man, as good as he is brave and they say that he is, in addition, an excellent statesman and diplomatist. I hope they will make him a King one of these days with a good liberal constitution, which is the truest and most practical form of liberty.

There are no titles allowed in this country except that of the Prince – His Highness and there is manhood universal suffrage. There are three and a half parties, the Radical, Liberal and Conservative, and a little Russian party, just now in bad odour with the masses.

People go about in sledges and the sun shines brightly most days. The intense cold has now passed away. Fancy when I had those long drives and when I was at the advanced post before Pirot to see the conditions of the men, the thermometer used to go down to 10 degrees Fahrenheit, that is 22 degrees below our freezing point.

No wonder that many poor fellows were frost-bitten when you consider that there was an army of 60,000 men holding an exposed position among the mountains under these conditions . . .

The most extraordinary operations have taken place here and those skilled German surgeons, Professor Gluck (with whom was our Dr Fetherstonhaugh) and Dr Langenbuch and others have simply saved lives by the dozen and also much suffering.

I shall be right glad to get home again and trust that no other war will disturb my rest yet awhile.

Adios – Give my best love to Ellinor [Vincent's new sister-in-law, Brackley's wife]. She will be interested in hearing that my Storekeeper and the assistant interpreter for N.A.S. surgeons are both 'preachers'. They took the two *Protestant* services on Sunday one preaching in the morning and other in the afternoon. The Bulgarian Church authorities are not quite pleased with the progress made by the Protestants I hear. The only state paid clergy here are the Archbishop of Sofia and the Bishop of Samakoff. Country priests or rather Popes are paid by voluntary offerings in the various villages.

The Govt. however subsidises the Mohamedans.

Sofia   11th January 1885 [*sic* 1886]

My own dear Alice,

Now for your letters – how shall I begin to answer them? I see you are much troubled about the one hundred pounds – I suppose that few people have so much difficulty in getting rid of 'filthy lucre', tho' we have managed to get rid of a tidyish lot this year! However I *quite agree* that I ought not to accept such a donation *on principle*, and this quite independently of any honorific reward. As a member of the council [of the National Aid Society] it would never do for me to accept presents from my colleagues of money which it is our business to guard jealously; moreover I quite disapprove of the heads of departments receiving gifts which are not shared by those under their command. It is all very well for Lord Wolseley etc. but not for V.K.B. or that ilk, and had I been Lord W. I should have distributed half among those who contributed to my success . . .

The world is the same all over and I am convinced that the spirit of Christianity does not necessarily co-exist with the blind acceptance of its impossible-to-be-comprehended mysteries handed down to us by uncertain traditions through men whose cruelty, ignorance and fanaticism in the middle ages converted what was once a pure, simple faith into cruel and superstitious idolatry. It is much the same old story out here. Before the *Protestants* established themselves the poor Bulgars never had much chance of reading the Bible for themselves. Now, thanks N.B. to the London Bible Society, the Bible is printed and circulated freely in Bulgaria. It will please the Madre and Aunt C. to know that my two Bulgar co-workers here, my storekeeper and Surgeons assistant are Protestants and Preachers! . . .

We had a grand dinner on Saturday night – I made a speech in French which was accepted with much satisfaction. All the great toasts being drunk I asked the president Caraialoff Prime Minister,[41] if I could propose a Toast. He said yes, of course, and so I rose and after remarking that we had drunk the health of their Prince 'si brave et si bien-aimé', of the foreign Red Crosses, of the Ministers etc. but that we must not forget the cause that brought us all together – the wounded. We were all leaving the country, not without regret, especially as we [were] leaving behind us many wounded still in hospital. I then moved my toast and proposed to empty our glasses to the 'health of the wounded'. This was received with cries of Bravo! Qu'ils vivent! Vivent les blessés!

Tonight I am to be the guest of the Bulgarian Red Cross Society at a public dinner and suppose that the spirit (not the champagne) will move me to utter winged words. I enclose you the invitations and même which may amuse you.

NOTES TO CHAPTERS ONE TO FIVE

1. Maurice-Adolphe-Charles, Vicomte de Flavigny (1799–1873), diplomat and moderate monarchist politician whose career spanned both the July Monarchy and the Second Empire between 1830 and 1871. A founding member of the Société de Secours aux Blessés.
2. Félix-Antoine-Philibert Dupanloup (1802–78), Bishop of Orleans from 1849. Celebrated liberal Catholic theologian and propagandist, and advocate of freedom of information and compromise with the secular authorities. Opposed the Doctrine of Papal Infallibility in 1869 and was elected to the National Assembly in 1871 where he sat as a monarchist.
3. Léon-Michel Gambetta (1838–82). Republican lawyer and opponent of Napoleon III who organized the defence of Paris from which he escaped by balloon. He became Minister of War and of the Interior in the Provisional Government and attempted to organize a continuing war effort.
4. Captain Burgess was the secretary to the National Aid Society. No C.J. Burgess appears in the Army List for this period.
5. Charles-Denis-Sauter Bourbaki (1816–97). A professional soldier of Greek origin and a military reformer under Napoleon III. Acted as a go-between with the Empress Eugénie in England before joining Gambetta to help organize the military resistance. Commander in the Besançon district.
6. Guiseppe Garibaldi (1807–82). Italian nationalist leader and general of irregular troops who played a leading role in the creation of a united Italy. Formed a volunteer corps in 1870 to aid the French and fought in the vicinity of Dijon. He was elected to the French National Assembly in 1871.
7. That is a Lieutenant Colonel or Colonel, or a naval Captain, in retirement.
8. Doña Margarita de Bourbon-Parma, the wife of Don Carlos.
9. Sir George Howland Beaumont (1828–82) and John von Sonnentag de Havilland (1827–86), both of whom were Knights of the Sovereign Military Order of Malta, the original, Catholic, Order.
10. The proclamation of General Arsenio Martínez de Campos (1831–1900) in support of Prince Alfonso, son of the deposed Queen Isabel II.
11. Don Domingo Moriones y Murillo (1823–81), commander of the Government forces who despite an initial failure to capture Pamplona was one of the most competent Government generals.
12. Don Fernando Primo de Rivera y Sobremonte (1831–1921), uncle of the future dictator and commander of the forces which took the Carlist centre of Estella in February, 1876.

13. Jesús Fendo y Valle (1849–1911), journalist and poet who was President of the Executive Committee of the Spanish Red Cross.

14. Lieutenant General Sir Andrew Clarke (1824–1902), soldier and politician, served variously in West Africa and Australia, Director of Works for the Royal Navy 1864–73, Inspector of Fortifications 1881–6, Minister of Public Works in the Government of India 1857–80.

15. Don José Gutiérrez de la Concha, Marqués de la Habana (1809–95).

16. Mikhail Grigor'evich Chernaiev (1828–98), served in Central Asia where captured Tashkent contrary to orders and was retired. An outspoken Panslav he volunteered to serve in Servia where he was made commander-in-chief of the Servian forces. Extremely popular in right wing nationalist circles in Russia.

17. For their activities, see E.M. Pearson and L.L. McLaughlin, *op. cit.*

18. Emily Anne, Viscountess Strangford (d. 1887). Widow of the 8th Viscount and orientalist who died in 1869. Had travelled extensively in the Near East and lived at Constantinople. After 1869 she trained as a nurse and spent the rest of her life promoting medical charities, especially in the Ottoman Empire.

19. Hafez Pasha, original entrepreneur of the Sofia–Salonika railway, was put in command of the regular Ottoman forces against the Bulgarian insurrectionists. Responsible for not stopping outrages against civilians. Commanded the Ottoman army in the 1876 war with Servia.

20. James Long, quaker active in the Franco–Prussian War and local representative in Bulgaria of the Manchester and Salford Relief Fund where he took carpenters displaced from Alsace after the German annexation. Vincent's comments are more explicable in the light of R.J. More, *Under the Balkans*, London, 1877, p. 52: 'He also joined security for the houses [built with the relief funds] by purchasing the freehold or an equivalent.'

21. Charles Augustus Hobart (1822–86). Entered Ottoman service after retiring from the British navy in 1862. Commander-in-chief in 1877 with particular charge of the blockade of the Russian Black Sea ports.

22. William Lehman Ashmead-Bartlett (1851–1921). First involved with philanthropic work in Ireland with Baroness Burdett-Coutts whom he later married and whose name he took. Special Commissioner for the Baroness's Turkish Compassionate Fund, based in Constantinople. Lady Kemball was the wife of Sir A.B. Kemball, Indian army political service and Military Commissioner with the Ottoman army in the Servo-Turkish War and with the Ottoman forces in Armenia, 1877–8.

23. Raouf Pasha, able and ingratiating Circassian confidant of the Sultan and Minister of Marine in 1877 and Minister of War in December, 1877. Negotiated with Ignat'ev at San Stefano.

24. Ghazi Ahmet Mukhtar Pasha (1837–1918). One of the two Ottoman generals to emerge from the war with credit and the title ghazi. Commanded in Bosnia, Hercegovina and Montenegro. In 1877 commanded the Ottoman forces in the Caucasus where he defended Kars until November 1877.

25. Either the Grand Duke Konstantin Nikolaevich, brother of the Tsar, or his son, Grand Duke Konstantin Konstantinovich.

26. The decision of the Conservative Cabinet to take powers to call out the militia if necessary.

27. The National Aid Society fitted out a special ship, the *Belle of Dunkerque*, to carry stores to Constantinople. It was plagued by delays.

28. Mauritz, Freiherr von Hirsch (1831–96), Jewish financier, railway promoter and philanthropist who became an Austrian citizen in 1870. Founded the Alliance Israelite

Universelle which provided aid to Ottoman Jews in the Russo-Turkish War.

29. Prince Hassan, second son of Khedive Ismail and Egyptian Minister of War. Born 1854. In command of the Egyptian contingent sent to Constantinople in June 1877.

30. Iosif Vladimirovich Gurko (1828–1901), commander of the advance south of the Balkan mountains in July and August 1877 which threw the Ottoman forces into disarray. Commanded the 2nd Guards Cavalry Division and spearheaded the final advance on Constantinople.

31. Sir Evelyn Baring, later Lord Cromer (1841–1917), since 1877 British Commissioner to the Egyptian International Debt Commission and British Agent and Consul-General in Egypt after 1883. Khedive Tawfiq Pasha, ruled 1879–92, was in the difficult position of being legally subordinate to the Ottoman Sultan but practically to the British occupying authorities.

32. Uthman Digna, born *c.* 1840, native of Suakin and member of the leading merchant family of Dignai. Was imprisoned and his wealth confiscated for slaving in 1877, at British insistence. After 1883 was the Mahdi's principal lieutenant on the Red Sea coast.

33. A system to assist the memorization of information, based on mnemonics.

34. The Panjdeh crisis arising from the Russian occupation of an area occupied by central Asiatic Turcoman tribes claimed by the British-protected Amir of Afghanistan, whose soldiers were defeated on 30 March 1885. The incident led to prolonged tension and a strong likelihood of war between Britain and Russia.

35. Major, later Sir, Herbert Charles Chermiside RE (1850–1929). Between 1876 and 1899 on continuous foreign service within the Ottoman Empire, and from 1884 to 1886 Governor of the Red Sea littoral, based at Suakin.

36. Themistocles Gluck (1853–1942), born at Jasny, Romania. Worked after 1878 under von Langenbeck at the surgical clinic of Berlin University where after 1883 he was Professor of Surgery.

37. The eminent surgeon and founding member of the German Red Cross Baron von Langenbeck (1810–87). Pioneer of twenty-one different surgical operations and *Generalartz* of the Prussian army in the wars of 1864, 1866 and 1870–1.

38. That is, the Queen's Messenger, the official courier of the Foreign Office.

39. Prince Alexander of Bulgaria.

40. Colonel J.K. Fraser of the 1st Life Guards, Military Attaché at the British Embassy in Vienna and British Commissioner with the International Frontier Commission for Bulgaria and Servia.

41. Presumably Petko Karavelov, leader of the Bulgarian Liberal Party since 1878 and Prime Minister from 1884 to 1886.